HOME

Also by Bryan Voltaggio

VOLTink. (with Michael Voltaggio)

HOME

RECIPES TO COOK WITH FAMILY AND FRIENDS

BRYAN VOLTAGGIO

WITH AKI KAMOZAWA

Photography by Ed Anderson

LITTLE, BROWN AND COMPANY

New York Boston London

Little, Brown and Company
Hachette Book Group
1290 Avenue of the Americas
New York, NY 10104
littlebrown.com

First Edition: April 2015

Little, Brown and Company is a division of
Hachette Book Group, Inc. The Little, Brown
name and logo are trademarks of Hachette
Book Group, Inc.

The publisher is not responsible for websites
(or their content) that are not owned by the
publisher.

ISBN 978-0-316-32388-8
Library of Congress Control Number: 2014944089

10 9 8 7 6 5 4 3 2 1

SC

Design by Gary Tooth / Empire Design Studio
Printed in China

Contents

Introduction

Thoughts on using your kitchen . . .

The kitchen is the heart of the home. People linger in kitchens if they feel welcome. Even those who don't love to cook have to eat, and therefore everyone ends up spending time in the kitchen. It's where people gather, it's where conversations take place, and it's where things happen. As a chef, I want everyone to feel welcome in my kitchen and I want to encourage you to use your kitchen as much as possible.

People love the idea of a big, spacious kitchen. In fact, smaller kitchens are easier to cook in. When you're working, you want everything to be within a few steps. You don't want to have to run all over the place to rinse parsley, grate some cheese, and then turn down a burner. Islands are great because you can have one side of the kitchen where people hang out and one side where you work. It's inclusive and efficient at the same time. My kids aren't all big enough to help with every task in the kitchen, but they can always climb up on a stool and keep me company while I cook. We've had many of our best conversations in that room while creating something delicious for the whole family to enjoy.

I'm not going to tell you that you need a fancy stove or sous vide equipment to cook well. I am going to tell you to buy a couple of inexpensive thermometers so you can keep track of your oven, refrigerator, and freezer temperatures. A few degrees here and there can make a big difference, and equipment that works perfectly when you bring it home from the store has a way of deteriorating over time. It's not the end of the world if your oven is off by 10 degrees, as long as you know it and can set your temperatures accordingly.

While we're on the subject of thermometers, having one or two digital probe thermometers around your kitchen can be a very useful thing. The basic model costs under $10, and there are even fancy probe thermometers that will send alerts to your smartphone letting you know when the roast is done. All of the cooks in my restaurant kitchens are required to carry digital thermometers, because they are a quick and foolproof way to know when your food is perfectly cooked.

Timers are almost as important as thermometers. In this age of smartphones, we all have timers in our pockets, so there's no excuse for letting things overcook. At home, if I don't want to carry my phone, old-fashioned kitchen timers work just as well. My oven may cook faster or slower than your oven, but if you have a timer and probe thermometer we should always be able to achieve the same results.

In my restaurants, we label everything, and I do a fair amount of this at home too. Get a roll of painter's tape and a Sharpie and keep them near the refrigerator. Label and date everything you put in there. That way, at the end of the week you won't wonder what something is and whether it's edible; you'll be able to

read the answer on the container. Trust me, this takes a few seconds and will make life for you and anyone else foraging in your refrigerator much easier. While you're at it, label dry goods with the date of purchase, especially things you use infrequently, and keep your shelves organized. You are more likely to cook if you can find the ingredients you are looking for.

Keep your knives sharp. It doesn't matter if you use a whetstone or one of those sharpening tools they sell in the stores. A dull knife is a dangerous knife. It doesn't cut properly, so it's more likely to slide off fruits and vegetables rather than into them. Dull knives also require you to use more pressure when you're cutting, which leads to accidents. A good knife slices through ingredients easily and your hands direct the motion without getting in the way. You don't need superexpensive fancy knives, though I confess that I own several. You just need knives that feel good in your hands. Pick them up and hold them before you buy them. Knives have different weights, shapes, and sizes. In order to use one well, you have to find one that fits your hand. A chef's knife, a paring knife, a serrated knife, and a peeler will do almost everything you need in the kitchen.

If you bake or cook often, you should own a digital scale. You can buy a good one at any home-goods store for less than $30. Once you start using one, you'll wonder how you lived without it.

You'll notice that we included weight equivalents, in grams and kilograms, for all the recipes in this book. That's because they are universal and allow you to see the ratio of ingredients in any recipe, which gives you the ability to make substitutions or scale them up or down. Furthermore, weights are easy to work with. Every digital scale has a tare function that zeros out the weight. What this means is that you can measure flour into a bowl and zero it out and then add cocoa powder and zero it out and then add sugar or whatever else you need. You'll have exactly the right amount of every ingredient and you'll end up with fewer dishes. What's not to love about that?

Pressure cookers are a chef's best friend, and they can be game changers for home cooks too. These are slightly more expensive than scales and thermometers—a good one costs around $100—but if you like to cook they can be invaluable. Pressure cookers exponentially reduce the amount of time spent cooking, so you can make traditional long-simmered braises in about 30 minutes. Electric pressure cookers, like the one from Cuisinart, allow you to load the ingredients, set the timer, and walk away. They don't take up any burner space and are quieter than stovetop models. You can "set it and forget it," and the results will be uniformly cooked every time. They're great for slow-cooked items like grits or sturdy root vegetables like beets. Pressure cookers braise beautifully and are my favorite piece of equipment for making stocks. Today's models are not your mother's pressure cookers. They are safe, quiet, and make any kitchen more efficient.

Finally, your kitchen needs a few good cookbooks to act as guides and help get things rolling in the kitchen. I wrote this book for my family. I spend more time in my restaurants than I do in my home kitchen. When this cookbook is on our kitchen shelf, it will be like a little part of me is always there with my wife, Jennifer, and the kids.

For me, cooking at home feels like an occasion, and often it is for some sort of a holiday or special meal. Thanksgiving, Christmas, and Super Bowl Sunday are days when I make it a point to be home. Sunday suppers are important to me too. I like to cook with my kids, and I love when we're all gathered around the table. Any chef will tell you that breakfast is the one meal every day that they can share with their family. It doesn't matter if I get only a few hours of sleep—I'm up in the morning for breakfast with Jennifer and the kids. It's a priority for me.

The recipes in this book reflect the spirit of the food I grew up with in Maryland, the things I learned in professional kitchens, and the meals I share with my family and friends today. Many of the holiday or special-occasion recipes later in the book can easily be adapted for Sunday suppers or even weeknight meals. Holiday meals are designed so you can do a lot of the preparation in advance and be able to enjoy your company on the big day. Cooking for the people you love is meant to be a pleasure rather than a chore. I've chosen straightforward preparations (for the most part!), bold flavors, and comforting dishes that I hope will inspire you to cook at home with your family and friends and to try something new, perhaps a fresh twist on an old favorite.

From my home to yours,

Bryan.

HOME

I do a lot of work with No Kid Hungry, a nationwide effort to end childhood hunger in America. Through my association with them I've come to appreciate the importance of breakfast; it really is the most important meal of the day. In the state of Maryland we've made it easier for any kid to come to school and get a good breakfast, regardless of whether or not he or she has the money to pay for it. For me, personally, breakfast is the one meal a day that I always spend with my family. It's a chance to connect and catch up with one another while we share a meal. It's special to me, and these recipes reflect my passion for the first meal of the day.

Breakfast

Cinnamon Roll Biscuits

PLUMPED GOLDEN RAISINS:

½ **cup** / 113 grams water

2 tablespoons / 28 grams Myers's Rum or other flavorful dark rum

½ **cup** / 100 grams granulated sugar

¼ **teaspoon** / 1.5 grams fine sea salt

¼ **cup** / 45 grams golden raisins

1 piece star anise

CANDIED PECANS:

2 large egg whites

1½ **tablespoons** / 30 grams sorghum syrup or molasses

1 tablespoon / 14 grams water

½ **cup** / 100 grams granulated sugar

2 teaspoons / 12 grams fine sea salt

½ **teaspoon** / 1 gram ground cinnamon

¼ **teaspoon** / 0.5 gram ground coriander

¼ **teaspoon** / 0.5 gram cayenne pepper

¼ **teaspoon** / 0.5 gram ground cumin

3 cups / 325 grams whole pecans

GLAZE:

Liquid from soaked raisins

1 cup / 225 grams unsalted butter, diced

10 tablespoons / 25 grams packed light brown sugar

CINNAMON BUTTER:

1¼ **cups** / 285 grams unsalted butter, room temperature

1 tablespoon / 12.5 grams granulated sugar

1 tablespoon / 6 grams ground cinnamon

¼ **teaspoon** / 1.5 grams fine sea salt

➡

When I was a kid, my mom would buy sticky pecan rolls and warm them up in the oven. I remember the smell of them wafting through the kitchen and what a treat it was to eat them warm from the oven. These cinnamon rolls are my way of re-creating that experience. This is one of those recipes that looks like a lot of steps but comes together quickly.

Golden raisins are my favorite. All too often the ones you buy in the store are shriveled and desiccated. My solution is to soak them in a sweet rum syrup. This plumps them up and brings back their natural snap. The candied pecans get a subtle heat from cayenne pepper to balance all the sweetness, and the cinnamon butter suggests a darned good cinnamon toast. You can prep **Cinnamon Roll Biscuits the day before and bake them off in the morning. That way, by the time everyone wakes up and wanders down the stairs, breakfast is already in the oven.**

Make the Plumped Golden Raisins:
Put the water, rum, sugar, and salt in a medium bowl and whisk until the sugar dissolves. Add the raisins and the star anise and stir gently to blend. Cover with plastic wrap or transfer to a lidded container and let the raisins soak overnight, at least 8 hours and up to 24 hours.

Make the Candied Pecans:
Preheat the oven to 250°F (120°C). Line a baking sheet with a silicone baking mat or buttered parchment paper.

Whip the egg whites, sorghum, and water in a stand mixer until soft peaks form. Meanwhile, in a small bowl, whisk together the sugar, salt, cinnamon, coriander, cayenne, and cumin. With the mixer running, add the sugar mixture 1 tablespoon at a time until it's all absorbed. Turn off the mixer and fold in the pecans, making sure that the nuts get fully coated with the egg white mixture. Spread them out on the prepared baking sheet and bake for 1 hour, rotating the pan every 15 minutes, or until they are golden brown and glossy. Remove from the oven and let cool completely before storing in an airtight container. Candied Pecans will keep for up to 6 weeks in an airtight container at room temperature.

Make the Glaze:
Drain the raisins and reserve them at room temperature. Put the raisin soaking liquid in a medium pot set over high heat and bring to a simmer. Whisk in the butter and brown sugar until they are

CINNAMON ROLL BISCUITS:

4 cups / 900 grams buttermilk

6 large egg yolks

¼ **cup** / 50 grams granulated sugar

9 cups / 1.35 kilograms all-purpose flour

3 teaspoons / 18 grams baking powder

2 teaspoons / 12 grams fine sea salt

1 teaspoon / 5 grams baking soda

½ **cup** / 55 grams chopped Candied Pecans

absorbed into the liquid. Divide the glaze between two 9-by-13-inch baking dishes and put them in the refrigerator to chill and set while you continue.

Make the Cinnamon Butter:
Put the butter, sugar, cinnamon, and salt in a small bowl. Mix well to blend. Reserve.

Make the Cinnamon Roll Biscuits:
Mix the buttermilk, egg yolks, and sugar in a stand mixer with a paddle attachment on low speed until smooth. Stop the mixer. Sift the flour, baking powder, salt, and baking soda into a medium bowl. Make a well in the center of the flour. Pour in one-third of the buttermilk mixture and fold it into the flour. Once the flour begins to clump, fold in half of the remaining buttermilk mixture, and then the remainder, gently folding and kneading the mixture just until it comes together as a soft dough. Wrap the dough in plastic wrap and chill in the

refrigerator for 1 hour.

Preheat the oven to 350°F (180°C).

Divide the dough in half. Roll out half of the dough on a floured surface into a rough rectangle, approximately ¼ inch thick. Spread half of the Cinnamon Butter over the top. Sprinkle half of the Plumped Raisins over the Cinnamon Butter. Roll the dough lengthwise into a tight cylinder and let it rest on a cutting board, seam side down, for a few minutes. Cut it into 10 even pieces. Pull the prepared baking dishes out of the refrigerator and sprinkle ¼ cup (27 grams) of the chopped Candied Pecans over the firm glaze. Arrange the cut biscuit rolls, flat sides down, over the glaze; it is okay for them to be touching each other. Repeat with the second batch of biscuits, if desired. Otherwise, they can be baked the next morning. Put the pan of biscuit rolls in the oven and bake for 1 hour, or until deep golden brown and cooked through.

Home Bryan Voltaggio

Cranberry-Corn Muffins

MAKES 12 MUFFINS

2 cups / 300 grams all-purpose flour

¼ cup / 70 grams ground John Cope's toasted dried sweet corn

1½ teaspoons / 9 grams baking powder

½ cup / 113 grams unsalted butter, room temperature

1½ cups / 300 grams sugar

½ teaspoon / 3 grams fine sea salt

¼ teaspoon / 0.6 gram ground nutmeg

3 large eggs

13 tablespoons plus 1 teaspoon / 200 grams Greek yogurt

6 tablespoons / 85 grams vegetable oil

1 teaspoon / 4 grams vanilla extract (or seeds from 1 vanilla bean)

1 cup / 113 grams chopped dried cranberries

⅓ cup / 50 grams chopped pistachios

Grated zest from 2 lemons

I am addicted to John Cope's toasted dried sweet corn. Francine Maroukian, a traditional American food advocate from the Workshop Kitchen in Philadelphia, brought me my first bag. It's a family-made product from Pennsylvania Dutch country (available online), and the flavor is incredible. Corn muffins so rarely taste like corn. Adding this toasted sweet corn to the muffin batter gives it a wonderful, fresh corn flavor. I add chopped dried cranberries for their sweet-tartness, and as an added benefit they give the muffins a festive confettilike appearance. Do not substitute whole dried cranberries because they tend to be too chewy and intense and their flavor can overwhelm the corn. These muffins will wake up your taste buds and brighten your day.

Preheat the oven to 350°F (180°C).

Butter a standard muffin pan or line it with cupcake papers. Sift the flour, corn, and baking powder together. In a stand mixer with a paddle attachment, cream the butter, sugar, salt, and nutmeg on low speed until light and smooth, 3 to 5 minutes.

Put the eggs, yogurt, vegetable oil, and vanilla in a medium bowl and whisk to blend.

With the mixer running on low, slowly pour the egg mixture into the butter, in 2 or 3 additions, and mix until it is fully incorporated. Stop the mixer and add the flour mixture. Mix until it becomes a smooth, silky batter. Fold in the chopped dried cranberries, pistachios, and lemon zest. Divide the batter equally among the muffin cups, about 4½ ounces (125 grams) batter per muffin. Bake for 30 minutes, or until a toothpick inserted in the center of a muffin comes out clean. Transfer to a wire rack to cool for 5 minutes before serving.

Blueberry Cake with Peanut Streusel

PEANUT STREUSEL:

¾ **cup** / 113 grams all-purpose flour

½ **cup plus 2 tablespoons** / 113 grams granulated sugar

7 ounces / 125 grams roasted unsalted peanuts

½ **cup** / 70 grams graham cracker crumbs

1½ **teaspoons** / 3 grams ground cinnamon

¼ **teaspoon** / 1.5 grams fine sea salt

¼ **teaspoon** / 0.5 gram cayenne pepper

½ **cup** / 113 grams unsalted butter, room temperature

BLUEBERRY CAKE:

2½ **cups** / 375 grams all-purpose flour

1½ **teaspoons** / 9 grams baking powder

½ **cup** / 113 grams unsalted butter, room temperature

1½ **cups** / 300 grams granulated sugar

½ **teaspoon** / 3 grams fine sea salt

3 large eggs

13 tablespoons plus 1 teaspoon / 200 grams sour cream

6 tablespoons / 85 grams vegetable oil

1 teaspoon / 4 grams vanilla extract (or seeds from 1 vanilla bean)

2 cups / 350 grams fresh or frozen blueberries

Grated zest from 2 limes

GLAZE:

½ **cup** / 120 grams sour cream

3 tablespoons / 45 grams buttermilk

2 tablespoons / 35 grams smooth peanut butter

2 teaspoons / 10 grams honey

Grated zest and juice of 1 lime

½ **cup** / 65 grams powdered sugar

½ **teaspoon** / 3 grams fine sea salt

Blueberry breakfast cake is a classic: moist, tender crumb; sweet, jammy berries; and soft, sandy streusel, usually served warm and sometimes accompanied by cold salted butter. My twist on the standard is using peanuts. Peanuts are a classic Southern ingredient and one I've personally never seen in streusel before. I thought their rich, nutty texture would be perfect against the cake. It seemed like a natural match, a riff off the classic PB&J in cake form. What better way to start off your morning?

Make the Peanut Streusel:

Preheat the oven to 350°F (180°C).

Put the flour, sugar, peanuts, graham cracker crumbs, cinnamon, salt, and cayenne in a food processor and pulse 3 or 4 times to blend and chop the peanuts. Add the butter and pulse until moist coarse crumbs form. Transfer to a bowl, cover, and refrigerate until needed.

➔

Make the Blueberry Cake:

Butter a 9-inch springform cake pan and set it on a baking sheet. Sift the flour and baking powder together. In a stand mixer with a paddle attachment, cream the butter, sugar, and salt on low speed until light and smooth, 3 to 5 minutes. Put the eggs, sour cream, vegetable oil, and vanilla in a medium bowl and whisk to blend. With the mixer running on low, slowly pour the egg mixture into the butter, in 2 or 3 additions, and mix until it is fully incorporated. Stop the mixer and add the flour mixture. Mix until it becomes a smooth, silky batter. Fold in the blueberries and lime zest. Pour the batter into the prepared cake pan. Take the streusel out of the refrigerator and sprinkle it evenly over the top of the cake batter. Bake for 50 to 65 minutes, until a toothpick inserted into the center of the cake comes out clean. Remove from the oven and transfer to a wire rack to cool for at least 20 minutes.

Make the Glaze:

Put the sour cream, buttermilk, peanut butter, honey, and lime zest and juice in a medium bowl and whisk until smooth. Add the powdered sugar and salt and whisk until smooth. Drizzle the glaze over the top of the cooled cake and let it set.

Glazed Bacon Biscuits

MAKES 8 BISCUITS

GLAZED BACON:

1 pound / 454 grams thick-cut bacon (12 slices)

¼ cup / 85 grams strawberry jam

1½ teaspoons / 9 grams sriracha

BISCUITS:

2 cups / 300 grams all-purpose flour

¼ cup / 50 grams sugar

1½ teaspoons / 9 grams fine sea salt

2 teaspoons / 12 grams baking powder

½ cup / 113 grams unsalted butter

1½ cups / 340 grams buttermilk

BISCUIT TOPPING:

2 tablespoons / 28 grams unsalted butter

2 tablespoons / 30 grams honey

¼ teaspoon / 0.75 gram ground cinnamon

For a fresh take on bacon, I make a quick glaze with strawberry jam and sriracha sauce. Sriracha is a slightly sweet Asian hot sauce punctuated with chiles and garlic that pairs beautifully with strawberries. I brush it on the bacon and cook it in the oven until it is crisp. While the bacon is cooking, I mix up a batch of biscuits and pop them into the oven too. The bacon comes out first and crisps as it cools. When the biscuits are done, I split them and stuff them with the bacon. Keep in mind it would not be a stretch to add a fried egg or scrambled egg in between. The contrast between the intensely flavored bacon and the soft, tender biscuits is brilliant. It's the best kind of breakfast: flavorful, comforting, and portable.

Make the Glazed Bacon:

Line a baking sheet with parchment paper and set a rack on top of the parchment. Lay the bacon slices out on the rack; they can be touching one another, since the bacon will shrink. Put the pan in the cold oven, and turn the oven temperature to 425°F (220°C). Put the strawberry jam and sriracha in a small bowl and stir them together with a small spoon. Set aside at room temperature. Once the oven comes to temperature, remove the bacon and spread the glaze over the slices, dividing it evenly among them. Return the bacon to the oven and cook until the bacon is a deep reddish brown color and dark brown around the edges, 12 to 15 minutes more.

Remove from the oven, transfer to a pan lined with paper towels, and keep in a warm spot. The bacon will crisp as it cools.

Make the Biscuits:

Spray a 9-inch round cake pan with nonstick cooking spray.

Put the flour, sugar, salt, and baking powder in a medium bowl and use a whisk to combine. Cut the butter into small dice and add it to the flour mixture. Use your fingers to work the butter into the flour until there are no lumps and the mixture looks sandy. Stir in the buttermilk. The mixture will be very sticky. Continue to work the mixture with your fingers until it comes together as a dough. Dump the dough onto a countertop and bring together into a large ball. Roll the ball into a 9-inch round, about 1 inch thick. Cut the dough into 8 triangles, like pie slices, and transfer them to the prepared cake pan, reassembling the round inside the pan. Bake until lightly browned, about 25 minutes.

Make the Biscuit Topping:

Melt the butter, honey, and cinnamon together in a small pot over low heat or in the microwave for about 30 seconds. Brush the biscuits with the honey butter, return them to the oven, and bake for 3 more minutes. Remove the biscuits from the pan and let cool for 5 minutes. Split the biscuits horizontally and stuff each with 1½ pieces of the glazed bacon. Serve immediately.

Sweet Potato Biscuits

2 medium sweet potatoes

½ **cup** / 113 grams unsalted butter, diced and chilled

3 **cups** / 450 grams all-purpose flour

1 **tablespoon** / 18 grams baking powder

2 **teaspoons** / 8 grams sugar

1¼ **teaspoons** / 7.5 grams fine sea salt

1 **teaspoon** / 5 grams baking soda

1 **cup plus 2 tablespoons** / 255 grams buttermilk, plus extra for brushing the biscuits

½ **cup** / 120 grams heavy cream

Baked sweet potatoes fill the kitchen with their sweet, earthy scent. When you cut one open, it has this luscious texture—tender and creamy, with soft fibers and slightly caramelized edges. I wanted to bring that flavor to a biscuit, making it hearty and aromatic but keeping the texture light and flaky. I happened to be making the Sausage Gravy (page 17) while rolling out the biscuits and absent-mindedly placed the punched-out biscuit trimmings in a baking dish filled with gravy. Something told me to bake this dish in the oven. It was a match made in heaven, and one you can easily replicate at home. You can also enjoy these biscuits on their own with pats of sweet butter melting into the nooks and sliding down over the crisp-tender edges.

Preheat the oven to 350°F (180°F). Line a baking sheet with parchment paper. Take two 8-inch pieces of aluminum foil, crumple each into a log, and form each into a doughnut shape. Place the foil doughnuts on a baking sheet and place the sweet potatoes on top of the foil. Bake for 45 minutes. Remove and cool. Peel and grate the sweet potatoes. Set aside.

Put the butter, flour, baking powder, sugar, salt, and baking soda in a large bowl, and work the butter in by hand until the mixture looks like coarse crumbs. Put the buttermilk, cream, and grated sweet potato in a bowl and stir to combine. Add the sweet potato mixture to the dry ingredients and fold in with a rubber spatula to combine.

Turn the dough out onto a lightly floured surface and dust the top with flour. Roll out the dough to a thickness of about ¾ inch. Use a 3-inch round cutter to punch out the dough, making 20 biscuits. Discard excess dough or save the trimmings to use with the Sausage Gravy (page 17). Arrange the biscuits on the prepared baking sheet, leaving 3 inches of space between each. Brush the tops of the biscuits with buttermilk. Bake for 10 minutes, rotate the sheet, and bake for 6 minutes more. Remove and cool for at least 5 minutes before serving.

Quick Breakfast Sausage and Sausage Gravy

SERVES 6 TO 8

QUICK SAUSAGE:

1 pound / 454 grams ground pork

½ medium onion, minced

1 teaspoon / 4 grams soy sauce

¼ teaspoon / 1 gram grated ginger
(I use a Microplane for this)

1 tablespoon / 14 grams bourbon

¾ teaspoon / 4.5 grams fine sea salt

SAUSAGE GRAVY:

5 tablespoons / 70 grams olive oil,
divided

½ medium onion, thinly sliced

½ bulb fennel, thinly sliced

1 pound / 454 grams small
button mushrooms

6½ ounces / 184 grams bacon,
cut into matchsticks

3 tablespoons / 26 grams
all-purpose flour

4 cups / 960 grams half-and-half

1½ teaspoons / 6 grams soy sauce

1 teaspoon / 5 grams malt vinegar

1 bay leaf

1 teaspoon / 1.5 grams chopped
fresh sage

Biscuits and gravy is a classic Southern breakfast dish. I like to make my own quick sausage because that way I know exactly what I'm feeding my children. It's easy, and the salt binds everything together so you don't need a lot of fillers to bulk it out. Sometimes I fry up sausage patties, and if I have extra time I like whipping up a batch of biscuits to serve alongside some rich, creamy gravy. Add a couple of poached eggs and you've got brunch.

Make the Quick Sausage:

Put the pork, minced onion, soy sauce, ginger, bourbon, and salt in a medium bowl and use a rubber spatula to mix everything together. The mixture will be slightly sticky. You want to mix it thoroughly until it forms a uniform sausage blend. Form the sausage into 1½-inch meatballs for gravy or 2-inch patties for frying, cover, and refrigerate for 2 hours before using. The sausage will keep for 3 days in the refrigerator, or you can freeze it for up to 2 weeks.

➔

Make the Sausage Gravy:

Add 2 tablespoons (28 grams) of the oil to a large sauté pan and set over medium-high heat. When the oil begins to shimmer, add the onion and fennel and cook, stirring, for 5 minutes, or until the vegetables soften and become aromatic. Add the mushrooms and turn the heat to high. Cook, stirring, until the mushrooms give off their liquid and then dry out again and start to brown. When the mushrooms are golden brown and tender, after 10 to 15 minutes, transfer the vegetables to a medium bowl. Wipe out the pan, add the bacon, and set it over medium heat. Let the bacon slowly render its fat, stirring occasionally, and then start to brown. Once the bacon is golden brown, transfer it to the bowl with the vegetables. Wipe out the pan and add the sausage. Brown the sausage and then transfer it to the bowl with a slotted spoon. Add the remaining 3 tablespoons (42 grams) oil and the flour to the pan. Set over medium heat and cook, stirring,

for 1 to 2 minutes, until the mixture smoothes out. Add the half-and-half, soy sauce, vinegar, bay leaf, and reserved meats and vegetables and bring to a simmer. Cook, stirring, until the mixture thickens. Remove the bay leaf. Stir in the sage and serve with Sweet Potato Biscuits (page 16) or Buttermilk Biscuits (page 116).

For baked biscuits and gravy, pour the gravy into a 9-by-13-inch baking dish and top with the cutout scraps of biscuit dough. Bake the casserole at 425°F (220°C) for 12 to 15 minutes, until the biscuits are golden brown and cooked through. Remove from the oven and let rest for 5 minutes before serving.

Coconut-Yogurt Parfaits

SERVES 4

**BLUEBERRY AND MADRAS
CURRY GRANOLA:**

¼ **cup** / 54 grams packed light
brown sugar

¼ **cup** / 60 grams maple syrup

2 **tablespoons** / 30 grams honey

½ **teaspoon** / 1 gram Madras
curry powder

½ **teaspoon** / 3 grams fine sea salt

1½ **cups** / 150 grams rolled oats

½ **cup** / 30 grams unsweetened
coconut flakes

½ **cup** / 50 grams slivered almonds

2 **tablespoons** / 20 grams sunflower seeds

1¾ **cups** / 275 grams dried blueberries

AERATED YOGURT:

½ **cup** / 120 grams coconut milk

2 **cups** / 570 grams Greek yogurt

¼ **cup plus 2 teaspoons** / 70 grams honey

⅛ **teaspoon** / 1.5 grams fine sea salt

Seeds from ½ vanilla bean

Fruit preserves, for serving

Fresh seasonal fruit, for serving

SPECIAL EQUIPMENT:

Whipped-cream canister and
2 NO₂ charges (optional)

I call this my commuter's breakfast. When I make the parfait, I layer everything into a mason jar. This way I can eat it with a spoon, screw the lid back on, and throw the empty jar into my bag to take back home. No muss, no fuss. It's also great for when you have a lot of houseguests or are putting on a holiday breakfast or brunch buffet. The combination of blueberries and curry is surprising, but if you think about classic Indian curries, they often incorporate fruits and nuts. They are also often made with coconut milk, and I add some coconut milk to Greek yogurt to lighten the texture. The resulting parfait has a great combination of textures and flavors to get your day off to a bright start.

**Make the Blueberry and Madras
Curry Granola:**

Preheat the oven to 325°F (165°F). Line a 12-by-18-inch baking sheet with parchment paper or a silicone baking mat.

Put the brown sugar, maple syrup, honey, curry powder, and salt in a small pot over medium heat. Bring to a simmer, stirring well to blend. Make sure that all the sugar has dissolved. Then remove from the heat.

Put the oats, coconut flakes, almonds, and sunflower seeds in a medium bowl. Pour the hot syrup over the dry ingredients and use a rubber spatula to gently fold everything together. Spread the granola on the prepared baking sheet and bake for 15 minutes. Rotate the pan and use a silicone spatula to gently mix the granola and then re-spread it evenly across the pan to promote even browning. Bake for another 15 minutes, and
➡

rotate the pan and mix again. Bake for another 8 to 10 minutes, until all of the granola is a deep golden brown. Immediately transfer the granola to a clean bowl and add the dried blueberries. Mix gently with a silicone spatula to blend. Cool completely before serving. The granola will keep in an airtight storage container or bag for several weeks.

Make the Aerated Yogurt:

Combine the coconut milk, yogurt, honey, salt, and vanilla in a large bowl. Cover the bowl with plastic wrap and let it sit overnight at room temperature to culture. The following morning, stir and refrigerate to chill.

Load the yogurt into a whipped-cream canister. Charge with 2 NO_2 charges. Divide the granola equally among 4 bowls. Place a large spoonful of preserves over the granola, layer some fruit over the preserves, and then discharge the whipped yogurt over the top of each one. Serve immediately. Alternatively, you could layer everything in small mason jars for breakfast on the go.

Granola Oatmeal with Bananas and Cream

SERVES 8

BANANA GRANOLA:

2 medium bananas

½ **cup plus 1 tablespoon** / 125 grams unsalted butter

2 pieces star anise

1 cinnamon stick

4½ **cups** / 454 grams rolled oats

½ **teaspoon** / 3 grams fine sea salt

⅔ **cup** / 125 grams packed light brown sugar

OATMEAL:

4 medium bananas

6½ **cups** / 1.5 kilograms almond milk

1 **teaspoon** / 6 grams fine sea salt

2 **cups** / 250 grams Banana Granola, plus extra for garnish

2 **cups** / 160 grams steel-cut oats

1 piece star anise

1 cinnamon stick

2 **cups** / 285 grams seasonal fresh berries or diced bananas

Fresh orange zest for garnish

SPECIAL EQUIPMENT:

Dehydrator (optional)

6-quart pressure cooker (optional)

As a kid, I would layer sugar and honey onto my bowl of oatmeal in the hope that the sugar rush would keep me going past homeroom. Now I know a little bit more about food, and I understand why the combination of instant oats and sugar never did take me very far. These days I use thick-cut rolled oats and steel-cut oatmeal in my porridge, and I toast them for extra flavor. The resulting oatmeal provides the perfect canvas for contrasting flavors and textures.

I begin the process by making homemade granola with dehydrated bananas. The granola is addictive, consisting of little chunks of crunchy goodness that disappear almost as fast as I can make it. I use it again in my pancake recipe on page 30, and you can eat it drenched with yogurt or milk for a quick breakfast on the run. For this oatmeal recipe, I also make a banana cream with cooked bananas and almond milk. I fold in the granola and some steel-cut oats before cooking it all in the pressure cooker. This is oatmeal as you've never had it before: Every bite is slightly different and the

flavors sing. It's a nourishing breakfast that will send your family out the door with full bellies and smiles on their faces.

Make the Banana Granola:
Peel the bananas and cut into medium dice. Lay the diced bananas out on a dehydrator tray or a baking sheet lined with a silicone baking mat. Dehydrate overnight in a dehydrator or in an oven set at the lowest temperature, 170°F (about 80°C). Remove from the dehydrator or oven when they are dry to the touch and still a little bit chewy, about 12 hours. Reserve in an airtight container.

Line a baking sheet with parchment paper or a silicone baking mat and set aside. Put the butter, star anise, and cinnamon in a medium saucepot over medium-low heat. Cook, stirring frequently, for 2 minutes, or until the butter foams and the spices become aromatic. Add the banana chips, rolled oats, and salt to the pot and cook, stirring often, until the oats are toasted and golden brown with a nutty aroma, 10 to 15 minutes. Add the brown sugar and

➲

continue to cook, stirring constantly, until the sugar melts and coats the oats. Pour the granola onto the prepared baking sheet to cool completely. Remove and discard the star anise pieces and cinnamon stick. The granola will keep in an airtight container for several weeks.

Make the Oatmeal:

Poke holes in the bananas with a cake tester or small skewer and put them on a microwave-safe plate. Microwave them on high power for 6 minutes. The bananas will be steaming hot and completely tender. Let them cool for 5 to 10 minutes, until you can comfortably scrape the cooked bananas into a blender.

Add the almond milk and salt. Turn the blender on low and increase the speed to medium-high for 30 seconds to puree them completely.

Set the rack that came with your pressure cooker inside it and add 1 inch of water. Transfer the banana puree to a bowl that fits inside your pressure cooker. Add the granola, oats, star anise, and cinnamon stick. Stir well and set on the rack inside the pressure cooker. Cook at high pressure for 10 minutes. Let the pressure dissipate naturally. Alternatively, you can put everything in a medium pot over medium-high heat, bring it to a simmer, reduce the heat to low, and cook, stirring occasionally so the oatmeal doesn't stick to the bottom of the pan, for 45 minutes.

Remove the bowl of oatmeal from the pressure cooker (if used). The oatmeal will look bumpy and slightly separated. Use a spatula to stir the mixture together until it smoothes out. Divide the oatmeal among 8 bowls. Top with a generous sprinkling of Banana Granola and fresh berries or diced bananas and fresh orange zest.

Country Ham Congee with Redeye Gravy

SERVES 8

CONGEE:

½ **cup** / 100 grams short-grain brown rice

½ **cup** / 85 grams brown basmati rice

2 **tablespoons** / 28 grams unsalted butter

1 medium onion, minced

3½ **ounces** / 100 grams country ham, minced

5¼ **cups** / 1.2 kilograms water

½ **teaspoon** / 3 grams fine sea salt

6 **tablespoons** / 30 grams finely grated Parmesan cheese (I use a Microplane for this)

REDEYE GRAVY:

11 **tablespoons** / 70 grams grated Parmesan cheese

1 **cup** / 240 grams brewed coffee

2 tablespoons / 28 grams unsalted butter

½ bunch scallions, chopped

Breakfast is the meal that sets you up for your day. Coffee is an automatic choice for me. There's a moment when I have a warm mug cradled in my hand and that rich aroma is curling through the air when everything is right with the world. Redeye gravy means a double shot of coffee, and what could be better than that?

Congee is Asian breakfast porridge, and it tends to be more savory than American oatmeal. The day I came up with this recipe I had two kinds of rice in the pantry, basmati and short-grain brown rice, and not quite enough of either one. So I blended them together, and the resulting porridge was revelatory. The brown rice added a great nutty flavor and the starch required to thicken the congee, while the basmati added a delicate texture and sweet, floral profile to the blend. Together they made this porridge something special.

When I make this I brown onions and small nuggets of country ham and then toast the rice grains in the rendered fat, scraping up all of those delicious caramelized bits, the *fond*, from the bottom of the pan. Then I simmer everything together. The finished rice porridge is studded with salty bits of ham and swimming in redeye gravy. This is a breakfast that wakes up all your senses.

Make the Congee:

Put the brown rice and basmati rice in a food processor and pulse for 1 minute. Set a large soup pot over medium heat and add the butter. Once the butter melts, add the onion. Cook, stirring frequently, for 5 minutes, or until the onion becomes tender and translucent. Add the ham and cook, stirring occasionally, until the meat is browned and caramelized, about 5 minutes. Add the processed rice and cook, stirring constantly, for 1 minute, or until it becomes fragrant. Add the water, salt, and Parmesan and stir, scraping the bottom as you go. Bring the mixture to a simmer. Turn the heat down to medium-low, cover, and cook undisturbed for 40 minutes, or until the rice is completely tender and the porridge has thickened.

Make the Redeye Gravy:

While the porridge is cooking, put the Parmesan in a small bowl and pour the hot coffee on top. Allow it to steep for 10 minutes. Strain the coffee into a small saucepot, discarding the cheese solids. Once the congee is almost finished, bring the Parmesan-infused coffee to a simmer and whisk in the butter.

Divide the porridge among 8 bowls, and top with Redeye Gravy and a sprinkling of chives. Serve immediately, with any extra gravy in a pitcher alongside. Top with a fried egg if you're feeling extra hungry.

Toad in
a Hole

SERVES 6

There are many variations of the hot ham, egg, and cheese sandwich, from the French croque madame to the American diner classic Monte Cristo sandwich. I like a good toad in a hole, American style, which means it's a sandwich with holes cut out of the middle and eggs fried in the hole. This sandwich is good at any time of day, whether it's first thing in the morning, midday brunch, breakfast for dinner, or a late-night snack.

It's my opinion that eggs are good all the time. The thing that makes this sandwich truly special is the Sorghum Sambal. It has a bright flavor with heat, acid, umami, and sweetness. I like to have a small puddle of sauce on my plate and swipe each bit through it. It pulls together the different elements: the sharp cheddar, the sweet ham, the soft eggs, and the gentle tang of the sourdough all accented by the complex hot sauce. It makes me hungry just writing about it.

Make the Sorghum Sambal:

Preheat the oven to 350°F (180°C). Line a 13-by-18-inch baking sheet with parchment paper.

Put the sorghum, sambal, soy sauce, and red wine vinegar in a medium bowl and whisk to combine. Reserve.

Make the Toad in a Hole:

Put 6 of the eggs, the egg yolks, cream, and salt in a large bowl and whisk until smooth. Transfer to a 9-by-13-inch baking dish and reserve. Lay out 6 slices of bread. Put 1 slice of cheddar cheese, followed by 2 pieces of ham, and topped with 1 more slice of cheddar, on each piece of bread and cover with another slice of bread to make 6 sandwiches.

Prepare 2 sandwiches at a time by soaking them in the egg mixture, then flipping them over 3 or 4 times until the bread becomes soft and spongy but is not falling apart. Transfer the sandwiches to a cutting board and use a 3-inch round cutter to punch out the center of each sandwich and separate that piece from the rest.

Put the butter in a microwave-safe measuring cup and microwave on high power for 1 minute, or until the butter separates. Reserve in a warm spot.

Set a large nonstick sauté pan over medium-high heat. Pour in enough melted butter off the top of the measuring cup to coat the bottom of the pan. Once the butter shimmers, put the sandwiches in the pan with their centers alongside. Crack an egg into the hole in the center of each sandwich.

Cook the sandwiches for about 2 minutes, until the bottoms are a deep golden brown. Carefully flip the sandwiches with the egg centers and then the middle pieces and cook for another 2 minutes, until the other side is golden brown as well. Remove from the heat, transfer the sandwich parts to the prepared baking sheet, and bake for 5 minutes.

Wipe out the pan and repeat the process 2 more times to make the remaining sandwiches. Arrange the sandwiches on a plate and drizzle the Sorghum Sambal on top.

Sometimes when I have larger slices of bread I will make larger sandwiches, with up to 3 eggs. These can be cut and shared or eaten by one hungry chef.

SORGHUM SAMBAL:

10½ **tablespoons** / 225 grams sorghum syrup or molasses

7 **teaspoons** / 42 grams sambal

1 **tablespoon** / 16 grams soy sauce

2 **tablespoons** / 28 grams red wine vinegar

TOAD IN A HOLE:

12 large eggs, divided

3 large egg yolks

2¼ **cups** / 500 grams heavy cream

¾ **teaspoon** / 4.5 grams fine sea salt

12 slices sourdough bread

12 slices sharp cheddar cheese

12 slices Black Forest ham

½ **cup** / 113 grams unsalted butter, sliced

Granola Pancakes

SERVES 4

When I was in middle school, my friend Malcolm Purdum and I would stage pancake-eating contests. It was just the two of us, and we would spend the morning carefully preparing stacks of pancakes to ensure a fair competition. Each one had to be the same size, and we experimented with various recipes and cooking methods to find the perfect pancake.

We learned that underdone cakes were pale and doughy, not fun to eat. Overcooked cakes were crispy and wouldn't properly absorb the butter and maple syrup with each bite. The best pancakes were light and fluffy, golden brown, with a tender crust that soaked up the toppings without falling apart. Looking back, it's easy to see how I became a chef—not only was I a competitive eater, but I also knew that each bite had to be consistently delicious.

It should come as no surprise that we are obsessed with pancakes at my house. We scrutinize every aspect of them, looking at how evenly they are browned, how much they rise on the griddle, and of course, how they taste. I love layering textures. It's so much fun to take something very familiar, like a pancake, and turn it at an angle to create something unusual and wonderful. There are myriad recipes for filled and stuffed pancakes out there. These granola pancakes are my personal favorite. The flavors are deep and rich and the recipe is very consistent. Every batch is a winner.

1 cup / 125 grams Banana Granola (page 23)

1 cup / 150 grams all-purpose flour

2 teaspoons / 12 grams baking powder

¼ teaspoon / 1.5 grams fine sea salt

1 large egg

2 tablespoons / 28 grams unsalted butter, melted, plus extra for serving

1 cup / 250 grams buttermilk

2 tablespoons / 40 grams maple syrup, plus extra for serving

Put the Banana Granola, flour, baking powder, and salt in a food processor and pulse about 8 times to grind. Put the egg, melted butter, buttermilk, and maple syrup in a large bowl and whisk to combine. Add the buttermilk mixture to the food processor and pulse until almost fully mixed. Do not overblend. Transfer the batter back to the bowl with a rubber spatula.

Preheat an electric griddle to 325°F (165°C), or set a heavy skillet over medium heat until a droplet of water skates across the surface. Ladle ¼ cup of batter onto the griddle for each pancake, being sure to leave a few inches around each one to facilitate flipping. Cook until the bottoms are set and bubbles appear on the surface of the batter, 2 to 3 minutes. Flip the pancakes and cook until they are a deep golden brown on both sides and the center feels firm when gently pressed with a fingertip, 2 to 3 more minutes. Serve hot off the griddle with maple syrup and butter alongside.

Loaded Hash Browns

SERVES 8

4 large russet potatoes

CHEESE SAUCE:

¾ **cup** / 180 grams evaporated milk

1½ **teapoons** / 9 grams sodium citrate (found in brewing-supply stores or online)

3½ **ounces** / 100 grams smoked Monterey Jack cheese, grated

5½ **ounces** / 160 grams pepper Jack cheese, grated

¼ **cup** / 56 grams unsalted butter, divided

1 small onion, diced

4½ **ounces** / 125 grams pepperoni, cut into matchsticks

8 **ounces** / 227 grams shiitake mushrooms, sliced

2 medium poblano peppers, peeled, seeded, and sliced

1 medium jalapeño pepper, peeled and thinly sliced

¼ **cup** / 56 grams Clarified Butter (page 57)

8 large eggs

Fine sea salt, for seasoning

Freshly ground black pepper, for seasoning

I have done my fair share of late-night eating at diners, bars, and greasy spoons. When you get out of work in the early hours of the morning, it just comes with the territory. On these occasions there are usually fried potatoes in some form on the table. Home fries, cheesy hash browns, French fries, stuffed potato skins, loaded tater tots, Irish nachos: You name it, and it's probably been done to a fried potato. It works because it almost always ends up tasting good, although the potatoes never seem to be crispy enough for me. When I took matters into my own hands, I parboiled thickly sliced potatoes to hydrate and set the starch. Then I gently mashed each slice so that it would have bumpy, uneven edges that would fry up super crisp. Once I had my crispy golden potatoes, I layered the top with pepperoni-fried vegetables and cheese sauce. These are truly loaded potatoes.

Peel the potatoes and slice them into rounds ½ inch thick. Put them in a large pot and cover them with cold water. Salt the water, stir, and set over high heat. Bring the water to a simmer and reduce the heat to medium-low. Simmer until the potatoes are tender, about 10 minutes.

Meanwhile, line a baking sheet with parchment paper. Drain the potatoes and lay them out on the prepared baking sheet, leaving 2 inches of space between each round. Cover with another sheet of parchment paper and let them cool for 10 minutes. Once cool enough to handle, use the palm of your hand to gently flatten the potato rounds so they spread a bit and have a bumpy, irregular surface. Let cool completely, cover, and refrigerate until ready to cook, up to 24 hours.

Make the Cheese Sauce:
Combine the evaporated milk and sodium citrate in a medium saucepot over medium heat and bring the mixture to a simmer. Slowly whisk in the cheeses until melted. Keep warm.

Set a large sauté pan over medium-low heat. Melt 2 tablespoons of the butter and add the onion. Cook, stirring occasionally, for 5 minutes, until the onions are soft and translucent. Transfer to a medium bowl and set the pan back over

❯

the heat. Add the pepperoni and cook, stirring occasionally, until it begins to render and release its fat into the pan, 5 to 7 minutes. Turn the heat up to medium-high and, when the fat begins to shimmer, add the mushrooms. Cook, stirring occasionally, until the mushrooms release their liquid and then dry out again and start to brown. Add the poblanos and jalapeño and sauté with the mushrooms until they are golden brown and tender. Return the onions to the pan and fold everything together. Keep warm.

Set another large sauté pan over medium-high heat and add the Clarified Butter. Once the butter is hot, put the potatoes in the pan and cook until they are a deep golden brown on the bottom, 5 to 7 minutes. Flip the potatoes and

cook until they are browned on the other side as well.

While the potatoes are cooking, set a large sauté pan over medium heat and add the remaining 2 tablespoons butter. Crack the eggs into a bowl, slide them into the pan, and season with salt and pepper. Reduce the heat to low, cover, and cook for 5 minutes, or until the whites are just set and the yolks are still soft. Uncover and remove from the heat.

When the potatoes are golden brown and crispy, transfer them to a large serving platter. Spread the mushroom-and-pepper mixture over the top. Slide the eggs onto the hash browns, and serve with a pitcher of warm Cheese Sauce alongside.

Crab Waffles Chesapeake

SERVES 6 TO 8, DEPENDING ON THE SIZE OF YOUR WAFFLE IRON

OUR BAY SEASONING BLEND:

1 dried shiitake mushroom

1 tablespoon / 7 grams black peppercorns

4 bay leaves

1 tablespoon / 3.5 grams coriander seeds

⅛ teaspoon / 1 gram yellow mustard seeds

½ teaspoon / 1 gram red pepper flakes

½ teaspoon /1 gram piment d'Espelette

2 teaspoons / 2.5 grams onion powder

2¼ teapoons / 6 grams paprika

2½ teaspoons / 7.5 grams celery seeds

½ teaspoon / 1 gram garlic powder

2 tablespoons plus 1 teaspoon /
42 grams fine sea salt

WAFFLE BATTER:

½ cup / 113 grams lukewarm water

1 package / 8.75 grams instant yeast

1 tablespoon / 12 grams sugar

2½ cups / 375 grams all-purpose flour

½ teaspoon / 3 grams fine sea salt

¼ teaspoon / 1.25 grams baking soda

2 cups / 480 grams buttermilk

2 large eggs

2 teaspoons / 8 grams vanilla extract

½ cup / 113 grams unsalted butter,
melted and cooled

BEER-NAISE:

1½ cups / 350 grams pilsner
or ale of your choice

¼ cup / 55 grams malt vinegar

1 medium shallot, thinly sliced

4 sprigs tarragon

1 cup / 225 grams unsalted butter, sliced

3 large egg yolks, room temperature

2 teaspoons / 6 grams Our Bay
Seasoning Blend

½ teaspoon / 3 grams fine sea salt

Juice of 1 lemon

Tabasco sauce, for seasoning

1 pound / 454 grams jumbo lump crabmeat,
picked through for shells and cartilage

6 to 8 poached eggs, for serving

Warm maple syrup, for serving

I'd been thinking about a Maryland eggs Chesapeake, so I changed the English muffin to a waffle. It's bigger and lighter, with the perfect built-in holes to catch runny egg yolks and creamy sauce. It made perfect sense to me.

Make the Our Bay Seasoning Blend:
Place all of the ingredients except the salt in a spice grinder and grind to a fine powder. Transfer to a bowl and whisk in the salt. If you have weighed the ingredients correctly, the mixture should be in between orange and brown in color and will be so delicious you'll want to put it on everything. Our Bay can be stored in an airtight container at room temperature for up to 1 year.

Make the Waffle Batter:
Put the water, yeast, and salt in a measuring cup and stir to combine. Put the flour, salt, and baking soda in a medium bowl and whisk to blend. Add the buttermilk, eggs, vanilla, and yeast mixture and whisk
➡

until just combined. Whisk in the melted butter. Cover with plastic wrap and rest at room temperature for 1½ to 2 hours, until it doubles in size.

Make the Beer-naise:
Put the beer, vinegar, shallot, and tarragon in a medium saucepot set over high heat. Bring to a simmer, adjust the heat to maintain a simmer, and reduce by half, about 15 minutes. Strain the mixture into a measuring cup.

Put the butter in a small pot set over medium heat and melt, stirring occasionally. Once the butter has melted, remove from the heat and keep in a warm spot on the stove. Put the egg yolks into a blender and start on medium speed. Blend until the yolks turn pale yellow and the outside of the blender feels warm. Drizzle in the beer reduction and puree until it is fully absorbed. Drizzle in the melted butter and puree until fully absorbed. Add the Our Bay Seasoning and salt, and then add lemon juice and Tabasco sauce to taste. Turn off the blender and transfer the sauce to a bowl. The Beer-naise sauce should be luscious and fluffy. Keep warm until ready to use.

Make the Waffles:
Fold half of the crabmeat into the waffle batter. Cook in a waffle iron according to the manufacturer's directions. Top each waffle with a spoonful of the remaining lump crabmeat, a poached egg, and Beer-naise, and serve with warm maple syrup alongside.

I think all chefs have a deep affection for soups and sandwiches because they are meals that we can eat standing up in our kitchens. They are also perfect for those late-night meals after work, when we are starving but don't want anything too heavy or complicated. As a kid, I watched my father layer potato chips into his sandwich and I wondered why he did that, when everyone else simply ate their chips on the side. The first time I tried sinking my teeth through layers of soft bread, crispy chips, creamy mayo, and tender lunch meats, I understood. It's all about the play of textures. In all of my recipes, I take to heart that philosophy of building a dish through a combination of textures and flavors, and this is especially true for soups and sandwiches, because this is where I learned the lesson first.

Soups and Sandwiches

Maryland Oyster Stew

SERVES 4

24 fresh oysters in the shell

½ **cup** / 113 grams
unsalted butter, sliced

1 medium sweet onion, minced

4 cloves garlic, minced

10 flat-leaf parsley stems,
finely chopped

⅓ **cup** / 160 grams crème fraîche

2 **cups** / 480 grams heavy cream

1½ **tablespoons** / 21 grams fresh
lemon juice

1 **teaspoon** / 5 grams extra-virgin
olive oil

1 **teaspoon** / 5 grams vinegar-based
hot sauce, like Tabasco or Crystal

2 **teaspoons** / 6 grams Our Bay
Seasoning Blend (page 35)

Fine sea salt, for seasoning

Our Bay Seasoning for garnish

Chopped dill for garnish

It should come as no surprise that the quality of your oysters will make all the difference in this stew. I like to use Rappahannock oysters from the Chesapeake region in my restaurants. For this stew, I prefer the Olde Salts. As the name indicates, they have a pronounced briny flavor, which works well to flavor the stew. Traditional oyster stew recipes often have you puree the oysters into the soup for flavor. I shuck the oysters (you can ask your fishmonger to do this, but make sure he or she saves every drop of liquid) and then use the oyster liquor as the base for a creamy, aromatic broth. Then I pour the hot broth over the oysters and they barely cook through. The texture of the oysters firms up a little bit but still remains silky, soft, and juicy. With oysters at their peak of texture and flavor, this dish is totally unforgettable.

Scrub the outer oyster shells in ice-cold water to remove sand and grit. Rinse them well. Hold an oyster over a bowl to catch the liquor. Insert an oyster knife into the rear hinge of a shell and pry it open. Cut off the top and then slide the knife underneath the oyster to cut the muscle holding it in the shell. Put the oyster in a clean bowl. Repeat with all of the oysters.

As you shuck, the oyster liquor will fall into the bowl you are shucking over. Once you are done, thoroughly check the shucked oysters for any small bits of shell. Then strain the oyster liquor through a fine-mesh sieve into a measuring cup.

Put the butter in a small saucepot over medium-high heat and, as it melts, begin whisking it continuously until you smell hazelnuts in the air and see the milk solids turn golden brown. This process should take no more than 3 minutes after the butter melts.

Add the onion, garlic, and parsley stems and cook, stirring, until the vegetables are tender and translucent, 5 to 7 minutes. Transfer to a blender and add the oyster liquor and crème fraîche. Puree until smooth, about 1 minute on high speed.

Strain the onion puree through a fine-mesh sieve into a clean saucepot. Add the heavy cream and set over medium heat. Bring to a bare simmer. Immediately add the lemon juice, olive oil, hot sauce, and Our Bay Seasoning. Taste and add salt to taste; the salinity of the stew will depend on your oyster liquor.

Warm 4 shallow soup bowls and put 6 oysters in each one. Divide the hot stew among the bowls; the heat from the stew will warm the oysters and cook them through. Garnish each bowl with Our Bay and chopped dill and serve immediately.

Stew of Blue Crabs and Shells

SERVES 6 TO 8

SHELLFISH COURT BOUILLON:

1 pound / 454 grams unsalted butter, diced

3 pounds / 1.36 kilograms blue crab bodies, meat reserved (12 crabs)

3 red onions, thinly sliced

3½ quarts / 3.15 kilograms Vegetable Stock (page 92, or store-bought) or water

Juice of 2 lemons, about ¼ cup / 56 grams

3 shallots, thinly sliced

8 cloves garlic, halved, germ removed

1 jalapeño pepper, charred and peeled

1 bunch tarragon

1 tablespoon / 9 grams Our Bay Seasoning Blend (page 35)

CRAB STEW:

4 quarts / 3.6 kilograms Shellfish Court Bouillon

5 tablespoons plus 2 teaspoons / 85 grams double-concentrated tomato paste (sold in tubes)

¼ cup / 56 grams unsalted butter

4 teaspoons / 20 grams balsamic vinegar

1 tablespoon / 16 grams soy sauce

1 teaspoon / 6 grams fine sea salt

2 teaspoons / 6 grams Our Bay Seasoning Blend (page 35)

⅓ teaspoon / 0.8 gram Aleppo pepper

1 cup / 240 grams heavy cream

1 pound / 454 grams small shell pasta

1 pound / 454 grams jumbo lump crabmeat, picked through for shells and cartilage

2 tablespoons / 28 grams dry sherry

SPECIAL EQUIPMENT:

Pressure cooker (optional)

This is a playful dish. My wife, Jennifer, loves Maryland crab soup. She orders it everywhere we go, so I took it as a challenge to make a great crab soup of my own. I've merged the idea of a traditional tomato-based Maryland crab soup with a classic French bisque. I cook the pasta shells in the pot with the soup and the starch from the shells helps thicken the broth, while the sherry gives it richness and complexity. I've found that the pasta takes longer than usual to cook this way, so cut into a shell to make sure they are tender before serving. I like to bring this to the table in the cooking vessel with a loaf of crusty bread and a simple green salad.

Make the Shellfish Court Bouillon:
Put the butter in a large soup pot set over medium heat. Once the butter melts, add the crab bodies and red onions. Cook, stirring, for 20 minutes to toast the shells.

Add the stock, lemon juice, shallots, garlic, jalapeño, tarragon, and Our Bay Seasoning. Bring the mixture to a simmer, reduce the heat to low, and cook for 1 hour.

Make the Crab Stew:
Strain the Shellfish Court Bouillon through a fine-mesh sieve and put it in a pressure cooker with the tomato paste, butter, balsamic vinegar, soy sauce, salt, Our Bay Seasoning, and Aleppo pepper and stir to blend. Cook at high pressure for 15 minutes, and let the pressure reduce naturally. Alternatively, put everything in a large pot set over high heat and bring to a simmer. Reduce the heat to low and cook, skimming occasionally, for 1 hour.

Strain the soup through a fine-mesh sieve into a large pot. (The soup base can be chilled at this point and finished the next day.) Add the heavy cream and set the pot over medium-high heat. Bring to a boil and add the pasta. Cook until the shells are al dente, usually 16 to 18 minutes. Taste one to be sure. Add the reserved and lump crabmeat and the sherry and gently fold them into the stew. Serve immediately.

Corn Chowder

PIMENTÓN OIL:

3 tablespoons / 42 grams light olive oil

1 tablespoon / 9 grams pimentón

CORN CREAM:

19 ears corn

6 cups / 1.44 kilograms heavy cream

6 cups / 1.56 kilograms whole milk

1¾ teaspoons / 10.5 grams fine sea salt

CHOWDER:

2 tablespoons / 28 grams light olive oil

5 ears corn, kernels only

4 leeks, cut into small dice

2 medium russet potatoes, peeled and cut into small dice

1 medium onion, cut into small dice

1 rutabaga, peeled and cut into small dice

1 celeriac, peeled and cut into small dice

2 cloves garlic, minced

½ cup / 113 grams unsalted butter, diced

2¼ teaspoons / 13.5 grams fine sea salt

4 ounces / 113 grams crumbled cotija cheese

In August, as you drive along Maryland's eastern shore, you can see fields of Silver Queen corn waving in the breeze. It's some of the best corn available in the region. I love the sweet, juicy flavor of fresh corn, and here I've paired it with earthy, smoky notes of *pimentón*. Otherwise known as Spanish smoked paprika, *pimentón* is a favorite ingredient of mine. The Spanish peppers are harvested, spread out on racks, and then dried over smoldering fires. The peppers absorb the flavor of the wood smoke, and once they are completely dry they are stone-ground into a flavorful powder. *Pimentón* is the perfect complement to the lighter sweetness of the corn and gives the soup a rich, smoky flavor that highlights the natural sweetness of the Silver Queen. This soup can be served warm or cold and is perfect for hot summer afternoons or those first chilly fall evenings.

Make the Pimentón Oil:

Put the oil and *pimentón* in a small pot set over medium heat. Cook, stirring, until the mixture comes to a simmer. Reduce the heat and toast the spice in the oil for 3 minutes, stirring constantly. Strain the oil through a fine-mesh sieve and let it cool to room temperature. Reserve until ready to use.

Make the Corn Cream:

Cut all of the kernels away from the ears of corn. Put the kernels and the cobs in a stockpot and add the cream, milk, and salt. Set over medium-high heat and bring to a simmer. Reduce the heat to low and cook for 20 minutes.

Use a pair of tongs to remove and discard the cobs. Puree the cream and corn kernels in batches in a blender until completely smooth. Be sure the lid is on securely before starting the blender and open the lid carefully afterward to avoid getting burned by the steam. Strain the Corn Cream through a fine-mesh sieve and reserve.

Make the Soup:

Set a large soup pot over medium-high heat and add the oil. When it begins to shimmer, add the corn, leeks, potatoes, onion, rutabaga, and celeriac and cook, stirring, for about 10 minutes, or until the vegetables are tender and translucent. Add the garlic and cook for another 2 minutes, or until it has softened and become aromatic. Add the Corn Cream and bring it to a simmer. Reduce the heat to low and whisk in the butter and the salt. Portion the soup into bowls and sprinkle some crumbled cotija cheese over the top. Drizzle each bowl with a teaspoon of Pimentón Oil and serve immediately.

Tomato and Watermelon Gazpacho

SERVES 6 TO 8

WATERMELON GRANITA:

½ large seedless watermelon
(about **6½ pounds** / 3 kilograms)

¼ **cup** / 50 grams sugar

1¾ **teaspoons** / 10.5 grams fine
sea salt

GAZPACHO:

1 (**28-ounce** / 794-gram)
can San Marzano tomatoes

3 red bell peppers, seeds and
stems discarded, roughly chopped

2 cucumbers, peeled, seeded,
roughly chopped

1 bulb fennel, roughly chopped

1 red onion, roughly chopped

1 jalapeño pepper, seeds and
stem discarded, roughly chopped

1 clove garlic, germ removed

Juice of 1 lime

1 teaspoon / 6 grams fine sea salt

1 teaspoon / 3 grams smoked paprika

1 tablespoon / 14 grams red wine vinegar

1 tablespoon / 14 grams sherry vinegar

SPECIAL EQUIPMENT:

Meat grinder or grinding attachment
for stand mixer

Tomatoes and watermelon are in season at the same time, and so they felt like a natural match. I grind the tomatoes and vegetables through a meat grinder to get a uniform chunky texture in the soup. It breaks everything up and allows the different flavors to merge and bloom as the soup marinates. I like to serve this soup in mason jars. It's perfect for making ahead, and if you have a crowd you can have the gazpacho ready to go in the jars and just add a scoop of the granita at the last second.

Make the Watermelon Granita:
Roughly chop up the red inner flesh of the melon. You should end up with about 4¾ pounds of fruit. Put the watermelon, sugar, and salt in a blender and puree until smooth. You may need to do this in batches. If so, mix everything together in a large pitcher or bowl when you're done.

Pour the watermelon puree into a large baking dish, cover, and put in the freezer. After 2 hours, scrape the semi-frozen watermelon with a spoon. It will be more frozen on the outside edges and more liquid toward the center. Just mix everything together. Cover and return to the freezer for another 2 hours.

Use a fork to scrape the granita again, slowly loosening all of the frozen particles from the edges and mixing everything together. Cover and return to the freezer for another 2 hours. It should be mostly frozen by now.

Use a fork again to scrape everything into small particles and mix it together. If it's not completely frozen, repeat the process one more time. The granita can be kept in a covered container in the freezer for up to 5 days.

Make the Gazpacho:
Pass the tomatoes through a food mill to break them up and remove the seeds. Grind the tomatoes, red peppers, cucumbers, fennel, red onion, jalapeño, and garlic through a meat grinder with a medium die. Add the lime juice, salt, and smoked paprika, and gently mix everything together. Cover and refrigerate overnight, or up to 24 hours.

Add the red wine vinegar and sherry vinegar and stir to blend. Taste to check seasoning, and add a touch more salt if necessary. Ladle the gazpacho into bowls and put a generous scoop of watermelon granita in the center of each one. Serve immediately.

Sandwich Bread

7 ounces / 200 grams water, room temperature

¼ cup / 50 grams sugar

2 tablespoons / 18 grams active dry yeast

¼ teaspoon / 2 grams molasses

4 large egg yolks

3⅓ cups / 500 grams bread flour

2 teaspoons / 12 grams fine sea salt

5 tablespoons plus 1 teaspoon / 75 grams light olive oil

1 large egg

2 tablespoons / 28 grams whole milk

FOR HAMBURGER BUNS:

½ cup / 64 grams sesame seeds

FOR HOAGIE ROLLS:

¼ cup / 56 grams unsalted butter

Maldon sea salt, for sprinkling

I use this one bread dough to make all of my different sandwich breads. I developed the recipe when I was the chef at Charlie Palmer Steak in Washington, DC, and I've been using it ever since. It's an adaptation of traditional French *pain de mie*. The bread is soft, tender, slightly sweet, and endlessly versatile. When I use it for hamburger buns and various rolls, it bakes up with a thin, crisp crust and a tender crumb, just what you want before getting to the good stuff inside.

Put the water, sugar, yeast, and molasses in a large bowl and whisk to combine. Cover and let sit in a warm spot in the kitchen for 10 minutes.

Put the egg yolks in a small bowl and whisk until smooth.

Mix the flour and salt in a stand mixer with the dough hook on low speed. Add the egg yolks, oil, and yeast mixture, and once it comes together and forms a dough, let it knead on medium speed for 10 minutes. Transfer to a greased bowl, cover with either a towel or plastic wrap, and let it rest at room temperature until it doubles in size, 60 to 90 minutes.

For Hamburger Buns:
Line at least 2 baking sheets with parchment paper and set aside. Use a scale to portion the dough into 75-gram balls. Put one piece of dough on a clean countertop and cup it with one or both hands, depending on the size of your hands. Press down gently and roll the balls in small (2- to 4-inch) circles, without lifting them, to stretch the tops and seal the bottoms, until they are smooth and nicely rounded. Place each ball on a prepared baking sheet, leaving 2 to 3 inches between each roll. Cover lightly with plastic wrap and let them proof at room temperature until they have doubled in size, about 30 minutes in a warm kitchen. They will look puffy.

Preheat the oven to 350°F (180°C).

Break the egg into a small bowl and add the milk. Whisk with a fork to blend.

Brush all of the hamburger buns with the egg wash and generously sprinkle the tops with the sesame seeds. You may not use them all. Bake for 7 minutes, rotate the pans, and bake for an additional 7 minutes, or until the buns are golden brown and cooked through.

For Hot Dog Buns:

Portion and shape the dough into 1½-ounce (45-gram) logs. Place each one into the well of a split-top baking pan or onto a baking sheet lined with parchment paper. Cover loosely with plastic wrap and let the dough rise until doubled in size, about 30 minutes in a warm kitchen. They will look puffy.

Break the egg into a small bowl and add the milk. Whisk with a fork to blend.

Brush with the egg wash. Bake at 350°F (180°C) for a total of 12 minutes, rotating them after 6 minutes, or until the hot dog buns are a deep golden brown. Let rest for 5 minutes in the pan, and then turn the buns out onto a wire rack to cool. Let them cool completely before breaking them apart into individual buns.

For Hoagie Rolls:

Portion the dough into 3½-ounce (100-gram) pieces. Without adding extra flour, use the palm of your hand to roll each portion into a sphere, and then use both palms to gently roll each sphere into a 6-inch log. Line 3 baking sheets with parchment paper and evenly space 4 logs on each pan. Cover loosely with plastic wrap and let rise until doubled in size, about 30 minutes in a warm kitchen. They will look puffy.

Melt the butter, brush over the rolls, and sprinkle with Maldon sea salt. Bake at 350°F (180°C) for 13 to 15 minutes, rotating the pans after 10 minutes, or until the rolls are golden brown. Remove from the oven and let cool on the baking sheets for 5 minutes. Transfer to wire racks and cool completely before using.

Chili Dogs with Aerated Cheese Sauce

MAKES 6 CHILI DOGS

My *chef de cuisine* at Volt, Graeme, is from Rochester, New York, and he introduced me to Zweigle's Pop Open hot dogs. They are stuffed into natural casings that pop open when you cook them. The hot dogs are seasoned with sweet spices and have great flavor and a smooth, creamy interior. Add some Texas chili and aerated cheese sauce and you have a sandwich that is delicious, messy, and fun to eat.

AERATED CHEESE SAUCE:

3½ cups / 900 grams whole milk

2 tablespoons / 36 grams sodium citrate (available from brewing-supply stores or online)

1 teaspoon / 6 grams fine sea salt

1 pound / 454 grams pepper Jack cheese, shredded

1 pound / 454 grams white cheddar cheese, shredded

CHILI DOGS:

6 Zweigle's Pop Open Texas Brand hot dogs

1 tablespoon / 14 grams rice bran oil or olive oil

Hot Dog Buns (page 48) or store-bought

Unsalted butter, for the buns

Chili with the Fixings (page 208)

½ bunch scallions, thinly sliced

Freshly ground black pepper, for seasoning

SPECIAL EQUIPMENT:

Whipped-cream canister and 2 NO₂ charges (optional)

Make the Aerated Cheese Sauce:
Put the milk, sodium citrate, and salt in a medium saucepot set over medium-high heat and bring to a simmer. Turn the heat down to low and whisk in the pepper Jack and cheddar cheeses a handful at a time. Once all of the cheese has been melted and incorporated, strain the sauce through a fine-mesh sieve. Pour half into a whipped-cream canister and charge twice with NO_2. Keep warm in a water bath set at 285°F (140°C). Alternatively, if you don't have a whipped-cream canister, you can simply spoon the warm cheese sauce onto the hot dogs without aerating it.

Make the Chili Dogs:
In a cast-iron pan set over medium-high heat, sear the hot dogs using the oil. Sear all sides until the hot dogs split or pop open. Spread the outside of each bun with butter and toast in a nonstick pan over medium heat. Stuff the hot dogs into the buns, and cover each dog with chili, Aerated Cheese Sauce, and sliced scallions. Sprinkle with black pepper.

Bryan's Burger

HAMBURGERS:

3½ pounds / 1.6 kilograms boneless chuck

8 ounces / 227 grams pepperoni, sliced

1¼ teaspoons / 7.5 grams fine sea salt

1 tablespoon / 14 grams light olive oil, divided

2 tablespoons / 28 grams unsalted butter, divided

SERVE WITH:

Hamburger Buns (page 48) or store-bought, griddled or toasted (optional)

8 slices pepper Jack cheese

8 slices Monterey Jack cheese

Fried eggs (optional)

Sliced avocado

SPECIAL EQUIPMENT:

Meat grinder or meat-grinding attachment for stand mixer

A great burger starts with good meat. The chuck shoulder is made up of a perfect blend of muscles and fat that grinds into an ideal burger. I enjoy the process of breaking down a chuck shoulder, separating the muscles, and removing any sinew or silverskin. If you follow the lines in the meat, it is pretty easy to do. That said, I understand that not everyone has the time or the inclination to butcher his or her own meat, and so this recipe calls for boneless chuck. The important thing here is grinding your own meat. The flavor is so much fresher and deeper—the burgers really taste like the beef they are made of. Try it once and you'll understand why I recommend that you do this; and you'll make a point of doing it again, because it tastes so good.

Cut the boneless chuck into pieces that will fit into your meat grinder. Grind the meat through a ⅛-inch or ¼-inch die into a medium bowl. Divide the meat in half and put half of the meat through the grinder again, with the pepperoni. Season the ground meat mixture with the salt and mix gently with your hands. Form into eight 8-ounce (225-gram) patties that are slightly larger than the buns and slightly indented in the centers, because they will shrink slightly and expand in the middle as they cook. Lay the prepared hamburgers on a large plate or baking sheet as you finish them.

Set a large sauté pan over medium-high heat and add 1½ teaspoons of the oil. Tilt the pan to coat the bottom. When the oil begins to shimmer but not smoke, add 4 of the hamburger patties. You can do this in 2 batches or you can get 2 skillets going at the same time. Care-ully flip the burgers every 30 seconds, cooking them for a total of 3 minutes. After 6 flips, add 1 tablespoon of the butter to the pan and baste the burgers continuously for about 30 seconds, until the butter begins to brown and stops foaming.

Remove the burgers from the pan and put each on the bottom of a bun. Return the pan to medium heat and add avocado slices. Cook 2—3 minutes until the bottoms are golden brown; flip the slices and cook 2—3 minutes until the tops are golden brown as well. Transfer to a plate lined with a paper towel to drain. Top each burger with 1 slice of the pepper Jack and 1 slice of the Monterey Jack. Add a fried egg, if using, and a layer of avocado slices. Add the top of the bun and serve immediately with condiments like ketchup, mustard, and mayo alongside.

Lobster Rolls

MAKES 6 TO 8 LOBSTER ROLLS

TRINITY SAUCE:

1 cup / 200 grams mayonnaise
(I prefer Duke's)

1 tablespoon / 20 grams sriracha

1 teaspoon / 4 grams soy sauce

½ teaspoon / 2.5 grams fish sauce

⅛ teaspoon / 0.5 gram sesame oil

1 tablespoon / 2 grams finely sliced
fresh chives

1 tablespoon / 2 grams chopped
fresh cilantro leaves

LOBSTER SALAD:

8½ quarts / 8 kilograms water

¾ cup / 165 grams white vinegar

½ cup plus 2 tablespoons / 160 grams
fine sea salt

¼ cup / 45 grams Our Bay Seasoning
Blend (page 35)

6 (1½-pound / 680-gram) lobsters

3 celery ribs, peeled and thinly sliced

½ head fennel, cut into small dice

¾ cup / 165 grams Trinity Sauce

1½ tablespoons / 21 grams fresh
lemon juice

6 to 8 Hot Dog Buns (page 48)
or store-bought, for serving

Unsalted butter, room temperature,
for griddling the buns

Potato chips, for serving

I've never been to Maine for a lobster roll, but the ones I've had in other places have been so good that I knew I needed to make one myself. Perfectly cooked lobster meat is plump and juicy, tender but firm, and slightly chewy. The trick to this recipe is soaking the lobster meat in the cooled cooking liquid to give it an extra burst of flavor and to rinse away any albumen from the surface, leaving nothing behind but sweet, briny lobster meat.

Make the Trinity Sauce:

Put all of the ingredients in a medium bowl and stir well to blend. Transfer to a covered container and refrigerate until needed. Trinity Sauce will keep for up to 10 days in the refrigerator.

Cook the Lobster:

Put the water, vinegar, salt, and Our Bay Seasoning in a large stockpot and bring to a boil. Remove from the heat and submerge the lobsters in the pot. Bring the mixture back to a simmer and cook for 12 minutes. Take out the lobsters and transfer to a large platter to cool. Reserve the cooking liquid.

Once they are cool enough to handle, use kitchen shears and a lobster cracker to remove all of the meat. Put the lobster meat in a large container and pour over just enough of the cooking liquid to cover the meat. Let the lobster meat macerate in the cooking liquid for 30 minutes.

Make the Lobster Salad:

Drain the lobster meat, pat dry, cut into bite-size pieces (roughly 1-inch dice), and put in a large bowl. Add the celery, fennel, Trinity Sauce, and lemon juice. Mix gently with a spatula to blend. Reserve the lobster salad in the refrigerator.

Prepare the Lobster Rolls:

Split open the hot dog buns and spread butter on the insides of the buns. Set a large nonstick pan over medium-high heat. Once the pan is hot, place the buns, butter side down, in the pan and cook for 3 to 5 minutes, until the insides of the buns are crisp and golden brown. You may need to do this in batches. Transfer to a large platter and fill generously with lobster salad. Serve with potato chips alongside.

Maryland Crab Cake Sandwiches

MAKES 6 SANDWICHES

CRAB CAKES:

2 pounds / 908 grams jumbo lump crabmeat

4 ounces / 113 grams mayonnaise (I prefer Duke's)

2 teaspoons / 12 grams Dijon mustard

1 tablespoon / 9 grams Our Bay Seasoning Blend (page 35)

2½ teaspoons / 10 grams Worcestershire sauce

3¾ teaspoons / 20 grams fresh lemon juice

½ teaspoon / 3 grams fine sea salt

6 drops Tabasco sauce

4 scallions, thinly sliced

2 large eggs

1 cup / 70 grams cracker crumbs

TARTAR SAUCE:

1 tablespoon / 14 grams grapeseed or olive oil

¼ cup / 35 grams celery, cut into small dice

¼ cup / 35 grams fennel, cut into small dice

¼ cup / 35 grams red onion, cut into small dice

¼ teaspoon / 1.5 grams fine sea salt, plus extra for seasoning

1 cup / 200 grams mayonnaise (I prefer Duke's)

¾ teaspoon / 4.5 grams whole-grain mustard

1 cup / 145 grams dill pickles, cut into small dice

½ cup / 60 grams capers, rinsed of brine, roughly chopped

¼ teaspoon / 1 gram soy sauce

¼ teaspoon / 1.5 grams red wine vinegar

1 tablespoon / 4 grams chopped fresh flat-leaf parsley

1½ teaspoons / 2 grams chopped fresh tarragon leaves

1½ teaspoons / 2 grams chopped fennel fronds (feathery green leaves of fennel)

Freshly ground black pepper, for seasoning

CLARIFIED BUTTER:

1 cup / 225 grams unsalted butter

Hamburger Buns (page 48) or store-bought

Unsalted butter, for griddling the buns

SERVE WITH:

Iceberg lettuce leaves

Sliced tomatoes

Crispy bacon strips

Potato chips

In blue crab country, every chef's challenge is making a crab cake with the least amount of filler that still holds together. The key to my crab cakes is forming them and then letting them chill for several hours before attempting to cook them. The second component of this sandwich is the tartar sauce. I make mine chunky with vegetables for texture and flavor and I add lots of fresh herbs for their bright, green flavors. I love a good sandwich, but these cakes are also great served on their own with a dollop of tartar sauce and a great salad. They are delicate and tender and stuffed full of sweet crabmeat.

Form the Crab Cakes:

Put the crabmeat in a bowl and gently pick through it to find and remove any bits of shells and cartilage. Try not to break it up too much as you do this. Put all of the remaining ingredients except for the cracker crumbs in a medium bowl and whisk to blend. Add the crabmeat one-third at a time and use a rubber spatula to gently fold it in. Be careful to keep the crabmeat in nice big chunks.

Use an ice cream scoop, a ring mold, or a scale to portion the mixture into six 6- to 7-ounce (170- to 198-gram) cakes. (You can also form the mixture into 10 individual 4-ounce [113-gram] cakes and skip the sandwich-making.)

Pour the cracker crumbs into a casserole dish or small baking sheet. Put 1 or 2 cakes in the pan, press them gently into the crumbs, and then flip them over and press them gently into the crumbs on the other side. Gently press crumbs along the sides if they are not already covered. Transfer the cakes to a clean baking sheet and continue coating the remainder in crumbs. At this point, the crab cakes can be covered and refrigerated until you are ready to cook them, up to 6 hours.

Make the Tartar Sauce:

Put the grapeseed oil in a small to medium sauté pan set over medium heat. As soon as the oil begins to shimmer, add the celery, fennel, and onion and season with the salt. Cook, stirring, until the vegetables are tender and translucent but have not started to color. Remove from the heat and let cool slightly.

In a medium bowl, combine the mayonnaise, mustard, dill pickles, capers, soy sauce, red wine vinegar, parsley, tarragon, and fennel fronds. Season to taste with salt and a generous amount of pepper. After the vegetables have cooled, fold them into the tartar sauce. Any extra tartar sauce can be stored in an airtight container in the refrigerator for up to 1 week.

Make the Clarified Butter:
Cut the butter into slices and put them into a 2-cup or larger microwave-safe measuring cup. The butter will rise as it melts and the container needs to be large enough to hold it without being too wide. Set the microwave for 2 minutes, and after 1 minute keep an eye on the butter until you see it melt completely and begin to rise in the container. Stop the microwave when the butter begins rising; there should be a layer of foam on top of the melted butter. If the butter has not melted completely, let the foam subside and then microwave it again for 15 to 30 seconds, without opening the door of the microwave, until it has completely melted and is rising again. Let the butter cool for 5 minutes in the microwave before removing the container. Skim off and discard the foam and transfer to a clean container. Clarified Butter can be used immediately or refrigerated in a covered container until needed, for up to several months.

Cook the Crab Cakes:
Use a large frying pan with a flat bottom. Heat the Clarified Butter slowly over medium heat to 325°F (165°C); use a thermometer to check. If you don't have a thermometer, you can take one of your leftover wooden chopsticks from the Chinese take-out place and stick it in the oil every so often. When the tip gives off a steady stream of bubbles, you are at the correct temperature.

Using a slotted metal or high-heat-resistant spatula, pick up the crab cakes, one at a time, and slide them into the butter. Be careful not to crowd them or they will not brown evenly. I like to keep ½ inch of free space on all sides of every cake. If you need to cook in multiple

batches, preheat your oven to its lowest temperature and set a wire rack on a baking sheet inside the oven. Cook the crab cakes for about 2 minutes on each side, or until they are a deep golden brown and heated through. If necessary, slide the finished crab cakes onto the prepared rack and keep them warm in the oven as you cook the next batch.

Once all of the cakes are cooked, spread the insides of each bun with butter. Set a griddle over medium heat and griddle the buns until the interior is crunchy and golden brown. Spread the buns with Tartar Sauce and add a crab cake and any of the serve-with suggestions. Serve warm. I like mine with potato chips.

Southern-Style Báhn Mì

MAKES 8 SANDWICHES

MARINATED CHICKEN:

8 boneless, skinless chicken thighs

1 (**15-ounce** / 425-gram) can coconut milk

1 cup / 240 grams buttermilk

3 tablespoons / 75 grams sambal

3 tablespoons / 50 grams soy sauce

1 teaspoon / 5 grams fish sauce

1 teaspoon / 4 grams finely grated
fresh ginger

1 teaspoon / 6 grams fine sea salt

CHICKEN MOUSSE:

3¼ **teaspoons** / 19.5 grams fine sea salt

4½ **cups** / 1 kilogram cold water

1¼ **pounds** / 567 grams chicken livers

1 cup / 225 grams unsalted butter, divided

4 medium shallots, thinly sliced

8 ounces / 227 grams button
mushrooms, thinly sliced

1 clove garlic, minced

½ **cup** / 113 grams bourbon

3 tablespoons / 55 grams whole-grain
mustard

1 tablespoon plus 2 teaspoons /
25 grams honey

½ **teaspoon** / 3 grams cider vinegar

Juice of 1 lemon

1½ teaspoons / 9 grams fine sea salt

2 teaspoons / 4 grams freshly ground
black pepper

1 teaspoon / 2.5 grams paprika

¼ **teaspoon** / 0.6 gram ground nutmeg

¼ **teaspoon** / 0.6 gram ground allspice

COLESLAW:

1 small head green cabbage,
thinly shaved

1½ medium carrots, grated

10 red radishes, grated

1 teaspoon / 4 grams finely grated
fresh ginger

Zest and juice of 3 limes

1 (**15-ounce** / 409-gram) can
coconut milk

½ **cup** / 100 grams mayonnaise
(I prefer Duke's)

1 tablespoon / 25 grams sambal

1 teaspoon / 4 grams soy sauce

½ **teaspoon** / 2.5 grams fish sauce

1 teaspoon / 6 grams fine sea salt

BREADING:

⅔ **cup** / 100 grams all-purpose flour

2 large eggs

3½ **cups** / 270 grams ground cornflakes

Peanut or canola oil, for frying

8 Hoagie Rolls (page 48) or (6-inch)
pieces French bread

Mint leaves for serving

Basil leaves for serving

This is my version of a fried-chicken sandwich. I use boneless, breaded thighs because that's the most flavorful piece, and I marinate them in a blend of buttermilk and coconut milk spiked with Asian seasoning. I make a rich chicken mousse and spread that over the bread instead of the classic mayonnaise. Extra mousse can be served with cheese and crackers for hors d'oeuvres or saved in small crocks in the refrigerator for several weeks under a layer of melted butter. Then I make an Asian-spiced slaw to dress the chicken. This is a hearty, satisfying sandwich. It's warm and cold, crunchy and creamy, and so darned good.

Marinate the Chicken:

Cut each chicken thigh in half. Put the thighs in a large zip-top bag. Put the coconut milk, buttermilk, sambal, soy sauce, fish sauce, and ginger in a medium bowl and whisk to blend. Reserve ¼ cup of the marinade for breading the chicken thighs later. Pour the remaining marinade into the bag with the chicken, squeeze out as much excess air as possible, and seal the bag. Gently move the thighs around in the bag so they are all exposed to the marinade. Set the bag in a bowl in the refrigerator and refrigerate for at least 16 hours and up to 24 hours.

Make the Chicken Liver Mousse:

Put the salt and water in a medium bowl and whisk until the salt dissolves. Add the chicken livers, cover, and refrigerate for 3 to 4 hours to draw out any blood and impurities.

Drain the livers and pat them dry. Trim the livers by separating the large and small lobes. Remove any whitish fatty pieces or dark spots from the large lobes. Carefully remove the stringy membrane from the smaller pieces and trim away any fat and fibrous or dark spots. Once you've cleaned all the livers, you should have about 1 pound left. Cut them into ½-inch pieces, rinse them under cold running water, and pat dry.

Set a large sauté pan over medium-high heat and add 2 tablespoons (28 grams) butter. Once the butter melts and begins to foam, add the shallots and cook, stirring, for 2 to 3 minutes, until tender and translucent. Add the mushrooms and continue to cook, stirring, until they give off their liquid and begin to dry out and brown. Once the mushrooms are golden brown and tender, after about 8 minutes, add the garlic. Cook, stirring, for 1 to 2 minutes, until it is aromatic and softened. Transfer to a large shallow bowl to cool slightly.

Wipe out the pan and add 2 more tablespoons (28 grams) of the butter. When the butter melts and begins to foam, add a handful of chicken livers, being careful not to crowd the pan. Cook for 2 to 3 minutes, until golden brown on the bottom. Flip the livers and cook for 2 to 3 minutes on the other side, until the tops are golden brown too. They

should still be pink in the centers, not cooked all the way through. Transfer the livers to the bowl with the vegetables to cool. Add more butter to the pan and continue to sear the livers until they are all in the bowl.

Set the pan back over medium heat and add the bourbon to deglaze. Cook, stirring, for 2 minutes, to let some of the alcohol cook out of the bourbon. If it ignites, let the flames burn out naturally. Pour over the cooked livers and vegetables and add any remaining butter. Transfer the mixture, including any juices, to a food processor. Add all of the remaining mousse ingredients and puree until smooth. Transfer to a mason jar or plastic container and gently rap it on the counter to make sure it settles completely with no air pockets in the mousse. Press plastic wrap onto the surface of the mousse or cover with a thin layer of melted butter. Refrigerate until needed.

Make the Coleslaw:

Put the cabbage, carrots, radishes, grated ginger, and lime juice and zest in a large bowl and mix gently to blend. Add the coconut milk, mayonnaise, sambal, soy sauce, fish sauce, and salt and mix well to blend. Cover and refrigerate until needed. The slaw will keep in a covered container in the refrigerator for up to 3 days. Be sure to mix it up and add additional lime juice, if needed, before using.

Cook the Chicken:

When you're ready to cook the chicken, put the flour in a shallow bowl. Put the eggs and reserved ¼ cup chicken marinade in another shallow bowl, whisk them together, and set them next to the flour. Put the ground cornflakes in a third bowl next to the eggs and set a baking sheet at the end. Drain the chicken thighs in a colander. One at a time, dredge the pieces of thigh in the flour, shaking off the excess. Then dip them in the egg, thoroughly coating them before gently shaking off the excess. Then roll them in the ground cornflakes, gently pressing them into the bowl to flatten out the meat, and coating them completely before shaking off the excess. Put the finished pieces of chicken on the baking sheet while you continue to bread the rest.

Preheat a deep fryer or large pot with 3 inches of oil to 350°F (180°C). Line a baking sheet with paper towels.

Fry each piece of chicken for 3 to 4 minutes, until golden brown and cooked through, and transfer to the prepared baking sheet to cool slightly. Split each piece of bread and spread it generously with the Chicken Liver Mousse. Lay 2 pieces of chicken on each sandwich and top with slaw. Add a few mint and basil leaves. Put the top on the bread, cut each sandwich in half, and serve immediately.

Soft-Shell Crab Tacos

MAKES 6 TACOS

RED CABBAGE SLAW:

½ medium red cabbage, shaved on a mandoline

6¼ ounces / 175 grams canned pureed tomatoes

1 bunch scallions, thinly sliced on the bias

1 jalapeño pepper, charred on a burner or grill and cut into small dice

¼ cup / 10 grams fresh cilantro leaves, chopped

½ cup / 113 grams red wine vinegar

Juice of 1 lime

½ teaspoon / 2 grams sugar

½ teaspoon / 3 grams fine sea salt

¼ teaspoon / 0.25 gram ground cumin

SMOKED GUACAMOLE:

4 avocados

2 tomatoes, cut into small dice

1 red onion, cut into small dice

1 jalapeño pepper, cut into small dice

Juice of 2 limes

¾ teaspoon / 4.5 grams fine sea salt

½ bunch / 13 grams cilantro, chopped

TEMPURA BATTER:

1 cup / 150 grams all-purpose flour

1 cup / 165 grams Wondra flour

⅛ teaspoon / 1.5 grams baking powder

⅛ teaspoon / 0.75 gram fine sea salt

2½ cups / 567 grams sparkling water

CRABS:

2½ quarts / 2.27 kilograms peanut or canola oil

½ cup / 83 grams Wondra flour

6 soft-shell crabs, cleaned

Fine sea salt, for seasoning

SERVE WITH:

Warm corn tortillas

Warm flour tortillas

Sour cream or Charred Lime Crema (page 208)

Pico de gallo (optional)

Sliced limes

SPECIAL EQUIPMENT:

Stovetop or outdoor smoker

Hickory wood chips

Soft-shell crabs are one of the few truly seasonal foods we have left. They have a sweet, briny flavor that is the essence of the sea. I like a delicate coating of tempura batter with them because it doesn't overwhelm the crab. Each element in this taco is designed to be flavorful and add to the dish without drowning out the flavors of the softies. I put a corn tortilla inside a flour tortilla to get flavor and flexibility and then add my tart, earthy red cabbage slaw and some creamy smoked guacamole. The crunchy crab goes in next, and if you're so inclined you can also add a drizzle of charred lime *crema* and/or fresh pico de gallo. It's like summertime in a sandwich and goes well with an ice-cold beer or fresh lemonade.

Make the Red Cabbage Slaw:

Put all of the ingredients in a medium bowl and mix well to blend. Reserve in a covered container in the refrigerator until ready to use, up to 3 hours. Mix well before serving.

Make the Smoked Guacamole:

Preheat a smoker according to the manufacturer's instructions and add the hickory chips. Use a serrated knife to cut the avocados in half around the pit, then twist the 2 halves in opposite directions and separate the 2 halves. Remove the pits and lay the avocados cut side down on the tray of the smoker. Smoke the avocados for 10 minutes, flip them over, and smoke for another 10 minutes. Take the avocados out of the smoker and put them in a medium bowl with the tomatoes, red onion, jalapeño, lime juice, salt, and cilantro. Mash everything together thoroughly with a spoon until completely combined. Reserve.

Make the Tempura Batter:

Set a medium bowl over an ice bath. Put the flour, Wondra, baking powder, and salt in the bowl and whisk to blend. Slowly pour in the sparkling water and whisk until smooth.

Fry the Crabs:

Preheat a deep fryer or large pot with 4 inches of oil to 350°F (180°C). Line a baking sheet with paper towels.

Put the Wondra in a shallow bowl large enough to hold a crab. Dredge each crab in the Wondra, coating it completely, and then dip each one in the batter and shake gently to remove any excess. Immediately slide the crab into the oil, gently swirling the legs as they enter the oil so they don't stick together, and fry for 4 to 5 minutes, until they are a deep golden brown. Transfer to the prepared baking sheet to drain for a minute, and season lightly with salt.

Arrange the cooked crabs on a platter and serve with warm tortillas, Red Cabbage Slaw, sour cream or Charred Lime Crema, Smoked Guacamole, and, if desired, pico de gallo.

Soups and Sandwiches

Cuban Sandwiches

MAKES 6 SANDWICHES

6 Hoagie Rolls (page 48) or store-bought

2½ **tablespoons** / 45 grams yellow mustard

2½ **tablespoons** / 30 grams mayonnaise
(I prefer Duke's)

12 slices Swiss cheese

3 large dill pickles, sliced lengthwise
into quarters

2 **pounds** / 908 grams pork shoulder,
thinly sliced (see page 118)

2 **pounds** / 908 grams country ham,
thinly sliced

SPECIAL EQUIPMENT:

Panini press

There's a little restaurant in Frederick, Maryland, called That Cuban Place Café. When I was opening Volt It was located on the corner of Third and Market Streets. During construction I literally lived on their Cuban sandwiches. I loved walking into that place. The owner was so warm and welcoming; he always asked about how construction was moving along, he was genuinely excited that we were opening nearby, and the sandwiches were great.

Cuban sandwiches are made on hoagie rolls or French bread. To my mind they are the quintessential leftover sandwich, combining roast pork with ham, Swiss cheese, and pickles. I like the salty bite of country ham paired with the spicy flavor of my leftover pork shoulder with Coffee BBQ Rub (page 118). Cuban sandwiches are always pressed so the bread crisps and the cheese melts and the aromas tickle your nose even before your take that first delectable bite.

Preheat a panini press to 400°F (200°C).

Slice each roll in half and evenly spread mustard on the bottom half of each bun. Spread mayonnaise on the top side of each bun and cover with 2 slices of Swiss cheese. Layer the bottom half with 2 slices of pickle, followed by slices of roast pork, and then slices of country ham, and cover with the top of the roll.

Put 1 or 2 sandwiches inside the panini press for 3½ minutes, flip the sandwiches over, and cook for 3½ minutes more, or until the sandwiches are deep golden brown on the top and bottom and the cheese has melted. Continue cooking the sandwiches in batches. If necessary, you can keep prepared sandwiches warm in a low (200°F/95°C) oven. Slice the sandwiches in half and serve immediately.

Salads and side dishes are easily the most flexible part of a meal. You may serve roast chicken all year long, but by changing what you put alongside it, you change the whole meal. It's no secret that I enjoy working with vegetables and fruits. They encompass such a wide array of colors, textures, and flavors that there is always something new to be discovered, like the mouthwatering flavor of Braised Kohlrabi and Lacinato Kale or the intensely sweet bite of Strawberry Mostarda. It's not always the protein that makes the meal.

Salads and Side Dishes

Spring Onions and Rhubarb

SERVES 6 TO 8

SPICY GOAT YOGURT:

1 cup / 225 grams goat's milk yogurt

1 tablespoon / 16 grams honey

¼ teaspoon / 1.5 grams fine sea salt

⅛ teaspoon / 0.25 gram piment d'Espelette

12 spring onions (or ramps in season)
Fine sea salt, for seasoning

RHUBARB PUREE:

8 ounces / 227 grams rhubarb

¼ cup plus 2 tablespoons / 75 grams sugar

¼ cup / 55 grams rice wine vinegar

¼ teaspoon / 1.5 grams fine sea salt,
plus extra for seasoning

2 tablespoons / 28 grams olive oil
Maldon sea salt, for sprinkling

When I was kid, my mom would occasionally make us cream cheese and jelly sandwiches for breakfast. This combination of rhubarb and goat yogurt reminds me of those long-ago sandwiches. Rhubarb is one of the very first crops to push through the spring soil. Here it gains a complex sweetness from the caramel, which plays off the natural tartness of the rhubarb and rice wine vinegar.

The grilled spring onions have a lighter but no less potent sweetness that is perfect against the yogurt sauce and the cooked rhubarb. Each component is good on its own and you experience different tastes as you eat. I love food that you can eat with your hands, and this dish is perfect, encouraging adults to bring their inner child to the table.

Make the Spicy Goat Yogurt:
Place all of the ingredients in a bowl and whisk until smooth. Reserve the yogurt in a covered container in the refrigerator until ready to serve.

Steam the Onions:
Trim the root end off of each spring onion. Trim the top 2 to 3 inches of greens from the onions. Cut each spring onion in half horizontally. Put the onions into a container full of cold water to soak, changing the water as needed to remove dirt and debris. Set a stovetop steamer with 2 to 3 inches of water in the bottom over medium-high heat. Once it comes to a boil, adjust the heat to medium. Remove the onions from the water and steam them for 10 minutes. Transfer the cooked spring onions to a large plate or tray and season lightly with salt. Let the onions cool.

Make the Rhubarb Puree:
Cut the rhubarb into ½-inch slices. Put the sugar in a pot set over medium heat. Cook, without stirring, though you can tilt the pan as needed to mix the caramel, until the sugar turns a dark amber (375°F / 190°C). Carefully add the vinegar—it will steam and sputter—and continue to cook, stirring with a silicone spatula until the caramel dissolves in the vinegar. Add the salt and stir in the rhubarb. Reduce the heat to medium-low and cook the rhubarb until it is just tender and starting to break down, stirring occasionally. Continue to cook the rhubarb until the liquid evaporates and the pan is mostly

dry, about 10 minutes. Remove from the heat. Transfer the rhubarb to a bowl and let it cool to room temperature.

Put the rhubarb in a blender and puree on low speed. Increase the speed to high and puree for 30 seconds, or until the rhubarb is smooth. Strain the rhubarb puree through a fine-mesh sieve. Reserve the rhubarb puree in a covered container in the refrigerator

Grill the Onions:
Preheat a charcoal or gas grill to medium-high.

Drizzle the spring onions with the olive oil. Grill the spring onions cut-side down until they begin to sizzle and lightly char, about 2 minutes. Turn the onions on the grill and cook for 1 more minute. Arrange the grilled onions on a platter. Sprinkle Maldon salt over the spring onions and serve the Rhubarb Puree and Spicy Goat Yogurt alongside.

Radishes and Olives

Radishes are so good, and they are seriously underutilized. Most people serve them as crudités or put them in salads, but these little vegetables aspire to so much more. I love the fact that they are sharp and crunchy when raw, and cooking softens them and brings out their natural sweetness, though not many people realize that. Combining them with earthy, briny olives creates a natural balance. I use the radish greens, normally discarded, to make a delicious green sauce to serve alongside.

2 bunches French breakfast radishes

8 ounces / 227 grams radish tops from 2 bunches radishes

1 bunch / 20 grams fresh mint leaves

⅔ cup / 150 grams olive brine

5 tablespoons plus 1 teaspoon / 75 grams olive oil, plus extra for cooking the radishes

⅛ teaspoon / 0.5 gram xanthan gum

Fine sea salt, for seasoning

2½ tablespoons / 35 grams fresh lemon juice

Grated zest from 1 lemon

5 ounces / 140 grams mixed pitted olives

Chopped mint leaves for garnish

Set a large pot of salted water over high heat and bring to a boil. Prepare 2 ice baths. Remove the tops from the radishes. Wash the radishes and their tops, keeping them separate. Blanch the radish tops in the boiling water for 2 minutes. Shock the radish tops in an ice bath, drain them, and squeeze the water out of the greens. Blanch the mint leaves for 30 seconds, and then shock them in an ice bath, drain them, and squeeze dry.

Put the radish tops, olive brine, and olive oil in a blender. Turn the blender on low and increase the speed to medium-high. When the radish-top puree is smooth, after about 30 seconds, turn the speed down to low and sprinkle in the xanthan gum. Increase the speed to high for 5 to 10 seconds, to fully disperse and hydrate the xanthan gum. Turn the blender off and reserve the radish-top puree.

Cut the radishes in half. Set a large sauté pan over medium heat. Add just enough oil to create a thin film on the bottom of the pan and sprinkle it lightly with salt. Put the radishes in the pan, cut side down, and cook until they are golden brown, 8 to 10 minutes. Remove from the heat and transfer to a large plate or a tray to cool. Once cool, put the radishes in a covered container in the refrigerator until ready to serve, for up to 24 hours.

To serve, put the radishes in a small bowl with the radish-top puree, lemon juice, and zest. Mix well and top with the olives. Sprinkle chopped mint leaves on the top. Serve family style.

Butter Lettuce with Blue Cheese and Strawberry Mostarda

SERVES 4 TO 6

STRAWBERRY MOSTARDA:

2⅔ ounces / 75 grams dried strawberries

⅓ cup / 75 grams balsamic vinegar

¼ cup / 72 grams Dijon mustard

⅓ cup / 75 grams white grape juice

¼ teaspoon / 1.5 grams fine sea salt

HONEY-ROASTED SUNFLOWER SEEDS:

¼ cup / 50 grams sugar

3 tablespoons / 50 grams honey

½ teaspoon / 3 grams fine sea salt

1¼ cups / 285 grams unsalted raw sunflower seeds

¼ teaspoon / 1 gram piment d'Espelette

THE REST OF THE SALAD:

4 heads butter lettuce

8 ounces / 227 grams fresh strawberries, washed, hulled, and cut into quarters

2 tablespoons / 28 grams olive oil

4 ounces / 113 grams Gorgonzola cheese, frozen

Butter lettuce has a wonderful, soft texture. The light green leaves are usually served whole so you can appreciate their delicate beauty and soft crunch. This salad uses dried strawberries in a spicy, tangy mostarda, along with fresh strawberries and Gorgonzola cheese.

The star of this dish is actually the sunflower seeds. They are cooked down with honey, sugar, and *piment d'Espelette*, creating a candied crunch that is almost like eating sweet sunshine on a plate. This may seem like a lot of sunflower seeds when you're cooking them, but once you taste them you'll understand. They have a habit of disappearing out of the pantry like magic.

Make the Mostarda:

The day before you want to serve the salad, make the Strawberry Mostarda. Place all of the ingredients in a container, mix well, cover with plastic wrap, and refrigerate overnight. The next day, put the strawberry mixture in a blender. Turn the speed on low and increase the speed to high. Puree until smooth, about 1 minute. Strain the mostarda through a fine-mesh sieve. Reserve.

Make the Honey-Roasted Sunflower Seeds:

Put the sugar, honey, and salt in a heavy-bottomed pot. Over medium heat, cook the sugar and honey together until the sugar melts, and then add the sunflower seeds. Cook and stir the seeds in the sugars until the sugars caramelize and the seeds become evenly roasted, about 10 minutes. Stir in the *piment d'Espelette*. Remove the honey-roasted seeds from the pan and cool them on a parchment-lined baking sheet. When the seeds are cool, store them in a zip-top bag.

Assemble the Salad:

Put the lettuce leaves in a large bowl. Add the strawberries and olive oil. Add the Strawberry Mostarda by the spoonful, so that it evenly coats and does not soak the leaves and strawberries. Put the salad into a large serving container. Break the Honey-Roasted Sunflower Seeds into clusters and sprinkle over the salad. Use a Microplane to grate the frozen Gorgonzola over the top of the salad.

Asparagus and Barley

SERVES 6 TO 8

4 ounces / 113 grams pecorino cheese

1¼ cups / 250 grams pearled barley

1 teaspoon / 6 grams fine
sea salt, divided

6 tablespoons / 84 grams olive oil, divided

1 teaspoon / 3 grams smoked paprika

1 bunch green asparagus

1 bunch white asparagus

1 cup / 240 grams buttermilk

¼ cup / 15 grams sorrel, thinly sliced,
plus several leaves to garnish the platter

2½ tablespoons / 35 grams fresh
lemon juice

SPECIAL EQUIPMENT:

Stovetop smoker

Wood chips

It may seem excessive to use two pots of water to blanch the asparagus, but it is necessary. The green asparagus makes the water green, and if you blanch the white asparagus in the same pot they will turn green as well. The white asparagus make the water bitter, so if you blanch the green after the white, the green vegetables become bitter too. You can use the same pot; just give it a good rinse between vegetables.

We created the smoked pecorino for this dish at my Italian restaurant, Aggio. In Italy they have very strict rules about what can be done to and with their cheeses. You will never see smoked pecorino there, which is a shame, because it is amazing. Sheep's milk cheese tastes more like the animal than any other variety. When I taste pecorino, I can taste lamb. Adding the smoke bumps up the meaty flavor while contrasting it with the creamy, salty experience of eating the cheese. Sprinkling it over the two very different types of asparagus and the earthy, tender barley makes for an unforgettable side dish.

Place wood chips in the bottom pan of a stovetop smoker and set over medium-high heat. When the wood begins to smolder and smoke, turn off the heat, put the base tray in place, and put the cheese in the smoker. Put on the lid and smoke the cheese for 10 minutes.

Remove the cheese and turn the heat on under the smoker to rekindle the wood. You don't want the cheese to melt in the smoker. When it is smoking again, turn off the heat and add the cheese. Leave the cheese in the smoker for 10 minutes. Remove the cheese again and turn the heat on under the smoker to rekindle the wood. When it is smoking, turn off the heat and add the cheese. Leave the cheese in the smoker for 10 minutes, for a total of 30 minutes. Remove the cheese and chill it.

Put the barley in a bowl and cover with 2 cups plus 3 tablespoons (500 grams) water. Cover the container and let it hydrate overnight.

Rinse the hydrated barley in cold water, drain, and put it into a medium pot. Cover the barley with 1 inch of cold water, add ¾ teaspoon (4.5 grams) of the salt, and set the pot over medium-high heat. When the barley comes to a boil, remove from the heat and drain in a colander. Put the barley into a large bowl and add the remaining ¼ teaspoon (1.5 grams) salt, 2 tablespoons (28 grams) of the olive oil, and the smoked paprika. Stir everything together to coat the grains and cool the mixture down.

Set a large pot of salted water over high heat. Prepare an ice bath. Remove the small triangular leaves from the stalks of the green asparagus. Sometimes there is a bit of dirt and grit hiding beneath them. Blanch the asparagus in the boiling water for 2 minutes, and then transfer to the ice bath. Set a fresh pot of salted water over high heat and, when it comes to a boil, repeat with the white asparagus. Cut the asparagus stems into ¼-inch rounds, leaving the tips 2 inches long.

In a bowl, mix the barley with the buttermilk and add the asparagus rounds, sliced sorrel, and lemon juice.

Set a large sauté pan over medium-high heat and put 3 tablespoons (42 grams) of the olive oil in the pan. When the oil shimmers, add the white asparagus tips and sauté for 1 minute. Turn the tips in the pan and sauté for 1 minute more. Transfer the white asparagus tips to a plate to keep warm. Add the remaining 1 tablespoon (14 grams) oil to the pan and then add the green asparagus tips. Sauté them for 1 minute, flip them over, and sauté for 1 minute more. Transfer them from the pan to the plate with the white asparagus tips.

Put the barley mixture onto a large platter. Top with the warm asparagus tips, shave the smoked pecorino on top, and garnish with sorrel leaves.

Cucumber-Cantaloupe Caponata

SERVES 6 TO 8

Classic caponata is a winter dish. It's made with eggplant, olives, onions, and tomatoes stewed down with fresh herbs and capers. This version is for the summertime. It takes the flavors of the herbs and the capers and the vinegar and applies them to golden raisins, cucumber, and cantaloupe. It is light and refreshing and still deeply flavored. The green pistachios add a bit of crunch and their rich nutty flavor to the mix. This caponata goes beautifully with grilled fish or seared shrimp or even grilled lobsters.

1⅔ **cups** / 250 grams golden raisins

1⅓ **cups** / 300 grams white grape juice

½ **cup** / 113 grams rice wine vinegar

3½ **ounces** / 100 grams capers in brine

1 tablespoon plus 1 teaspoon / 5 grams freshly cracked coriander seeds

2½ **teaspoons** / 5 grams freshly ground cumin seeds

1 teaspoon / 2 grams red pepper flakes

10 Persian cucumbers, peeled

1 teaspoon / 6 grams fine sea salt

1 medium cantaloupe

1 bunch cilantro, leaves only

3½ **ounces** / 100 grams pistachios, roasted and chopped

Extra-virgin olive oil, for drizzling

Several hours before you want to serve this salad, put the raisins, grape juice, vinegar, capers, coriander, cumin, and red pepper flakes into a bowl. Let the raisins hydrate for at least 4 hours and up to 24 hours.

Cut the tips off each cucumber and discard. Cut the cucumbers in half lengthwise. Cut each half of cucumber into bite-size oblique (rough triangular) pieces. Put the cucumbers in a large bowl and season with the salt.

Use a chef's knife to cut the top and bottom off the cantaloupe. Stand it up on a cutting board and pare away the rind and skin, cutting from the top to the bottom of the melon. Cut the cantaloupe in half from top to bottom and scrape out the seeds. Cut each half of cantaloupe into quarters lengthwise, and then cut those quarters into bite-size oblique pieces; add to the bowl with the cucumber. Add the raisin mixture. If not serving immediately, refrigerate until ready to serve.

Thinly slice the cilantro leaves. Fold the cilantro and chopped pistachios into the caponata. Drizzle olive oil over the top and serve immediately.

Beets and Burrata

SERVES 6 TO 8

2 bunches medium beets,
with greens attached

13 tablespoons / 195 grams prepared
horseradish

3½ tablespoons / 50 grams
balsamic vinegar

¾ teaspoon / 4.5 grams fine sea salt

⅜ teaspoon / 1.5 grams xanthan gum

8 bunches mâche

3 (**4-ounce** / 113-gram) pieces
burrata cheese

Extra-virgin olive oil, for drizzling

Maldon sea salt, for sprinkling

SPECIAL EQUIPMENT:

Pressure cooker (optional)

This is an incredibly simple dish that delivers big flavors. *Burrata* means "buttered" in Italian. It's like fresh mozzarella to the extreme. It's a thin skin of cheese encasing soft curds blended with fresh cream. It practically melts in your mouth. As always, I love using the entire vegetable, and the grilled beet greens add a smoky element to the sauce that brings out the sweetness in the burrata. People expect to see fresh tomatoes with slices of fresh mozzarella cheese, but once they taste these sliced beets with creamy burrata, they'll know what they've been missing.

Remove the leaves and stems from the beets. Wash the beets and their greens separately and spin the greens dry in a salad spinner. Set a grill pan over medium-high heat and sear the beet greens on both sides, 2 to 3 minutes per side. Transfer to a bowl and reserve at room temperature.

Put the beets into a pressure cooker with 3⅓ cups (750 grams) water. Cook the beets at high pressure for 15 minutes. Let the pressure dissipate naturally. Let the beets cool to room temperature. Peel the warm beets and reserve in a covered container in the refrigerator. Alternatively, you can set up a stovetop steamer. When the water comes to simmer, add the beets, cover, and steam for 45 minutes, or until tender when tested with a cake skewer. Use the steaming liquid instead of the beet stock below and, if needed, add enough water to make 500 grams.

Strain the cooking liquid through a fine-mesh sieve and weigh out 500 grams. Discard the rest. Put the grilled beet greens in a blender. Add the beet cooking liquid, horseradish, balsamic vinegar, and salt. Turn the blender on low speed and increase the speed to medium-high. Puree the mixture until it is smooth, about 1 minute. Turn the blender down to low and sprinkle in the xanthan gum. Increase the speed to medium-high to disperse and hydrate the xanthan gum. Strain the beet-top sauce through a fine-mesh sieve. Reserve the sauce in the refrigerator.

Slice each beet into 5 or 6 slices horizontally. Arrange the beets on a platter. Put 3 piles of mâche between the beets. Top each pile of mâche with a piece of burrata. Spoon the beet-top sauce over the beets. Drizzle with olive oil and sprinkle Maldon salt over each piece of burrata.

Potato and Eggplant Puttanesca

SERVES 6 TO 8

BASIL OIL:

3½ ounces / 100 grams fresh basil leaves

⅔ cup / 150 grams olive oil

THE REST:

1¾ pounds / 800 grams eggplant, peeled and cut into large dice

1 tablespoon / 18 grams fine sea salt, divided

1¾ pounds / 800 grams fingerling potatoes

1 head of garlic, cut in half horizontally

2 large onions

2 tablespoons / 28 grams cloves garlic, peeled

4½ tablespoons / 65 grams olive oil

12¼ ounces / 350 grams pitted spicy olives

2 (28-ounce / 794 gram) cans plum tomatoes

2 tablespoons / 30 grams fish sauce

Grated lemon zest, for sprinkling

Freshly ground black pepper, for sprinkling

When I was working on my last book, *VOLTink.*, I was fascinated by the many family relationships to be found in classic dishes. Potatoes and eggplant are from the same family of nightshades, and so it's no surprise that they go well together in dishes. Puttanesca is an Italian sauce made with tomatoes, onions, garlic, anchovies, olives, and herbs. It is aromatic and strongly flavored, perfect for flavoring both potatoes and eggplant. This warm salad is wonderful in winter or summer and brings a taste of Italy to your table.

Make the Basil Oil:

Prepare an ice bath and set a bowl in it. Put the basil and olive oil in a blender. Turn the blender on low speed and increase the speed to high. Puree the basil until it is smooth. Pour the basil-oil puree into a small pot set over medium heat. Bring the mixture to a simmer. Remove the pot from the heat and immediately strain the basil through 4 layers of damp cheesecloth into the bowl set over the ice bath to cool it immediately. Reserve the basil oil in the refrigerator for up to 3 days. The color will begin to darken over time, so it is best used the first day.

Cook the Vegetables:

Put the eggplant into a bowl and season it with 1 teaspoon (6 grams) of the salt. Stir the eggplant to coat evenly with the salt. Put the eggplant into a colander set over a bowl to drain.

Put the potatoes and head of garlic into a pot and cover with cold water. Set the pot over medium-high heat and bring the potatoes to a boil. Turn the heat down to low and cook the potatoes until they are tender, about 25 minutes. Remove the potatoes from the heat, drain them, discarding the garlic, and lay them onto a baking sheet to cool. When they are cool enough to handle, peel the potatoes, cut them into ½-inch rounds, and reserve.

Put the onions and garlic cloves into a food processor and pulse to mince them. Put the olive oil into a large pot set over medium heat. When the oil is hot, add the onion and garlic mixture, stirring, and cook for 5 minutes.

Mince the olives in the same food processor (no need to clean it from the onions), and add them to the onion mixture. Cook them together for 5 minutes. While the olives cook, crush the tomatoes with your hands. Add the tomatoes, fish sauce, eggplant, and remaining 2 teaspoons (12 grams) salt and then stir until the mixture is evenly blended. Cook over low heat for 30 minutes, stirring occasionally to make sure that nothing sticks. Remove the pot from the heat and fold in the peeled and sliced potatoes. Transfer to a serving bowl. Drizzle with the Basil Oil, sprinkle lemon zest over the top, and grind some black pepper over the top. Serve warm.

Spaghetti Squash Frittata

SERVES 8 TO 10

ROASTED SPAGHETTI SQUASH:

1 medium spaghetti squash

PARSLEY PESTO:

⅓ **cup** / 50 grams Marcona almonds

3 tablespoons / 42 grams olive oil

2⅔ ounces / 75 grams fresh flat-leaf parsley, blanched

1 ounce / 28 grams Parmesan cheese

¼ **teaspoon** / 1.5 grams fine sea salt

DIJON MUSTARD VINAIGRETTE:

¼ **cup** / 30 grams finely chopped shallot (from 2 shallots)

1 cup / 225 grams apple cider vinegar

1 bay leaf

1 sprig thyme

¼ **cup** / 65 grams honey

1 tablespoon / 15 grams Dijon mustard

¼ **teaspoon** / 1.5 grams fine sea salt

½ **cup** / 113 grams light olive oil

FRITTATA:

4½ ounces / 125 grams Parsley Pesto

15 large eggs

¾ **teaspoon** / 4.5 grams fine sea salt

8 ounces / 227 grams Roasted Spaghetti Squash

10½ ounces / 300 grams ricotta cheese

9 cups / 250 grams baby arugula

4 ounces / 113 grams ricotta salata cheese

This frittata is great for Sunday brunches or any kind of a buffet. The arugula can be kept on the side and people can add the salad as they take their portion of frittata. Frittatas have the advantage of holding well at room temperature. In fact, in Italy they are often served at room temperature rather than straight from the pan. The combination of roasted spaghetti squash and parsley pesto is so flavorful, earthy, and herbaceous against the tender sweetness of the eggs. Alongside I like a sharp salad of arugula and Dijon vinaigrette to wake up the palate.

Roast the Squash:
Preheat the oven to 350°F (180°C).

Cut the top and bottom off the spaghetti squash. Cut the squash in half and remove the seeds. Put the squash, cut side down, into a roasting pan and add 2 inches of water. Cook the squash for 1 hour and 15 minutes, or until it is tender. Remove the squash from the oven and turn the halves cut side up. Let them cool till they are easily handled. Use a fork to scrape the filaments of squash flesh into a bowl. Cool the squash and reserve.

Make the Parsley Pesto:
Put the Marcona almonds and olive oil into a small pot set over medium heat. Cook the almonds until they are a light golden brown. Remove the pot from the heat. The almonds will continue to darken as they cool in the oil. Put the parsley, cooled almonds, and oil into a food processor. Pulse until the mixture is finely minced. Add the Parmesan and the salt and pulse to combine. Reserve the pesto in the refrigerator.

Make the Dijon Mustard Vinaigrette:
Put the shallots, vinegar, bay leaf, and thyme into a small pot set over medium heat. Cook the vinegar until it is reduced to a syrup. Remove the thyme stem and bay leaf. Put the reduction into a mixing bowl. Set the mixing bowl on a kitchen towel shaped into a circle to prevent the bowl from wobbling. Whisk in the honey, mustard, and salt. Slowly drizzle in the oil, whisking constantly to emulsify the vinaigrette. If the vinaigrette appears to thicken too much, add a teaspoon of cold water.

Make the Frittata and the Salad:

Preheat the oven to 300°F (150°C).

Put the Parsley Pesto, eggs, and salt in a large bowl and whisk until smooth. Put the Roasted Spaghetti Squash and ricotta in a separate bowl and mix them together. Stir the spaghetti squash into the egg mixture.

Spray a 9-by-13-inch baking dish with nonstick cooking spray. Pour the frittata mixture into the pan. Put the baking dish into a larger roasting pan and pour hot water into the roasting pan to come halfway up the sides of the smaller pan. Bake the frittata for 50 minutes. Gently shake the pan, and if it still appears loose in the center, return to the oven for another 5 minutes. It should be set and only slightly jiggly in the center.

Remove the frittata from the water bath and let it rest at room temperature. Cut the frittata into long slices. Put 1 slice on each plate. Put the arugula in a bowl and dress with the Dijon Mustard Vinaigrette. Use a vegetable peeler to shave the ricotta salata into the arugula. Stir to combine. Arrange a portion of salad next to the sliced frittata and serve immediately.

John Cope's Corn Dumplings Succotash

SERVES 6 TO 8

DUMPLINGS:

1 cup / 260 grams whole milk

7 tablespoons / 100 grams unsalted butter, sliced

1 teaspoon / 6 grams fine sea salt

1 cup / 140 grams all-purpose flour

2⅔ ounces / 75 grams John Cope's toasted dried sweet corn, finely ground

2 teaspoons / 12 grams baking powder

3 large eggs

RED PEPPER SAUCE:

1 large red bell pepper, seeded, stemmed, and diced

9 tablespoons / 125 grams water

1½ teaspoons / 7 grams red wine vinegar

SUCCOTASH:

¼ cup / 56 grams olive oil, divided

1 cup / 120 grams baby chanterelle mushrooms

1 cup / 200 grams shelled peas

1 cup / 150 grams shelled fava beans

Fine sea salt, for seasoning

Parmesan cheese, for serving

I've said it elsewhere: I love the flavor of John Cope's toasted sweet corn. You can order it online or you could substitute freeze-dried corn; the important thing is capturing the flavor of fresh sweet corn. I like to pulverize the dried corn and use it as flour to add flavor to these dumplings. Then I combine the corn dumplings with fresh peas, fava beans, and chanterelles for my personal interpretation of succotash. It makes for a hearty side dish, or you could turn it into a main dish for a vegetarian meal. I love the way the fresh vegetables, sweet earthy mushrooms, and tender dumplings all come together in the red pepper sauce.

Prepare the Dumplings:

Put the milk, butter, and salt in a medium pot set over medium-high heat and bring to a simmer. Use a silicone spatula or wooden spoon to stir in the flour, ground corn, and baking powder, and cook, stirring constantly, until the liquid is absorbed and the mixture dries out a bit. Transfer to a stand mixer and mix with the paddle attachment on low speed until cool, about 10 minutes.

Line a baking sheet with parchment paper. Add the eggs to the mixer one at a time, mixing on low speed, until each one is fully incorporated before adding the next. Transfer the dumpling dough to a piping bag fitted with a large plain tip. Pipe the dough into long ropes on the prepared baking sheet. Let cool completely, about 15 minutes. Use a paring knife to cut the ropes into 1-inch pieces. Roll each piece into a ball. Set them back on the parchment paper, cover with plastic wrap, and reserve in the refrigerator until ready to cook.

Make the Red Pepper Sauce:

Put the red pepper, water, and vinegar in a blender and puree until smooth. Pass the mixture through a fine-mesh sieve, discarding the solids. Reserve in a covered container in the refrigerator.

Make the Succotash and Cook the Dumplings:

Set a large pot of salted water over high heat and bring to a boil. Meanwhile, set a large sauté pan over medium-high heat and add 2 tablespoons (28 grams) of the olive oil. Once the oil shimmers, add the mushrooms and sauté until they start to brown, 3 to 5 minutes. Add the peas and fava beans, season lightly with salt, and cook, stirring, until the vegetables are just tender. Keep warm.

Once the water comes to a boil, set a large skillet over medium heat. Drop the dumplings into the boiling water and add the remaining 2 tablespoons (28 grams) olive oil to the skillet. Blanch the dumplings until just tender, 2 to 3 minutes, and transfer them to the hot skillet. Sear the dumplings on one side, 2 to 3 minutes, and flip them over. Add the Red Pepper Sauce and deglaze the pan, stirring gently to loosen the dumplings from the bottom. Add the mushrooms and beans to the stew, stir to combine, and transfer to a shallow serving bowl. Grate Parmesan cheese over the top and serve immediately.

Braised Kohlrabi and Lacinato Kale

SERVES 6 TO 8

When I first came back to Frederick, Maryland, to open Volt, I would drive along the roads and see fields full of kohlrabi. Oddly enough, I never saw it in any of the local restaurants. After talking to a few farmers, I discovered that it was all going to Baltimore and Washington, DC. I knew there was a lot I could do with it, so I immediately began reserving my share. Here I've braised it in cream with peanuts and Tuscan kale. It's a surprising dish and all of the ingredients work well together, with their varying degrees of sweetness and earthiness. It's a vegetarian side that will satisfy everyone at your table.

½ **cup** / 113 grams unsalted butter

4 ounces / 113 grams shelled and skinned raw peanuts

1 large onion, halved, core removed, and thinly sliced lengthwise

2 medium or 1 large kohlrabi (about **2½ pounds** / 1.1 kilograms), cut into medium dice

1 teaspoon / 6 grams fine sea salt

¼ **teaspoon** / 0.5 gram red pepper flakes

3 cups / 720 grams heavy cream

2 bunches kale, stems removed, leaves cut into bite-size pieces

Put the butter in a large sauté pan set over medium heat. Once the butter melts, add the peanuts and cook, stirring, until both the nuts and the butter start to brown. When the peanuts are a deep golden brown, after 5 to 7 minutes, lower the heat, add the onion, and cook until tender and translucent, 3 to 5 minutes. Add the kohlrabi, salt, and red pepper flakes and cook for 2 to 3 minutes, stirring, until everything is well blended. Add the cream and bring to a very low simmer. Stir in the kale leaves, cover with a tight-fitting lid, and braise the kale and kohlrabi over very low heat for 12 to 15 minutes, stirring occasionally.

Check the tenderness of the kohlrabi using a cake tester or by tasting a piece. Once the kohlrabi is tender, remove the lid and let the liquid reduce to half its original volume, about 5 minutes. It should form a syrupy glaze. Serve immediately.

Celeriac and Green Apple Slaw

SERVES 6 TO 8

1 cup / 240 grams buttermilk

2 tablespoons / 28 grams extra-virgin olive oil

2 tablespoons / 25 grams mayonnaise (I prefer Duke's)

1 tablespoon / 14 grams champagne vinegar

Grated zest from 1 lemon

1 teaspoon / 6 grams fine sea salt

½ teaspoon / 1 gram freshly ground black pepper

1 medium celeriac (about 1 pound / 454 grams), peeled and thinly shaved with a mandoline and cut into matchsticks

1 medium green apple, peeled, thinly sliced, and cut into matchsticks

4 celery ribs, thinly sliced on a long bias

¼ cup / 30 grams capers

½ cup / 32 grams fresh chervil, minced

½ cup / 32 grams fresh flat-leaf parsley, minced

¼ cup / 32 grams celery heart leaves, chopped

This is my favorite coleslaw. I played around with it for years before I was satisfied with the recipe. I love the variety of textures and flavors in this salad. Sweet, mellow celeriac dug from the ground and crisp, juicy apples plucked from the trees come together in a tart buttermilk dressing. The capers add salt, the herbs add brightness, and the fresh celery leaves complement the deeper flavor of the celeriac. I like this slaw with everything, alongside my Cuban Sandwiches (page 67) or with Maryland Crab Cake Sandwiches (page 56) or on a turkey sandwich the day after Thanksgiving.

Combine the buttermilk, olive oil, mayonnaise, vinegar, and lemon zest in a medium bowl and whisk until smooth. Season with the salt and pepper and whisk until the salt has dissolved. Add the celeriac, green apple, celery, and capers and mix well. Cover and let the vegetables marinate in the refrigerator for at least 2 hours and up to 12 hours.

Add the chervil, parsley, and celery leaves and mix well. Transfer to a serving bowl and serve immediately.

Sunchokes with Bacon, Caramelized Onions, and Thyme

`SERVES 6 TO 8`

VEGETABLE STOCK:

1 celeriac, peeled and diced

1 medium yellow onion, peeled and diced

1 medium carrot, peeled and diced

1 cup / 85 grams mushroom trimmings or diced cremini mushrooms

2 turnips, peeled and diced

2 parsnips, peeled and diced

3 celery ribs, diced

1 bay leaf, split

2 cloves garlic, smashed

4 black peppercorns

2½ tablespoons / 50 grams white soy sauce

8½ cups / 1.9 kilograms water

SUNCHOKES:

2½ pounds / 1.1 kilograms sunchokes, peeled or scrubbed, cut into bite-size chunks

4½ cups / 1 kilogram Vegetable Stock or water

3½ tablespoons / 56 grams honey

1½ teaspoons / 9 grams fine sea salt

8 ounces / 227 grams double-smoked bacon, cut into 1-inch rectangles

2 medium onions, halved, core removed, and thinly sliced lengthwise

2 tablespoons / 10 grams fresh thyme leaves

Sunchokes are also known as Jerusalem artichokes. They look a little bit like fresh ginger and have a sweet, nutty flavor. Some people shy away, thinking that it's too much work to peel them, but I've found that fresh sunchokes from the farmers' market do well with just a firm scrubbing with a vegetable brush. Then their skins are thin enough to be edible and disappear into the dish. Inspired by the classic Lyonnaise potatoes, I've cooked them with bacon, onions, and fresh thyme. The finished dish is sweet and earthy, smoky from the bacon, and infused with the herbal flavor of the thyme leaves. This is one of my favorite fall side dishes, and I happily serve it with my Meat Loaf (page 133) or alongside Monketta (page 184) or with a great roast chicken. The kids love it, and that makes my table a happy place to be.

Make the Vegetable Stock:
Place all of the stock ingredients in a pressure cooker and cook at high pressure for 15 minutes. Let the pressure dissipate naturally and uncover. Alternatively, place all of the ingredients in a large pot and set over high heat. Bring to a simmer, reduce the heat to low, and cook, skimming occasionally, for 45 minutes. Strain the stock through a fine-mesh sieve. Use immediately or chill and refrigerate until needed, up to 1 week.

Make the Sunchokes:
Put the sunchokes in a pot with the Vegetable Stock, honey, and salt and set over high heat. Bring to a boil and turn off the heat. Use a slotted spoon to transfer the sunchokes to a baking pan, laying them out in a single layer to cool. Reserve the liquid for the glaze.

Put the bacon in a large sauté pan set over medium-low heat to render. Stir often, lowering the heat if it begins to brown too quickly. Once the fat has rendered from the bacon, after 10 to 15 minutes, add the onions. Cook, stirring, until they become translucent and then slowly caramelize, about 10 minutes. Do not raise the heat to try to speed up the process. The onions will start to take on a golden brown hue. Take care that they don't burn, as that will make the dish

bitter. Once the onions are uniformly golden brown, add the reserved sunchoke liquid to deglaze any browned bits stuck to the pan. Bring the liquid to a simmer and reduce it to approximately half of its original volume. Stir in the sunchokes and reduce the heat to start to warm them through, being careful not to over-reduce the glaze. The glaze should cling to the sunchokes and onions like maple syrup. If it gets too thick, add a tablespoon or two of water. Once the sunchokes are warmed through, add the thyme leaves and salt and transfer to a large bowl. Serve family style.

Vadouvan Brown Rice Pilaf

SERVES 8

½ **cup** / 113 grams unsalted butter, sliced

1 tablespoon plus 1 teaspoon / 12 grams vadouvan spice blend

1 large clove garlic, minced

2 cups / 390 grams short-grain brown rice

1 medium onion, cut into small dice

1 bay leaf, cut into 4 pieces

½ **cup** /113 grams white wine

7½ cups / 1.7 kilograms Vegetable Stock (page 92, or store-bought) or water

2 teaspoons / 12 grams fine sea salt

Vadouvan refers to a French spice blend, with curry powder built on a base of dried onions, shallots, and garlic, giving it an unusually savory flavor. As a young professional cook, one of the first techniques you are expected to master is that of a rice pilaf. A perfect pilaf is flavorful, the rice has a light and fluffy texture, and every grain is firm yet tender. Here I've browned the butter, toasted the spices in it, and then added the rice to toast in the aromatic butter. The spices infuse into the rice and the finished pilaf is like eating curry without the stew. I like to serve this with the fried soft-shell crabs from the Soft-Shell Crab Tacos (page 62) or with the Whole Roasted Sea Bass and Cranberry Sea Beans (page 177) or with simple grilled or broiled lamb chops.

Preheat the oven to 350°F (180°C).

Take a piece of parchment paper and cut it into a circle that just fits inside a large pot. Cut a small circle in the center of the parchment and set the parchment aside.

Put the butter in the pot and set over medium heat. Once the butter starts to melt, begin stirring, and cook until it browns and becomes fragrant. Turn the heat to low, add the vadouvan, and cook, stirring, until the spices become fragrant, 1 to 2 minutes. Add the minced garlic and cook for another 1 to 2 minutes. Add the rice, increase the heat to medium, and cook, stirring, for 5 to 7 minutes, until it toasts and begins to smell nutty. Add the onion and cook, stirring, for 3 to 5 minutes, until tender and translucent. Add the bay leaf and white wine. Bring to a boil, and then add the Vegetable Stock and salt. Bring to a low boil, cover the liquid with the reserved parchment paper circle (it will rest on top of the liquid, and the center hole will allow steam to escape), and cover the pot with the lid. Transfer the pot to the oven and cook for 1 hour, or until the rice is fully cooked and tender. Stir the rice to fluff it up, transfer to a bowl, and serve family style.

Baked Applesauce

MAKES ABOUT 3 QUARTS

This was one of the very first things I put on the menu at my restaurant Family Meal. Baked applesauce is so easy to make and so delicious. I like to use a blend of Granny Smith apples for acidity and Gala apples for sweetness, but once you get the hang of the recipe you can use whatever apples are your favorites. That little bit of bourbon at the end adds its own sweetness and gives the sauce a lingering finish. At home I like to serve this warm with baked ham or fried pork chops. I also use it in my Applesauce-Apple Pie (page 225). It's the most flavorful applesauce you'll ever taste.

8 medium Granny Smith apples
(about **2 pounds 2 ounces** / 965 grams)

8 medium Gala apples
(about **2 pounds 2 ounces** / 965 grams)

1 pound / 454 grams unsalted butter, diced

2 cups / 525 grams apple cider

Seeds from ¾ vanilla bean

1½ teaspoons / 5 grams ground cinnamon

1 teaspoon / 6 grams fine sea salt

2 tablespoons / 28 grams bourbon

Preheat the oven to 350°F (180°C).

Lay the apples on a baking sheet and roast until the skins begin to peel away and the flesh is completely tender, 45 to 60 minutes. Remove from the oven and let the apples cool for 30 minutes. Peel off the skins and then remove and discard the seeds and core. Pass the apples through a food mill fitted with the largest disk. Reserve.

Put the butter in a large pot set over medium heat. Once the butter has melted, add the pureed apples, apple cider, vanilla seeds, cinnamon, and salt. Bring to a simmer, reduce the heat to low, and cook for 15 minutes, stirring occasionally.

Remove from the heat and stir in the bourbon. Cool the applesauce and keep in a covered container in the refrigerator until ready to serve, up to 2 weeks.

Sundays are my day off. It's family day, and we try to do something fun that everyone can participate in. This often involves cooking, because we generally make dinner together on Sundays. The kids love to help out in the kitchen, peeling potatoes, punching out biscuits, or rolling pasta dough. Very often other family members and friends show up for the evening meal, so these recipes are easily stretched or doubled to include unexpected guests. Sunday suppers may take a little extra effort to prepare, but once you and your family are gathered around the table, you'll know it was worth it.

Spaghetti and Meatballs

Pasta Dough for Tagliolini

**Focaccia with Mozzarella
   and Roasted Garlic**

Fried Chicken with Hot Sauce

Bread-and-Butter Pickles

Buttermilk Biscuits

Pork Shoulder and Pumpkin Sauerkraut

Cheese Grits

Braised Greens with Smoked Turkey Tails

Pork Ribs with Kimchi and Dr Pepper

Bacon-Wrapped Corn on the Cob

Skirt Steak Fajitas

Grilled Watermelon "Ribs"

Potato and Egg Salad

Meat Loaf

Everything Mashed Potatoes

Mushroom Confit

Steak Dinner with Steak Sauce

Broccoli with Anchovy Dressing

Ranch Duchess Potatoes

Sunday Suppers

Spaghetti and Meatballs

SERVES 6

MEATBALLS:

4 cups / 200 grams cubed day-old bread, preferably brioche

1 cup / 260 grams whole milk

1 pound / 454 grams ground pork

1 pound / 454 grams ground veal

1 pound / 454 grams ground beef

1 medium onion, minced

5 cloves garlic, thinly sliced

1 teaspoon / 2 grams freshly ground black pepper

1 teaspoon / 2 grams red pepper flakes

3 large eggs

1 cup / 80 grams grated Parmesan cheese, plus extra for serving

1 teaspoon / 3 grams Worcestershire sauce

1½ teaspoons / 9 grams fine sea salt

1 teaspoon / 2 grams crushed fennel seeds

⅓ cup / 50 grams all-purpose flour

SAUCE POMODORO (TOMATO SAUCE):

2 (**28-ounce** / 794 gram) cans whole peeled San Marzano tomatoes

¼ cup / 56 grams olive oil

1 medium onion, minced

3 cloves garlic, minced

1½ teaspoons / 9 grams fine sea salt

2 teaspoons / 8 grams sugar

6 fresh basil leaves, plus extra for serving

¼ cup (56 grams) olive oil

Focaccia with Mozzarella and Roasted Garlic (page 108)

Fresh Tagliolini (optional; page 104)

Grated Parmigiano-Reggiano for serving

Mom always made homemade meatballs and sauce from scratch. Now that I am a chef, how could I do any less? My meatballs are fried and then braised in the sauce for an hour. They soak up some of the liquid and become plump and juicy, tender, and super flavorful. This is a meal that all three of my kids love. They can help shape the meatballs or roll out the pasta dough. It makes for a fun afternoon cooking at home.

Make the Meatballs:

Soak the diced dried bread in the milk in a mixing bowl until soft and tender. Meanwhile, put the pork, veal, beef, onion, garlic, black pepper, and red pepper flakes in a stand mixer fitted with a paddle attachment. Mix on low speed until just combined.

In a medium bowl, whisk together the eggs, Parmesan cheese, Worcestershire sauce, salt, and crushed fennel seeds. Add to the meat mixture. Add the soaked bread. Start the mixer on low speed. Increase the speed to medium for 30 seconds, or just until the meat mixture is completely combined. Do not overwork the meat mixture or it will become a paste; you just want it to hold together.

Portion the meat mixture into 3½-ounce (100-gram) meatballs. Lay them out on a parchment-lined baking sheet; you should end up with about 20 meatballs. Use a small strainer to dust the meatballs with the flour, giving them a light, even coating. Refrigerate for at least 2 hours. The flour will absorb moisture from the meatballs and create an outer layer that will form a nice crust when you fry the meatballs.

Make the Tomato Sauce:

Use a food mill to press the tomatoes into a large bowl, discarding the seeds. Alternatively, you can pulse the tomatoes in a food processor and then pass them through a mesh strainer to remove the seeds. Put the olive oil in a heavy bottomed saucepot or Dutch oven set over medium-high heat. When it begins to shimmer, add the onion and garlic and cook, stirring constantly, until they are translucent and aromatic, 2 to 3 minutes. Add the tomatoes, salt, and sugar to the pot, bring them to a simmer, and reduce the heat to low. Cook the sauce for 30 to 45 minutes, stirring occasionally, until the sauce thickens and looks homogenous. Remove from the heat and add the basil. Cover and steep for 20 minutes.

➲

Cook the Meatballs in the Sauce:

Preheat the oven to 325°F (165°C).

Heat the ¼ cup olive oil in a large Dutch oven set over medium-high heat until the oil shimmers in the bottom of the pan. Carefully add the meatballs one at a time, being careful not to crowd the pan. You can do this in batches if necessary. Let the meatballs brown on the bottom before turning them. Get a nice crust on the outside of the meatballs, and then transfer them to the pot of warm sauce while you continue to sear the remainder. Once all the meatballs are in the sauce, put the lid on the pot and put it in the oven to cook for 1 hour.

Serve 3 meatballs per person in a pool of sauce, and garnish with grated Parmesan and fresh basil leaves. Serve with the Mozzarella and Roasted Garlic Focaccia. Or serve 2 or 3 meatballs per person on a bed of fresh Tagliolini, garnishing with grated Parmesan and fresh basil leaves.

Or you can make meatball sandwiches by splitting long loaves of Italian bread and layering them with meatballs, sauce, and mozzarella cheese. Place the tops back on the bread, wrap the sandwiches in aluminum foil, and bake for 20 minutes to melt the cheese before serving.

Note Sandwich Bread from page 48 and Broccoli Rabe with Anchovy Dressing from page 141.

Pasta Dough

MAKES 6 TO 8 PORTIONS (PLUS 1 EXTRA SHEET)

5¼ cups / 560 grams "00" artisan pasta
flour, plus extra for rolling out the dough

4 large eggs

2 tablespoons / 28 grams water

Semolina flour, for nesting the cut noodles

SPECIAL EQUIPMENT:

Pasta-rolling machine or attachment
for stand mixer

I love making fresh pasta, so much so
that I was compelled to open my Italian
restaurants. It's a soothing process to
knead and roll dough. Even better,
when people realize that you've made
it yourself, it makes them feel special.
They know you've taken extra care with
their supper. This recipe makes more
than enough pasta for 6 to 8 people,
but feel free to freeze the extra because
fresh pasta keeps very well when frozen.
Once made, these noodles will keep for
up to a week in the fridge and up to a
month in the freezer. Frozen noodles
can go directly into a pot of boiling
water; it will just take an extra minute
or two to cook them.

Pour the "00" flour onto a counter or into
the center of a large mixing bowl and use
a clean hand or spoon to make a well in
the center of the flour. In a smaller mixing
bowl, combine the eggs and water and
beat them with a fork or whisk until
smooth. Pour the eggs into the well in a
slow, steady stream, while stirring them
into the flour with a fork, rubber spatula,
or wooden spoon. Switch over to mixing
with your hands when the mixture starts
getting stiff. The finished dough will feel
tacky; transfer to a lightly floured countertop and begin to knead the dough. Try
not to add much additional flour; it
should be moist, but after kneading a
few times it should no longer be sticky.
If it becomes too dry, it will be hard to

roll out later. As you knead, the dough will become smooth and silky. This process should take about 5 minutes. The gluten in the flour will begin to pull in the surface moisture, and what once felt tacky will become quite dry. Wrap the pasta in plastic wrap and refrigerate for at least 1 hour and up to 12 hours.

Divide the dough into 6 equal pieces. Take one piece and cover the rest with plastic wrap. Use your hands to press the first piece of dough into a flattened rectangle, roughly 4 by 8 inches, to prepare it for a pasta-rolling machine. This rectangle should fit into your pasta machine at the widest setting, usually #1; if not, simply flatten it a little bit more with your hands so you can begin

running it through the machine. Dust the dough with a small amount of flour on both sides. Roll it through the machine on the first setting 2 times. Dust the outside of the pasta sheets, as needed, with a small amount of flour to prevent sticking. Move to the next setting on the pasta machine and run the dough through it twice, dusting with flour as needed. Repeat until you have run the dough through the second-to-last setting 2 times.

Attach a cutter to the machine and place a parchment-lined baking sheet coated with a light dusting of semolina flour nearby for the cut noodles. Run the dough through the cutter and coil the noodles into small nests on the baking sheet. Repeat with the remaining pieces

of dough until all of the noodles have been cut. Use immediately, or let dry at room temperature for up to 4 hours before cooking or freezing. If freezing, transfer to an airtight container, and, when ready to serve, cook from frozen.

Focaccia with Mozzarella and Roasted Garlic

MAKES 1 (9-BY-13-INCH) LOAF

BIGA:

7 tablespoons / 100 grams room-temperature water, preferably distilled

¼ teaspoon / 0.75 gram active dry yeast

4¼ ounces / 170 grams bread flour

ROASTED GARLIC PUREE:

1 head garlic

2 tablespoons / 28 grams olive oil

DOUGH:

5½ tablespoons / 78 grams olive oil, divided

1 cup plus 7 ounces / 425 grams room-temperature water, preferably distilled

1 teaspoon / 3 grams active dry yeast

2¼ teaspoons / 14.5 grams fine sea salt

1¼ pounds / 567 grams bread flour

8 ounces / 227 grams mozzarella cheese, diced

2 tablespoons / 30 grams Roasted Garlic Puree or store-bought

1 teaspoon / 5 grams olive oil

¼ cup / 20 grams finely grated Parmesan cheese (I use a Microplane for this)

Who doesn't like cheesy garlic bread? It's the perfect accompaniment for spaghetti and meatballs. Some people think that making bread is complicated, but it's mostly weighing the ingredients, mixing, and shaping. Everything else happens on its own while you do other things. This bread is great because you can make the biga in the morning, mix the dough in the afternoon, and have crusty, delicious bread for dinner. It's so much better than what you can buy in a store; you'd be crazy not to try it.

Make the Biga:

Put the water and yeast in a medium bowl and stir them together with a wooden spoon. Add the flour and stir until completely blended. Cover loosely with a kitchen towel and leave on a countertop for at least 5 hours and up to 12 hours.

Make the Roasted Garlic Puree:

Preheat the oven to 375°F (190°C).

Wrap the garlic in aluminum foil, set it in a small baking dish, and roast for 30 to 45 minutes, until it feels tender when gently squeezed with your hands (in oven mitts). Let the garlic cool for 15 minutes, or until cool enough to handle. Peel the garlic and put the cloves in the small bowl of a food processor along

with the olive oil. Puree until smooth. Use immediately, or transfer to a clean container and chill. Roasted Garlic Puree may be kept in a covered container in the refrigerator for up to 2 weeks.

Make the Dough:

Use 1 tablespoon (14 grams) of the olive oil to coat the inside of a medium bowl. Mix the water, 3½ tablespoons (50 grams) of the olive oil, and the yeast in a stand mixer with the paddle attachment on low speed until the yeast dissolves, 30 to 45 seconds. Add the Biga and salt to the mixture and mix for 30 seconds. Stop the mixer and add all of the flour, and then mix on low speed until the flour is incorporated. Turn the mixer up to medium speed and mix for 2 minutes. The dough will still look wet and start to pull away from the sides of the bowl. Transfer the dough to the prepared bowl and cover with plastic wrap. If your oven has a proofing setting, proof the dough at 90°F (32°C) for 45 minutes, or until the dough has doubled in size; or set it in a warm spot in the kitchen until the dough has doubled, 60 to 90 minutes.

Once the dough has proofed, press your hand down gently in the center of the dough to deflate it, turn it out onto the countertop, and use a bench scraper to divide it in half. Oil a 2-quart baking

dish with the remaining 1 tablespoon (14 grams) olive oil, put one piece of dough in the bottom of the dish, and press it out into an even layer from edge to edge with your fingers. Sprinkle the diced mozzarella over the top and then lay the second piece of dough over the cheese. Gently stretch and press it out to fit the inside the baking dish so the cheese is enclosed between the top and bottom layers of dough. Cover with plastic wrap and let the dough proof for another 30 to 40 minutes, until it has risen and looks puffy.

Preheat the oven to 425°F (220°C).

Put the garlic puree and the 1 teaspoon olive oil in a small bowl and mix them together. Brush the garlic over the top of the dough, using all of the puree. Sprinkle the Parmesan cheese over the garlic. Bake for 15 minutes, and then reduce the oven temperature to 350°F (180°C) without opening the oven door, and bake for an additional 25 to 30 minutes. The bread should be a deep golden brown around the edges and look set and cooked through.

Fried Chicken

SERVES 4

CHICKEN BRINE:

9 cups / 2.02 kilograms brown chicken stock

1 cup / 225 grams pickle brine

2 tablespoons / 36 grams fine sea salt

1 teaspoon / 1.2 grams coriander seeds

1 teaspoon / 2.3 grams fennel seeds

½ teaspoon / 2.6 grams yellow mustard seeds

1 bay leaf

½ bunch thyme

½ head garlic, split horizontally

1 orange, quartered

1 (**4- to 5-pound** / 1.8- to 2.26-kilogram) whole chicken

CHICKEN SPICE:

2 tablespoons / 18 grams Our Bay Seasoning Blend (page 35)

4 teaspoons / 24 grams fine sea salt

4 teaspoons / 12 grams paprika

2 teaspoons / 2.5 grams chili powder

2 teaspoons / 4.5 grams onion powder

2 teaspoons / 4.5 grams garlic powder

2 teaspoons / 2.5 grams ground celery seeds

1 teaspoon / 2 grams freshly ground black pepper

CHICKEN DREDGE:

4 cups / 600 grams all-purpose flour

1 cup / 140 grams cornmeal

½ cup / 56 grams cornstarch

2 tablespoons / 18 grams Chicken Spice

Peanut or canola oil, for frying the chicken

I named one of my restaurants Family Meal because I love the idea of gathering the family around a table, whether at home or in a restaurant, to enjoy each other's company along with a good meal. I love to bring people together. This fried chicken was developed for the opening menu of Family Meal and, funnily enough, when we were testing recipes for it we served the fried chicken for "family meal" to the staff at my other restaurant Volt. Everybody weighed in on what they liked best about each version, and this recipe is the culmination of all those tests. The secret is the pickle juice in the brine. It's like a magic elixir, and it kills me whenever I see someone throw it away. In this crunchy, juicy, fried chicken, it makes everything taste better. Depending on the season, the Celeriac and Green Apple Slaw (page 90) or the Baked Applesauce (page 95) would be a great way to round out this meal.

Make the Chicken Brine:
Put all of the ingredients in a large pot set over high heat. Bring to a boil, adjust the heat to maintain a simmer, and cook for 15 minutes. Strain and cool the liquid to 40°F (4°C) and reserve in the refrigerator until you are ready to brine your chicken.

Cut Up the Chicken:
Use kitchen shears to cut along one side of the backbone of the chicken from the head to the tail. The hardest piece to cut will be at the top of the neck. Then cut along the other side of the backbone to remove it from the bird. Set aside to use for stock. Open up the chicken and pat down the cavity with paper towels to remove any excess moisture. Cut away any excess skin from the bottom of the thigh area and remove any pocket of fat. Add them to your stock trimmings.

Beginning from the tail end of the bird, use the shears to cut through the center of the breast, dividing the chicken in half.

➔

Flip over one piece so that it is breast side up and gently lift the leg. Cut through the skin at the bottom of the breast and down to the bone, sliding it horizontally under the bone and toward the leg, separating it from the breast. Lay the leg on a cutting board and look at the skin; you will see a line where the skin changes from the leg to the thigh. That line indicates where to separate the leg and thigh. Cut through the joint to separate the pieces. Set them aside.

Pull the wing slightly out and away from the breast so you can see where it attaches to the body. Slide the tip of your knife around the top of the wing where it attaches to the breast and expose the joint. Cut through the joint and remove the wing. Use the shears to trim any excess bone from around the breast and reserve for stock. Repeat with the other side so that you end up with 8 pieces of chicken. Alternatively, you can ask your butcher to break the chicken down for you or substitute 4 to 5 pounds of your favorite part of the chicken. Put the chicken in a large container with a lid and pour the brine over it. Cover and refrigerate for 12 hours.

Make the Chicken Spice:
Put all of the ingredients in a small bowl and whisk to blend. Chicken Spice can be stored in an airtight container for up to 1 year.

Make the Chicken Dredge:
Place all of the ingredients in a medium bowl and whisk to blend. Drain the chicken from the brine and set it on a rack set over a baking sheet. Line another baking sheet with parchment paper. Dredge the chicken 1 piece at a time, rolling it in the bowl and then shaking it gently to remove any excess. Put each piece on the parchment-lined baking sheet. When all the pieces are dredged, put the baking sheet in the refrigerator for 30 minutes. Reserve the remaining dredge in the bowl.

Fry the Chicken:
Preheat a deep fryer or heavy skillet with 3 inches of oil to 350°F (180°C).

Preheat the oven to 200°F (95°C). Place a wire rack on a baking sheet and set aside.

Dredge the chicken pieces one more time, returning them to the parchment-lined baking sheet. If you don't have a thermometer, you can check the temperature of the oil by adding a pinch of flour. If it fries up immediately, you're good to go. Put 2 or 3 pieces of chicken at a time in the hot oil, beginning with the larger pieces, and fry for 8 minutes on each side, or until golden brown all over. Transfer to the wire rack, put it in the oven, and continue to fry the remaining chicken. Once the last batch of chicken has spent 10 minutes in the low oven, you are ready to serve.

Hot Sauce

4 pounds / 1.8 kilograms red bell peppers, seeded and stemmed

1 pound / 454 grams jalapeño peppers, seeded, stemmed, and cut into small dice

5 fish peppers (or Arbol peppers), seeded, stemmed, and cut into small dice

4 cloves garlic, minced

4 bunches thyme, leaves picked and finely chopped (about 6 tablespoons)

1 cup / 225 grams rice wine vinegar

3 tablespoons / 40 grams packed light brown sugar

Zest and juice of 4 limes

½ teaspoon / 2 grams xanthan gum (optional)

2¼ teaspoons / 13.5 grams fine sea salt

2 teaspoons / 4 grams ground white pepper

SPECIAL EQUIPMENT:

Masticating juicer (optional)

It should come as no surprise that I wanted to try my hand at making hot sauce. I'm all about reinventing things in my kitchen. At the height of their season peppers are abundant, and I'm always searching for new ways to use them. Fish peppers, sometimes referred to as Baltimore fish peppers, are grown locally from an heirloom seed. The peppers are spicy and hot and when fully ripe are a deep and brilliant red. They make a great hot sauce, especially when blended with jalapeño peppers and sweet red bell peppers for balance. My sauce is quickly made and unfermented, retaining the fresh, bright flavor of the peppers. I've added a small amount of xanthan gum to keep the sauce from separating, but if you don't have it, just give the sauce a good shake before using it. It's easy to make and a great staple to have in your culinary arsenal.

Use a masticating juicer to juice half of the red bell peppers. If you don't have a juicer, you can puree them in a blender until completely smooth, then line a sieve with 3 or 4 layers of cheesecloth and let the juice drip through overnight into a bowl in the refrigerator. Or you can ask your local juice place to juice them for you.

Cut the rest of the red bell peppers into small dice. Put the diced red bell peppers, jalapeño peppers, fish peppers, garlic, and thyme in a medium pot set over medium heat and cook, stirring occasionally, until tender and fragrant, about 10 minutes. Add the vinegar and brown sugar. Bring to a simmer and cook for 15 minutes. Transfer to a blender and add the red pepper juice, lime zest and juice, xanthan gum (if using), salt, and white pepper, and puree until smooth. Strain through a fine-mesh sieve into a bowl and cool. The hot sauce may be stored in a bottle in the refrigerator for up to 3 months.

Bread-and-Butter Pickles

MAKES ABOUT 4 QUARTS

Here's an opportunity to make your own pickle brine. Sweet pickles are a staple in the South. This version has a little kick from the jalapeño peppers and a little more spice than those bright green pickle slices you can buy at the supermarket. If there are any leftovers from supper, I like to make a midnight snack or breakfast sandwich with them. Split a biscuit, slide in a piece of (boneless) fried chicken, top with hot sauce and pickles, and lay on the top of the biscuit. Sink your teeth in and enjoy.

5 pounds / 2.26 kilograms
Kirby cucumbers, cut crosswise into
¼-inch rounds (about 8 cups)

2 large Spanish onions, thinly sliced
(about 4 cups)

5 cloves garlic

2 jalapeño peppers, stems removed
and split in half lengthwise

1 cup / 288 grams fine sea salt

4 cups / 900 grams apple cider vinegar

4 cups / 900 grams distilled white vinegar

3 cups / 600 grams sugar

3 tablespoons / 24 grams yellow
mustard seeds

3 tablespoons / 10.5 grams coriander seeds

1 tablespoon / 9 grams celery seeds

1 tablespoon / 7.5 grams allspice berries

1 tablespoon / 9 grams ground turmeric

1 tablespoon / 6 grams red pepper flakes

3 whole cloves

2 bay leaves

Mix the cucumbers, onions, garlic, and jalapeño peppers with the salt and put them in a heatproof container large enough to hold them and 3 quarts of liquid. Let them macerate overnight at room temperature.

Put all of the remaining ingredients in a large pot set over high heat. Bring to a boil, and then adjust the heat to maintain a simmer for 15 minutes. Strain the liquid over the cucumbers, cover, and let cool to room temperature.

Transfer to a covered container and refrigerate. The pickles will be ready to eat after at least 12 hours in the brine, and they may be stored in their liquid in a covered container in the refrigerator for up to 6 months.

Buttermilk Biscuits

MAKES 20 BISCUITS

These buttermilk biscuits require a light touch. At my restaurant Family Meal, where we make these in giant batches, we grate the butter and freeze it with liquid nitrogen before putting all of the ingredients in a large plastic container and then gently shaking it until the dough comes together. It doesn't get mixed at all. This version doesn't require liquid nitrogen; just be sure your butter is well chilled and you'll get light, flaky biscuits that will practically melt in your mouth.

1½ pounds / 680 grams
all-purpose flour

1½ tablespoons / 27 grams
baking powder

1½ tablespoons / 19 grams sugar

2 teaspoons / 12 grams fine sea salt

1½ teaspoons / 7.5 grams baking soda

2 cups plus 2 tablespoons / 510 grams
chilled buttermilk

4 large egg yolks, divided

10 tablespoons / 140 grams chilled
unsalted butter, diced

1 cup / 113 grams grated cheddar
or Jack cheese

½ cup / 32 grams chopped fresh chives

2 tablespoons / 33 grams whole milk

Put the flour, baking powder, sugar, salt, and baking soda in a medium bowl and whisk to blend. Put the buttermilk and 3 of the egg yolks in a large measuring cup and whisk to blend. Cut the butter into the flour using 2 knives or a pastry blender until the mixture resembles coarse meal. Pour the buttermilk mixture into the flour and add the cheese and chives. Use a rubber spatula to gently mix everything together until all of the flour has been absorbed. Do not overwork the dough. You should be able to see bits of butter throughout the dough. Cover and chill for at least 30 minutes and up to 2 hours.

Turn the dough out onto a lightly floured countertop. Gently roll it out into a rectangle approximately ½ inch thick. Fold the top third down over the middle third and the bottom third up over the two layers, as you would fold a letter. Give the dough a quarter turn and repeat rolling and folding the dough. Wrap with plastic wrap and return to the refrigerator for 10 minutes to rest.

Preheat the oven to 375°F (190°C).

Put the remaining egg yolk and the milk in a small bowl and whisk with a fork until smooth. Take the dough out of the refrigerator, unwrap, and put it on a lightly floured countertop. Roll it out to a thickness of ½ inch and use a 2-inch biscuit cutter to cut out biscuits. Arrange them on a baking sheet, leaving 2 inches of space between each one. Brush the tops with the egg wash and bake for 8 minutes, or until they rise and turn golden brown. Let rest for 5 minutes before serving.

Pork Shoulder and Pumpkin Sauerkraut

SERVES 6 TO 8

COFFEE BBQ RUB:

½ **cup** / 106 grams packed light brown sugar

3 tablespoons plus 1 teaspoon / 20 grams ground coffee

2¾ tablespoons / 50 grams fine sea salt

2½ tablespoons / 20 grams smoked paprika

2½ teaspoons / 5 grams ground ginger

2½ teaspoons / 5 grams red pepper flakes

PORK SHOULDER:

1 (**8- to 10-pound** / 3.6- to 4.5-kilogram) pork shoulder

2 pounds / 908 grams prepared sauerkraut

15 ounces / 425 grams canned pumpkin puree

3 medium onions, thinly sliced

4 cups / 900 grams apple cider

This pork is amazing. I don't know how else to describe it. The Coffee BBQ Rub goes on the night before. As it soaks into the pork, it forms a layer of brine on the surface. This denatures the surface proteins just enough to ensure that an amazing crust will form when you roast the pork. The combination of pumpkin and sauerkraut may sound unusual, but the ingredients work together to make something sweet and tangy and full of great flavors. The apple cider in the pan steams just enough to help tenderize the meat, and the long rest ensures that it is tender and juicy when you carve it up for dinner. It's the taste of fall.

Make the Coffee BBQ Rub:
Put all of the ingredients into a bowl. Whisk to blend.

Season the Pork Shoulder:
Put the pork shoulder in a large bowl or container. Rub the shoulder all over with the Coffee BBQ Rub. Wrap the bowl with plastic wrap and refrigerate the shoulder for 12 to 18 hours.

Cook the Pork Shoulder:
Preheat the oven to 250°F (120°C).

Remove the pork shoulder from the refrigerator. Put the prepared sauerkraut and its juices, the pumpkin puree, and sliced onions in a large roasting pan. Use a spoon to stir the pumpkin puree into the sauerkraut and onions. When the mixture is evenly combined, lay the pork shoulder on the bed of vegetables. Pour any juices and spices from the pork shoulder over the meat and spread them evenly over the top. Put the roasting pan in the oven and cook for 1 hour.

Remove the pan from the oven and stir the sauerkraut, onion, and pumpkin mixture. Use a rubber spatula to scrape down the sides of the pan so that nothing begins to stick and burn. Put the shoulder back in the oven and cook for another hour. After the second hour, remove the shoulder from the oven and stir the apple cider into the sauerkraut, onion, and pumpkin mixture. Put the shoulder back into the oven and cook for 2 hours longer.

Remove the shoulder from the oven and stir the vegetable mixture, scraping the sides of the roasting pan. Put the shoulder back in the oven and cook for 1 more hour. After a total of 5 hours, remove the shoulder from the oven. A rich crust will have formed on the meat. The bone will be loose but not quite falling out of the meat. The vegetable mixture will be a deep, caramelized orange. Put the roasting pan in a warm place to rest for 35 to 45 minutes. Do not skip the resting step. Cover loosely with aluminum foil and go do something else so you're not tempted to cut into it too soon. When the meat is fully rested, carve the shoulder, and serve it with the pumpkin sauerkraut alongside.

Cheese Grits

SERVES 6 TO 8

CHEESE STOCK:

3 quarts / 2.7 kilograms water

2 medium carrots, cut into chunks

1 celery rib, diced

½ large onion, cut into chunks
with the skin on

4 large cloves garlic

1 ounce / 28 grams Parmesan
cheese rind

1 teaspoon / 6 grams fine sea salt

GRITS:

8 cups / 1.8 kilograms Cheese Stock

1 cup / 225 grams unsalted butter

2 cups / 340 grams stone-ground
yellow grits

1 bay leaf

1 teaspoon / 6 grams fine sea salt

1 cup / 260 grams whole milk

1 cup / 113 grams shredded
cheddar cheese

SPECIAL EQUIPMENT:

Pressure cooker (optional)

Cheese grits are one of those staple items that everyone should know how to cook well. Locally grown stone-ground grits are becoming more common, and that's a good thing. These grits are coarse and retain all of their natural oils. What this means is that they may take a little longer to cook, but they will be creamy and full of flavor when they're done. The Parmesan cheese stock adds umami and helps amplify the natural nutty flavor of the cornmeal. Use your favorite cheddar cheese here, because the flavor will shine through and complement the natural corn flavor of the grits.

Make the Cheese Stock:
Put all of the ingredients in a pressure cooker and cook on high pressure for 30 minutes. Let the pressure dissipate naturally. Strain through a fine-mesh strainer. Alternatively, put everything into a large pot set over high heat and bring to a simmer. Reduce the heat to low and cook, skimming occasionally, for 1 hour. Strain and reserve.

Make the Grits:
Put the 8 cups Cheese Stock in a medium pot and bring to a simmer. Melt the butter in a medium Dutch oven set over medium heat until it foams and starts to brown. Add the grits and cook, stirring until they smell slightly nutty, 1 to 2 minutes. Whisk in the hot Cheese Stock and add the bay leaf and salt. Bring to a simmer, then reduce the heat to low and cook for 30 to 45 minutes, until the grits are completely tender. Add the milk and cheddar and mix thoroughly to make sure everything is incorporated.

Braised Greens with Smoked Turkey Tails

SERVES 6 TO 8

Smoked turkey tails are one of those ingredients you stumble across in Wegmans and wonder why you never thought of them yourself. There are many who consider the tail to be the best part of the bird. It's a tiny nugget, with more fat than meat, that roasts up crispy and juicy. Smoked tails are perfect for braising, adding fat and flavor to the greens, but if you can't find them at your local market, smoked turkey necks or wings will work in this recipe too. I like to pair the sweet flavor of Tuscan kale with spicy mustard greens to wake up the palate. I use the pressure cooker here to expedite the cooking process while making sure the greens are tender and full of flavor. This also helps free up your hands to get everything else on the table.

2 bunches Tuscan kale

2 bunches mustard greens

1⅓ **cups** / 300 grams apple cider vinegar

1 **tablespoon** / 6 grams Tabasco sauce

¼ **cup** / 54 grams packed light brown sugar

1½ **teaspoons** / 9 grams fine sea salt

1 **tablespoon** / 12.5 grams light olive oil

1 medium onion, thinly sliced, preferably with a mandoline

3 cloves garlic, thinly sliced, preferably with a mandoline

4 smoked turkey tails

SPECIAL EQUIPMENT:

8-quart pressure cooker (optional)

Trim and discard any fibrous stems from the greens. Combine the vinegar, Tabasco, sugar, and salt in a small saucepan and set over low heat just until the sugar dissolves. Put the oil in the base of an 8-quart stovetop pressure cooker and set over medium heat. Once the oil shimmers, add the onion and garlic cook for 2 to 3 minutes, stirring, until the onions soften. Add half of the greens. Wilt the greens by folding from the bottom to the top of the pot with a silicone spatula. Pour over one-quarter of the cider-and-sugar mixture to help the wilting process. Add more greens and continue wilting until you can fit all the greens in the pressure cooker. Add the turkey tails and pour in any remaining vinegar mixture. Close the lid securely and bring to full pressure. Cook at full pressure for 30 minutes. Let the pressure dissipate naturally for 20 to 30 minutes. Open the cooker and remove the turkey tails.

Alternatively, you can use a large pot instead of the base of a pressure cooker to wilt the greens. Once the turkey tails and remaining vinegar have been added, set the pot over high heat and bring the liquid to a simmer. Reduce the heat to low, cover, and cook for 90 minutes.

Pick the meat from the turkey tails and fold it back into the greens. Transfer to a large bowl and serve immediately.

Pork Ribs with Kimchi and Dr Pepper

SERVES 6 TO 8

In 2011 my brother Michael and I went on a "Fire Smoke & Flavor" BBQ tour thanks to Williams-Sonoma. We were lucky enough to eat at some of the very best BBQ joints in the country, and when I got home I was fired up to create some great meals of my own. I had some of the best ribs at Charlie Vergo's Rendez-vous restaurant, known for their ribs cooked over charcoal. I love that smoky flavor, but it's hard to find the time to cook them that way at home. I want to be able to spend that time with my family. So instead I pressure-cook these ribs so they are tender and juicy, and then I finish them on the grill to get a hint of char and some of that smoky flavor.

2 full slabs (about **6¾ pounds** / 3 kilograms) St Louis pork ribs (each slab cut into thirds)

2 (**30-ounce** / 850-gram) jars kimchi

2 (**12-ounce** / 340-gram) cans Dr Pepper

¼ **cup** / 75 grams ketchup

4 scallions, thinly sliced (about ¼ cup)

SPECIAL EQUIPMENT:

Pressure cooker (optional)

Charcoal grill

Put the pork, kimchi, and Dr Pepper in a pressure cooker and cook at high pressure for 15 minutes. Alternatively, put the pork, kimchi, and Dr Pepper in a covered baking dish and braise for 3 hours at 300°F (150°C), or until the meat is tender.

Preheat a charcoal grill to high heat.

Once the ribs are cooked, let the pressure release naturally (if using a pressure cooker) and then transfer the ribs to a baking sheet to cool. Strain the cooking liquid from the pressure cooker or baking dish, reserving the kimchi and the broth separately. Put the broth and the ketchup in a medium saucepot set over low heat and simmer until the sauce thickens enough to coat the ribs. Put the cooked kimchi in a casserole pan large enough to hold the ribs and keep warm in a low (200°F / 95°C) oven.

When you are ready to serve, take the ribs out to the grill and sear them on both sides, being sure to heat them through. Baste them with the sauce, and serve with the kimchi and a small bowl of the sliced scallions for sprinkling on top.

Bacon-Wrapped Corn on the Cob

SERVES 8

As long as you've got the grill fired up you may as well use it. Corn on the cob comes with a natural handle that makes it easy to turn the cobs on the grill. I line the bacon with basil and jalapeño pepper before I wrap it around the corn. The bacon crisps and the corn steams inside. Some of that smoky flavor penetrates, and as you bite into the corn you get bright bursts of aromatic basil and the sweet heat of the jalapeño pepper. This corn is so good it's practically a meal all by itself.

3 pounds / 1.36 kilograms bacon slices

1 bunch basil, leaves only

2 jalapeño peppers, thinly sliced

8 ears corn, shucked

Charred Lime Crema (page 208)

Line a baking sheet with parchment paper.

Lay a 13-by-18-inch piece of parchment paper on your countertop and lay 6 or 7 slices of bacon alongside each other, slightly overlapping one another, fat side against meat side, to form a rough rectangle that is as wide as an ear of corn is long. Cover with another sheet of parchment paper and pound lightly with a meat mallet or small sauté pan to flatten the bacon and press it together. Remove the top parchment sheet and decorate the bacon with 10 to 12 small pieces of basil (you can tear up the larger leaves) and a few slices of jalapeño pepper. Lay 1 ear of corn across the bottom of the rectangle and roll the corn up in the bacon. Transfer the bacon-wrapped corn to the prepared baking sheet, laying it seam side down on the parchment paper. Repeat the process with the remaining 7 ears of corn (you can use the same 2 pieces of parchment paper) until all are wrapped in bacon. Cover with plastic wrap and refrigerate for at least 8 hours and up to 24 hours.

Preheat a grill to medium heat.

If you have a larger grill with an upper rack, use that to cook the bacon. Grill the corn, starting with the bacon seam side down. Give them a quarter turn every 5 minutes, until all of the bacon is crisp and caramelized and the corn is tender, 25 to 30 minutes total. Alternatively, you can lay the bacon-wrapped corn on a rack set over a baking sheet and cook it in a 350°F (180°C) oven for 25 to 30 minutes, until the bacon is crisp and the corn is tender. I recommend serving these with the Charred Lime Crema alongside.

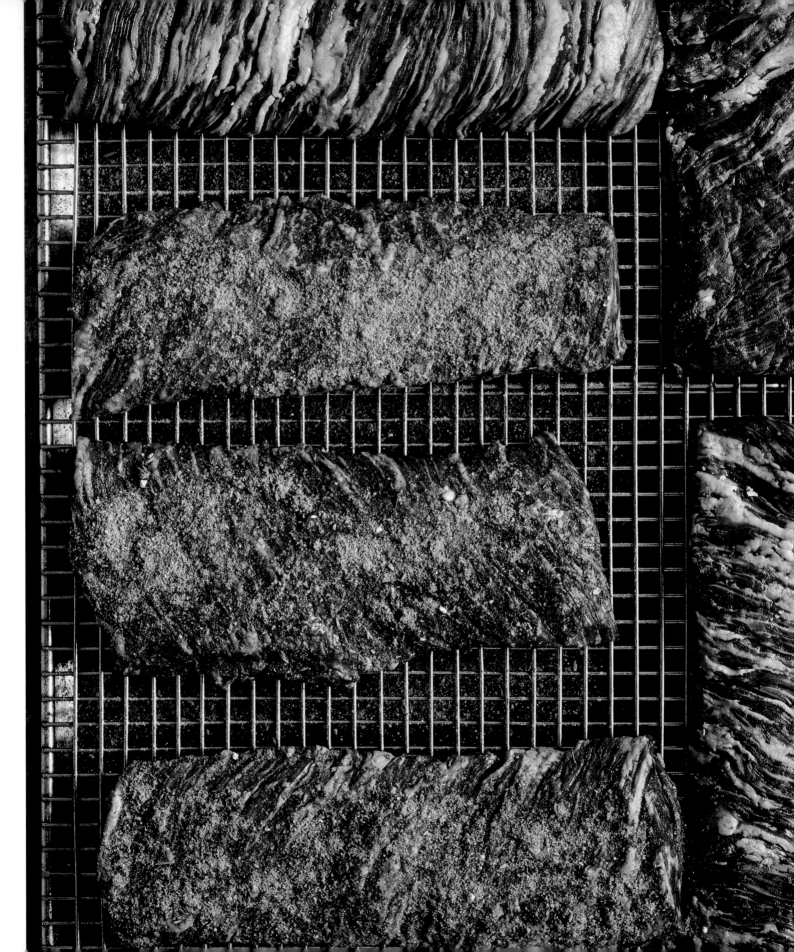

Skirt Steak Fajitas

SERVES 6

FAJITA SEASONING:

5 teaspoons / 12 grams chili powder

1 tablespoon / 12 grams sugar

1 tablespoon / 7 grams cornstarch

2 teaspoons / 5 grams onion powder

2 teaspoons / 5 grams garlic powder

2 teaspoons / 4 grams ground cumin seeds

1½ teaspoons / 8 grams smoked paprika

1 teaspoon / 6 grams fine sea salt

½ teaspoon / 1 gram cayenne pepper

FAJITAS:

3 pounds / 1.36 kilograms skirt steak

1 tablespoon / 9 grams Fajita Seasoning

1 teaspoon / 6 grams fine sea salt

FOR SERVING:

Flour or corn tortillas

2 tomatoes, diced

½ head iceberg lettuce, shredded

2 limes, cut into wedges

Charred Lime Crema (page 208)

Smoked Guacamole (page 62)

Salsa

I love Tex-Mex cooking. If we go out on a Friday night, I'm heading to a Tex-Mex joint and ordering fajitas. They are fun to eat: the sizzling platter as it comes to the table, the container of warm tortillas, and the array of vegetables and condiments that range alongside the meat. I also enjoy the way meat is served in South American countries, well spiced and with an abundance of lime juice or other citrus to cut through the fat and the spice. I've married those two approaches in my fajitas. The meat gets seasoned and left overnight so the flavors can really penetrate, and then it's seared and served alongside an array of tortillas and condiments so people can build their own meal.

Make the Fajita Seasoning:

Put all of the ingredients in a large mortar and grind them together into a uniform mixture. Alternatively, you can put everything in a medium bowl and whisk to blend. Fajita Seasoning can be stored in an airtight container at room temperature for up to 1 month.

Make the Fajitas:

Set a small rack on a plate or a smaller baking dish. Trim any silverskin and large pieces of fat from the skirt steak and cut it into 4 equal pieces. Mix the Fajita Seasoning with the salt and then use the mixture to season the meat on both sides. Lay the meat on the rack and refrigerate, uncovered, overnight, or up to 24 hours.

Preheat a grill so that it is very hot. Sear the steaks on the grill for 2 to 3 minutes per side, and then transfer to a plate. Invert another plate on top to cover the meat and let it rest for 10 minutes. Slice the skirt steak about ½ inch thick and serve with warm tortillas, diced tomatoes, shredded lettuce, lime wedges, Charred Lime Crema, Smoked Guacamole, and salsa alongside.

Grilled Watermelon "Ribs"

SERVES 6 TO 8

I love serving grilled watermelon rind with fajitas. I season it with the same Fajita Seasoning a few hours before I'm ready to cook it and then squeeze fresh lime over the melon after it's cooked. The melon rind firms up a bit on the grill and absorbs some rich, smoky flavors. The texture of the cooked meat and melon is actually quite similar, though one is chewy and spicy while the other is tangy and sweet.

1 (**8- to 10-pound** / 3.6- to 4.5-kilogram) watermelon

¼ cup Fajita Seasoning (page 127)

2 tablespoons / 28 grams olive oil

2 limes, cut into wedges

Cut the small ends of the watermelon on both sides. Stand it up on a cutting board and use a serrated knife to shave off the skin, leaving the pale green rind and the red center. Once you have pared away all of the skin, cut away the green and white rind, along with the lightest inner section of the fruit, leaving the deep red center intact. This can be reserved to serve on its own. Try to remove the rind in 4 pieces.

Place each piece on a cutting board and score them in slightly diagonal lines, ¼ inch deep, horizontally across the slabs so they resemble a rack of ribs. Season each piece on both sides with 1 tablespoon of the Fajita Seasoning. Wrap the watermelon "ribs" in plastic wrap and refrigerate for at least 4 hours and up to 24 hours.

Preheat a grill so that it is very hot.

Rub each slab of watermelon rind on both sides with 1 ½ teaspoons of the olive oil. Place the ribs diagonally on the grill and cook for 1 to 2 minutes, until grill marks form on the fruit. Give each melon a half turn and cook for another 1 to 2 minutes, so that crosshatch marks appear. Flip the watermelon over and repeat on the other side. Transfer the watermelon to a large platter and squeeze lime juice over the slabs. Carve the watermelon into "ribs" and serve.

Potato and Egg Salad

SERVES 6 TO 8

I love potato salad. It's one of those must-haves at family gatherings and BBQs. There's always at least one potato salad and sometimes as many as four. Each one is different, and most of them are pretty good. My potato salad incorporates the flavors of a deviled egg. The yolks absorb the dressing and make the salad creamy, while the whites add a contrasting texture to the soft, creamy potatoes. I like to serve this ice cold so that it balances out all the hot and spicy food that comes off the grill.

12 large eggs

3⅓ **pounds** / 1.5 kilograms Yukon Gold potatoes, peeled and cut into 1-inch dice

1¼ **cups** / 300 grams buttermilk

1 cup plus 2 tablespoons / 225 grams mayonnaise (I prefer Duke's)

3 tablespoons plus 1 teaspoon / 56 grams yellow mustard

5 teaspoons / 30 grams pickle juice (from your favorite pickles)

2 teaspoons / 8 grams soy sauce

1 teaspoon / 6 grams Tabasco sauce

1 teaspoon / 5 grams apple cider vinegar

1 teaspoon / 6 grams fine sea salt

⅓ cup / 80 grams minced pickles (sweet or sour, as you like)

2½ ounces / 70 grams country ham, minced

2 tablespoons / 6 grams chopped fresh chives

1 tablespoon / 4 grams chopped fresh dill

Put the eggs in a single layer in a large pot and cover with at least 2 inches of cold water. Set the pot over high heat and, once it comes to a boil, reduce the heat to medium and cook for 7 minutes; use a timer. When the time is up, remove from the heat, drain the eggs, and cover the eggs with ice water. Let them cool in the pot for about 15 minutes, and then peel the eggs. Cut each egg in half and use a small spoon to scoop the yolks out into a bowl. Set aside. Finely chop the whites and reserve in a separate bowl from the yolks.

Put the potatoes in a medium pot and cover with at least 2 inches of cold water. Bring the potatoes up to a simmer, then reduce the heat to medium-low and cook for 10 minutes, or until just tender. Drain the potatoes in a colander and transfer them to a large bowl to cool.

Put the egg yolks, buttermilk, mayonnaise, mustard, pickle juice, soy sauce, Tabasco, vinegar, and salt in a food processor and process until smooth, about 30 seconds. Pour over the potatoes and add the egg whites, pickles, ham, chives, and dill. Mix gently but thoroughly. Cool the salad completely and refrigerate in a covered container until ready to serve.

Meat Loaf

SERVES 8 WITH LEFTOVERS

When I was a kid, my mom would top her meat loaf with pineapple and ketchup. It was a sweet glaze, and I always have that in the back of my mind. My meat loaf also has a sweet glaze, minus the pineapple, and features a different kind of ketchup. Sir Kensington's ketchup has become a favorite of mine. They have a classic version and a spicy version made with chipotle peppers, and you can use either depending on your taste. I like the fact that they don't use processed ingredients, and the ketchup tastes delicious. I use ketchup in the loaf and in the glaze. Meat loaf just doesn't seem like meat loaf without it. And in case there are actually any leftovers, there's nothing like a cold meat loaf sandwich. I try to make enough to ensure that happens.

MEAT LOAF:

4 bacon slices, minced

2 medium carrots, cut into small dice

3 celery ribs, cut into small dice

1 medium onion, minced

1 clove garlic

½ cup / 140 grams Sir Kensington's ketchup

5 pounds / 2.26 kilograms ground beef

2 pounds / 908 grams ground pork

3 cups / 150 grams panko bread crumbs

½ cup / 130 grams whole milk

4 large eggs

4¼ teaspoons / 25 grams fine sea salt

GLAZE:

½ cup / 140 grams Sir Kensington's ketchup

½ cup / 80 grams sorghum syrup or molasses

1 tablespoon / 14 grams apple cider vinegar

½ teaspoon / 3 grams fine sea salt

Prepare the Meat Loaf:

Put the bacon in a large heavy-bottomed sauté pan set over medium-low heat. Render the bacon and cook until it becomes crispy, stirring occasionally to prevent sticking, 10 to 15 minutes. Next add the carrots, celery, onion, and garlic and cook, stirring occasionally, until they are slightly caramelized, 7 to 8 minutes. Stir in the ketchup, reduce the heat to low, and cook for 15 to 20 minutes, until all of the vegetables are completely tender. Transfer to a bowl and let the vegetables cool completely.

Preheat the oven to 350°F (180°C).

Put the beef, pork, and bread crumbs in a large bowl. Whisk together the milk, eggs, and salt until smooth and pour over the meat. Add the cooled vegetables and mix everything together using your hands or a rubber spatula. Shape into two loaves in cast-iron or regular loaf pans.

Make the Glaze and Bake the Meat Loaf:

In a small bowl, whisk together the ketchup, sorghum syrup, vinegar, and salt. Reserve a small amount separately for brushing over the finished meat loaf. Brush some of the glaze over the meat loaf and bake for 30 minutes. Brush with the glaze again, rotate the pan, and bake for another 15 minutes. Brush with the glaze again, rotate the pan, and bake for another 15 minutes, for a total cooking time of 1 hour. Remove from the oven, finish with a final coat of the reserved glaze, and let the meat loaf rest for 10 minutes before serving.

Everything Mashed Potatoes

SERVES 6 TO 8

In my last book, *VOLTink.*, my brother Michael created a recipe for seaweed mashed potatoes that changed the way I thought about mashed potatoes. When I was starting out as a cook, everyone was serving rosettes of garlic mashed potatoes with a sprig of rosemary stuck in them. Sometimes you saw cheddar mash, but mainly it was plain or garlic mashed potatoes. Somehow chefs never really pushed past those flavors. Mashed potatoes are the perfect medium for flavor. They have their own slightly sweet earthiness that soaks up butter and cream. You can add almost anything to mashed potatoes, good mashed potatoes, and still know you're eating potato. These Everything Mashed Potatoes are one of my favorite variations. I also serve them at Thanksgiving, because you have to have mashed potatoes in addition to stuffing. It's a rule.

EVERYTHING BUTTER:

5½ tablespoons / 27.5 grams nonfat milk powder

3¾ tablespoons / 30 grams sesame seeds

2½ tablespoons / 24 grams dried minced onions

2 tablespoons / 14 grams poppy seeds

4½ teaspoons / 10 grams garlic powder

1 teaspoon / 2 grams caraway seeds

1 pound / 454 grams unsalted butter, sliced

POTATOES:

5 pounds / 2.26 kilograms russet potatoes, peeled and diced

2½ quarts / 2.25 kilograms cold water

1 cup / 240 grams heavy cream

8 ounces / 227 grams cream cheese, diced

1¾ teaspoons / 10.5 grams fine sea salt

Make the Everything Butter:

Put the nonfat milk powder, sesame seeds, dried onions, poppy seeds, garlic powder, and caraway seeds in a medium sauté pan set over medium heat. Toast, stirring, for 2 to 3 minutes, until the mixture becomes aromatic. Remove from the heat and let cool to room temperature.

Put the butter in a stand mixer fitted with the paddle attachment and add the spice blend. Turn the mixer on low speed and gradually increase the speed to medium. Beat for 1 to 2 minutes, until smooth. Transfer to a covered container and reserve at room temperature.

Make the Potatoes:

Put the potatoes and water in a large pot set over high heat. Once the water comes to a boil, adjust the heat to maintain a simmer and cook until fork-tender, 12 to 15 minutes.

Meanwhile, put the cream, cream cheese, and salt in a medium pot set over low heat and bring to a simmer, stirring occasionally. Once the potatoes are done, remove from the heat. Remove 1 cup of the cooking liquid and add it to the pot of cream. Drain the potatoes in a colander and return to the pot. Set over low heat to dry any surface moisture.

Put the Everything Butter in a 6-quart saucepot and set a food mill over the top. Rice the potatoes into the pot and use a silicone spatula or wooden spoon to stir them into the butter. Set the pot over low heat and pour the warm cream into the potatoes. Stir until smooth. Cover and keep warm until ready to serve.

Mushroom Confit

I love mushrooms. When I go turkey hunting in the spring, we always finish up foraging for morels. They say that in warm weather, after two good rains, when there are violets, mustards, and wood apples in the woods, you can look for morels. This recipe call for cremini and button mushrooms, but if you are lucky enough to have wild mushrooms, feel free to substitute them, though I still like to have a small amount of creminis or buttons (say, ¼ pound of the total) for their texture and flavor. This is a classical mushroom preparation. Slowly cooking the mushrooms in a bath of aromatic fat gives them a silky texture and full flavor that you can't get any other way. Duck fat is traditional, and it has a wonderful flavor, but if you can't find it you can use all bacon fat. The mushrooms will still be delicious.

1¼ pounds / 567 grams cremini or button mushrooms

1¾ teaspoons / 10 grams fine sea salt

¼ teaspoon / 1 gram sugar

2 cups / 450 grams rendered bacon fat

½ cup / 113 grams rendered duck fat

1 tablespoon / 5 grams juniper berries

Put the mushrooms in a large bowl and mix with the salt and sugar. Cover and let stand at room temperature for 1 hour.

Put the bacon fat, duck fat, and juniper berries in a heavy-bottomed 4-quart saucepot set over medium heat. Once the fat melts, add the mushrooms and cook until the mushrooms begin to release their liquid and become very fragrant. Once the mushrooms begin to shrink, remove from the heat and cool to room temperature. The mushrooms may be stored in the fat in the refrigerator for up to 6 months as long as there is an unbroken layer of fat on top of them.

Steak Dinner

SERVES 6 TO 8

There's nothing like a good steak. Good meat has become so expensive that a steak dinner like this is usually a celebratory occasion. With that in mind, I've developed this bulletproof recipe. The only kicker is that you do need a good thermometer that has a roasting alert. This will ensure that your steak is perfectly cooked every time. Once you have one in your kitchen, you'll find that you use it all the time, so it's an investment worth making.

I was the chef at Charlie Palmer Steak for five years, so trust me when I say that you need to buy the best-quality meat you can find. Searing a thick steak is always my choice over grilling. Don't be afraid of a little smoke—turn on the fan or open a window, because the finished steak is going to be worth it. This is a meal fit for a king.

2 (2¼-pound / 1-kilogram) bone-in rib-eye steaks

Fine sea salt, for seasoning

1 tablespoon / 14 grams olive oil

2 tablespoons / 28 grams unsalted butter

2 cloves garlic, sliced

2 sprigs thyme

1 sprig rosemary

Set a wire rack over a baking sheet. Season the steaks generously with salt on both sides and refrigerate on the rack, uncovered, for at least 12 hours and up to 14 hours.

Preheat the oven to 250°F (120°C). Set a clean wire rack over a baking sheet and reserve.

Remove the steaks from the refrigerator and let rest at room temperature for 30 minutes. Set a large cast-iron pan over medium heat, rub each steak on both sides with 1½ teaspoons olive oil, and, when the pan is hot, lay them in the pan. Sear the meat for 4 to 6 minutes, until a deep brown crust forms on the bottom. Flip the steaks, add the butter, garlic, thyme, and rosemary, and baste the meat for 3 minutes. Transfer the steaks to the prepared rack, slide a probe thermometer in the thickest part of the meat, and put the setup in the oven. When the steak reaches 120°F (49°C), remove from the oven and let rest for 10 minutes before slicing and serving.

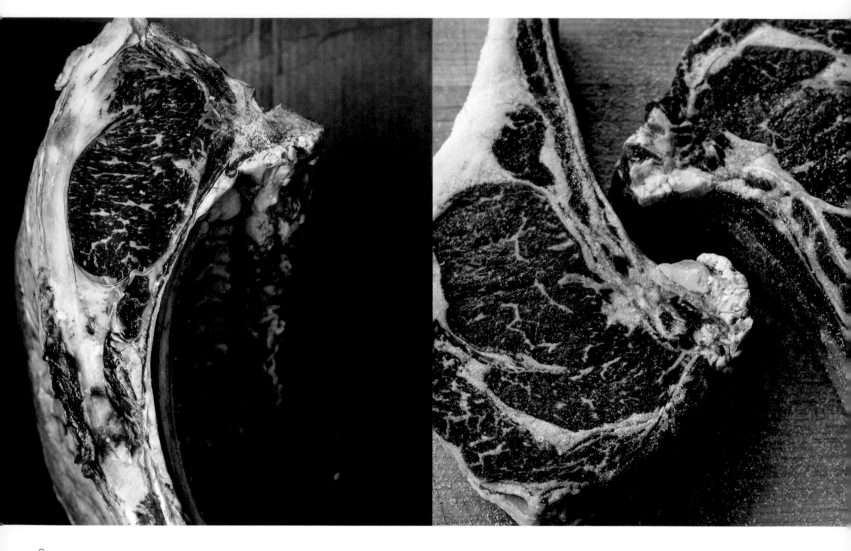

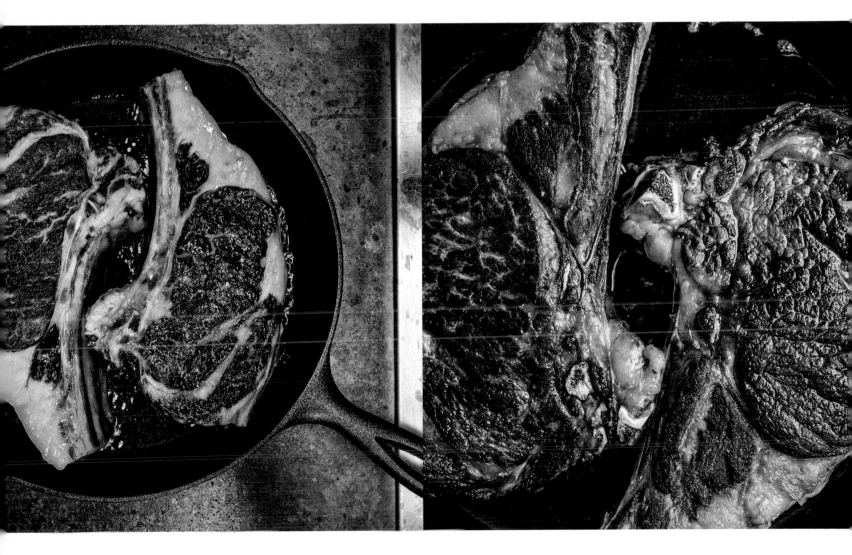

Steak Sauce

MAKES ABOUT 8 CUPS

1 medium onion

1 medium red bell pepper

2 teaspoons / 10 grams light olive oil

2 cinnamon sticks

6 whole cloves

2¼ teaspoons / 6 grams mustard seeds

28 ounces / 794 grams tomato puree

2¼ cups / 570 grams prune juice

9 ounces / 255 grams mango puree

1 cup / 225 grams apple cider vinegar

1 cup / 225 grams water

7 ounces / 200 grams
Worcestershire sauce

½ cup / 120 grams maple syrup

⅓ cup / 100 grams tamarind paste

2½ tablespoons / 15 grams minced
fresh ginger

6 cloves garlic

2½ teaspoons / 15 grams fine sea salt

¼ teaspoon / 0.5 gram cayenne pepper

One of the many stations I mastered during my tenure at the restaurant Aureole was that of *saucier*. During that time I was in charge of making all of the stocks and sauces. It was a challenge that I enjoyed, and it left me with a lifelong fascination with sauces. I always appreciate tasting a good one, and I always wonder how I can make it even better. This is my version of steak sauce. It's rich with fruit and aromatic with spices, unctuous and the perfect foil for a great crusty steak. I also use it for sandwiches, and I've even been known to fold it into salad dressings. This steak sauce is better than anything I've ever poured out of a bottle.

Preheat a cast-iron grill pan or skillet or a charcoal grill so that it is very hot. Peel the onion and cut it in half vertically so that the core holds the pieces together. Rub the bell pepper and onion halves with the olive oil. Place each onion half cut side down on the grill and sear until completely charred. Transfer to a heatproof bowl and cover the top tightly with plastic wrap so the onion steams. Sear the pepper on all sides, rotating every 5 minutes, until it is blackened. Add the pepper to the bowl with the onion and cover with fresh plastic wrap. Once the vegetables are cool enough to handle, remove and discard the skin and seeds from the pepper.

Use cheesecloth to make a sachet for the cinnamon sticks, cloves, and mustard seeds and tie it securely with butcher's twine. Set a large pot on the stove and add the sachet and all of the remaining ingredients. Set over medium-high heat and bring to a simmer. Adjust the heat to maintain a simmer and reduce by half, 45 to 60 minutes.

Remove the sachet and transfer the sauce to a blender. Puree until smooth; you may need to do this in batches. Cool and store in a covered container in the refrigerator until needed.

Broccoli with Anchovy Dressing

SERVES 6 TO 8

3 bunches broccoli rabe or broccoli

3 quarts / 2.7 kilograms water

1¾ teaspoons / 10.5 grams fine sea salt

7 tablespoons / 100 grams extra-virgin olive oil

2 tablespoons / 36 grams minced garlic

1 ounce / 28 grams anchovy fillets, chopped

2½ teaspoons / 5 grams red pepper flakes

¼ cup / 56 grams fresh lemon juice

2 tablespoons / 28 grams light olive oil

1 lemon

This warm side dish is imbued with the flavors of Italy. Broccoli rabe and broccoli are both sweet, earthy vegetables that can stand up to big sauces. I like the hint of bitterness and mustard that you can taste in the broccoli rabe, though I must admit my kids prefer regular broccoli. Both vegetables go well with the addictive sauce, which is made with garlic, olive oil, anchovies, red pepper flakes, and fresh lemon juice. It hits all the high notes and has a deep, rich umami flavor to complement both the broccoli and the steak.

Trim off the bottom of each piece of broccoli rabe and cut into 6 even pieces (or cut the regular broccoli into large florets). Put the water and salt in a large pot, set over high heat, and bring to a rapid boil. Prepare an ice bath. Blanch the broccoli rabe in batches for 3 to 4 minutes, until the color sets and the vegetable becomes just tender. Transfer immediately to the ice bath to cool. Once the broccoli is cold, drain and let air-dry. Reserve at room temperature.

Put the extra-virgin olive oil and garlic in a small pot set over low heat just until it starts to bubble. Add the anchovies and red pepper flakes and cook for 3 minutes, to infuse their flavor into the oil. Remove from the heat and transfer to a food processor. Add the lemon juice and pulse just until smooth.

Set a cast-iron skillet over medium heat and add the light olive oil. When the oil begins to shimmer, add the broccoli rabe and sauté until slightly caramelized, 5 to 7 minutes. Transfer to a serving bowl and drizzle the anchovy dressing over the broccoli. Zest the lemon over the top and squeeze its juice over all. Stir gently and serve immediately.

Ranch Duchess Potatoes

SERVES 6 TO 8

Duchess potatoes are seasoned mashed potatoes that are baked in the oven until the tops turn golden brown. I like to bake mine in greased muffin tins to get a nice crust all over the outside that you can break through with a fork to get to the creamy goodness inside. Kids love the individual portions, and everyone loves the golden crust. It's almost like combining ranch potato chips with potato puree.

RANCH SEASONING:

1 cup / 80 grams buttermilk powder

5 teaspoons / 10 grams freshly ground black pepper

4½ teaspoons / 10 grams onion powder

3¼ teaspoons / 1.6 grams dried parsley

1½ teaspoons / 3 grams garlic powder

1½ teaspoons / 8 grams smoked paprika

½ teaspoon / 1 gram cayenne pepper

Grated zest of 1 lemon

POTATOES:

4 pounds / 1.8 kilograms russet potatoes

1 cup / 225 grams unsalted butter, diced

8 ounces / 227 grams cream cheese, diced

10 large egg yolks

4 teaspoons / 20 grams soy sauce

2 tablespoons plus 1 teaspoon / 21 grams Ranch Seasoning

2 teaspoons / 12 grams fine sea salt

Grated Parmigiano-Reggiano for serving

Make the Ranch Seasoning:
Put all of the seasoning ingredients in a bowl and whisk to blend. Ranch Seasoning may be stored in an airtight container at room temperature for up to 1 month.

Make the Potatoes:
Preheat the oven to 300°F (150°C).

Rinse and peel the potatoes. Cut them into large dice. Put them in a large pot with enough water to cover them by 2 inches. Set over medium-high heat and bring to a boil. Reduce the heat to maintain a simmer and cook until tender, about 13 minutes. Drain the potatoes, lay them out on a baking sheet, and put them in the oven to dry out for 5 minutes. After you remove them from the oven, increase the oven temperature to 350°F (180°C).

Spray the wells of a muffin tin with nonstick cooking spray. Use a ricer or food mill to press the potatoes into a warm bowl that fits your stand mixer. Add the butter, cream cheese, egg yolks, soy sauce, Ranch Seasoning, and salt. Mix in the stand mixer with the paddle attachment on low speed until smooth. Transfer the mixture to a piping bag fitted with a star tip. Pipe the mixture into each well of the prepared muffin tin and bake for 16 minutes, or until golden brown and hot throughout.

Sprinkle with cheese and serve.

Thanksgiving is the chef's holiday, so there is a certain amount of irony in the fact that most of us spend it working in our restaurants. When I was coming up through the ranks, I worked every single holiday and most weekends. I always knew that when I had my own restaurant it would be closed for the big holidays so that my staff could enjoy that time with their families, and so could I. The recipes in this chapter, and many others in this book, are designed so that they can be mostly prepped in advance and finished on the big day. That way you can spend your time with the people you love instead of in the kitchen. While sharing a kitchen with many cooks can be fun, holidays are a time to be at the table enjoying a delicious meal. These recipes will help make that a reality.

Whole Roasted Cauliflower with Pearl Onions and Grapes

Green Bean Casserole

Roasted Carrots with Chimichurri

Turnip and Rutabaga Salad

Cast-Iron Pan-Fried Brussels Sprouts with Pickled Raisins and Sunflower Seeds

Corn Bread Stuffing

Orange Creamed Butternut Squash

Cranberry Compote

Thanksgiving Turkey

Turkey Gravy

Thanksgiving Dinner

Whole Roasted Cauliflower with Pearl Onions and Grapes

SERVES 10 TO 12

CAULIFLOWER:

1 medium cauliflower
(about 1¾ **pounds** / 800 grams)

8 cloves garlic, split lengthwise

1 lemon, cut into 8 wedges

2 bay leaves, sliced into quarters

6 **tablespoons** / 84 grams olive oil,
divided

2 **tablespoons** / 18 grams za'atar
spice blend

1½ **teaspoons** / 9 grams fine sea salt

PEARL ONIONS AND GRAPES:

8½ **cups** / 2 kilograms cold water

1 **pound** / 454 grams red pearl onions

3 **tablespoons** / 60 grams sorghum
syrup or molasses, divided

1 **tablespoon plus** ¼ **teaspoon** / 20 grams
fine sea salt

¼ **cup** / 56 grams unsalted butter

½ **cup** / 57 grams pecans

2 **tablespoons** / 28 grams apple
cider vinegar

2 **tablespoons** / 28 grams red wine vinegar

1 **pound** / 454 grams seedless red grapes

2 **teaspoons** / 3.4 grams chopped fresh
rosemary

YOGURT SAUCE:

1 **cup** / 227 grams goat's milk yogurt

¼ **teaspoon** / 1.5 grams fine sea salt

¼ **teaspoon** / 0.75 gram za'atar
spice blend

I love the idea of putting vegetables at the center of a platter. Everything on the Thanksgiving table has to be delicious and has to work with the turkey. This whole roasted cauliflower is beautiful, with a haunting aroma from the za'atar. It makes a statement. It's served with a warm relish of pearl onions and grapes that is sweet and tart and has a rich herbal note from the rosemary.

Prep and Cook the Cauliflower:
Trim the leaves off the cauliflower. Wedge the garlic cloves, lemon wedges, and bay leaf slices into the nooks and crannies underneath the cauliflower. Put a steamer insert inside a large pot. Put 2 inches of water into the bottom of the steamer and set over high heat. Once the water is boiling, put the cauliflower into the steamer and cover with a lid. Steam for 30 minutes, or until completely tender. Remove from the heat and use a large skimmer or slotted spoon to gently transfer the cauliflower to a large baking dish to cool.

Preheat the oven to 350°F (180°C).

Cut the cooled cauliflower in half vertically. Set a large sauté pan over high heat. Add 2 tablespoons (28 grams) of the olive oil and, when the oil begins to shimmer, put the cauliflower in, cut side down. Depending on the size of your pan, you may need to sear the halves one at a time. Transfer back to the baking dish. Put the remaining 4 tablespoons (56 grams) olive oil, the za'atar, and salt into a small bowl and mix together. Use a pastry brush to thoroughly coat each half of the cauliflower with the mixture. At this point, you can cook the cauliflower immediately or cover and refrigerate it overnight.

If necessary, remove the cauliflower from the refrigerator 30 minutes before cooking. Use a pastry brush to brush on any spice blend that has dripped off the cauliflower. Roast the cauliflower in the baking dish for 30 minutes, or until golden brown and caramelized.

Make the Pearl Onions and Grapes:
Put the water, onions, 2 tablespoons (40 grams) of the sorghum, and the salt in a medium saucepot set over high heat and bring to a boil. Immediately drain the onions, reserving all of the onion broth, and lay them out on a baking sheet to cool completely.

Put the butter in a large sauté pan set over medium heat. Let it melt and cook, stirring, until it browns and froths. Immediately add the onions and let them slowly caramelize, stirring occasionally, for 5 to 7 minutes, until they are a deep golden brown. Add the pecans and let them toast for a minute or two, until they become fragrant. Add the apple cider vinegar, red wine vinegar, and remaining 1 tablespoon (20 grams) sorghum and turn the heat up to high. Add ½ cup of the reserved onion liquid and let it reduce to a syrupy glaze, about 10 minutes. Add another ½ cup of the onion liquid and

reduce to a glaze, 10 to 15 minutes more. Add the grapes and let them cook for about 4 minutes, or until they soften and plump. Add the rosemary and the remaining 2 tablespoons of the onion liquid to loosen up the glaze.

Remove the cauliflower from the oven and let it rest on top of the stove for 5 minutes.

Make the Yogurt Sauce:

Put the yogurt, salt, and za'atar in a small bowl, and mix well to blend. Transfer to a small serving dish. Put the onion-grape mixture onto a serving platter. Carve the cauliflower into pieces and place over the onion-grape mixture. Serve the Yogurt Sauce on the side.

Green Bean Casserole

2¼ **pounds** / 1 kilogram green beans, trimmed and split lengthwise

1 **cup** / 225 grams unsalted butter, sliced

3 medium to large sweet onions, thinly sliced (about 4½ cups)

2 **pounds** / 908 grams cremini mushrooms, quartered

1½ **teaspoons** / 9 grams fine sea salt, divided, plus extra for the blanching water and seasoning

¼ **cup** / 37 grams all-purpose flour

1½ **cups** / 250 grams reserved onion broth or vegetable stock (from Pearl Onions and Grapes, page 146)

12½ **ounces** / 340 grams shredded white cheddar cheese (6½ cups)

1 **cup** / 15 grams dried shiitake mushrooms

14 **tablespoons** / 310 grams Clarified Butter, divided (page 57)

2 shallots, sliced ⅛-inch thick

1 **cup** / 225 clarified butter (page 57)

9 **ounces** / 260 grams fresh shiitake mushrooms, stems removed, thinly sliced

Green bean casserole is on almost everybody's Thanksgiving table, either because people love it or maybe because they just love that fried-onion topping. Thanksgiving dinner at our house wouldn't be the same without it. I use the onion liquid from the Pearl Onions and Grapes in the Whole Roasted Cauliflower recipe on page 146 because it has wonderful flavor and I'll be cooking them at the same time anyway. I like to get the most out of my ingredients. This gives my green bean casserole a deep onion flavor without the traditional store-bought topping. Instead I make a mushroom and shallot topping.

Set a large pot of water over high heat. Season with salt (I like to use 20 grams [¾ ounce] of salt for every quart of water), and bring to a boil. Prepare an ice bath. Blanch the green beans in the boiling water for 30 seconds. You will need to do this in batches so you don't crowd the pot. Immediately use a skimmer to transfer the beans to the ice bath to cool. Drain the green beans and reserve.

Put ½ cup (113 grams) of the butter in a large skillet that has a lid and set over low heat. Once the butter melts, add the onions and mix them thoroughly to coat the onions with the butter. Cover and cook undisturbed for 30 minutes. You don't want the onions to take on any color.

Meanwhile, cook the cremini mushrooms. Set a large sauté pan over medium-high heat. Put the remaining butter in the sauté pan and let it melt. Add the mushrooms, season with ¾ teaspoon (4.5 grams) salt, and cook, stirring, until they turn a deep golden brown. Use a slotted spoon to transfer to a plate lined with paper towels to drain and cool. Pour any remaining butter from the sauté pan into the pan with the onions and mix it in.

After 30 minutes, season the onions with the remaining ¾ teaspoon (4.5 grams) salt and continue to cook for another 30 minutes, stirring every 8 to 10 minutes so they don't start to stick to the bottom of the pan. At the end of 1 hour, there still should be no color on the onions or the bottom of the pan. Add the flour and lightly stir to incorporate. The mixture will start to form a lumpy mass in irregular patterns throughout the pan. Add the onion broth and stir to incorporate completely. Cook the mixture, stirring gently, for 6 minutes, or until the raw flour taste is gone. Remove the pan from the heat and transfer the onions to a blender. Blend on high speed until the mixture is smooth. Pour into a clean saucepot, set over medium heat, and bring to a simmer. Whisk in the cheddar cheese a little bit at a time until it is totally incorporated and the mixture has thickened.

Preheat the oven to 350°F (180°C).

Arrange the green beans in a large baking dish or casserole. Sprinkle the cremini mushrooms throughout the beans. Pour the cheese sauce over

the green beans and mix gently to thoroughly coat the vegetables. Cover with aluminum foil or a lid and bake for 35 minutes.

While the casserole is baking, put 1 cup (225 grams) of the Clarified Butter in a medium pot and set over medium-high heat. Add the sliced shiitake mushrooms and cook, stirring, until they become golden brown and crisp. Use a slotted spoon to transfer the mushrooms to a plate lined with paper towels to drain and cool. Once cooled and crisp, put the mushrooms in a blender or spice grinder and pulverize.

Put the shallots in a medium pot and pour the clarified butter over them. Stir the shallots and set the pot over medium-low heat. Cook, stirring occasionally, until the shallots begin to fry and brown, about 10—15 minutes. Once the shallots are a deep golden brown, use a slotted spoon to transfer them to a plate lined with paper towels. Season them lightly with salt and let cool. Strain the butter into a clean pot and add the mushrooms. Set the pot over medium-low heat and cook, stirring occasionally, until the mushrooms begin to fry and brown, about 10—15 minutes. Once the mush-rooms are crisp and brown, use a slotted spoon to transfer them to a plate lined

with paper towels. Season lightly with salt and let cool. Onec the shallots and mushrooms are completely cool, mix them together.

After 35 minutes, take the green beans out of the oven and uncover them. Sprinkle the fried shallots and mushrooms evenly over the top and bake, uncovered, for 20 minutes, or until they are golden brown.

Roasted Carrots with Chimichurri

SERVES 10 TO 12

I love roasting carrots. They soften and sweeten and develop a slightly chewy, caramelized crust. It's important that all your carrots are about the same size. Medium carrots, not thicker than your thumb, are perfect for this recipe. I roast them with cinnamon and Szechuan peppercorns for a combination of sweet and spice and then serve them with a chimichurri sauce made with the carrot greens. This dish hits all the high notes and is perfect alongside moist, juicy pieces of turkey.

CARROTS:

13 medium carrots
(about 2¼ pounds / 1 kilogram)

2 tablespoons / 28 grams light olive oil

¾ teaspoon / 1.5 grams ground cinnamon

1 teaspoon / 3 grams ground Szechuan peppercorns

¾ teaspoon / 4.5 grams fine sea salt

CHIMICHURRI SAUCE:

2½ ounces / 70 grams carrot greens

1 ounce / 28 grams fresh flat-leaf parsley or baby spinach

1 clove garlic

2½ tablespoons / 35 grams light olive oil

1 tablespoon / 14 grams red wine vinegar

½ teaspoon / 3 grams fine sea salt

½ teaspoon / 1 gram piment d'Espelette

Small carrot greens for serving

Cook the Carrots:

Preheat the oven to 350°F (180°C).

Peel the carrots and trim the ends. Set a large skillet with a lid or a Dutch oven over high heat and add the olive oil. When it begins to shimmer, add the carrots and cook, stirring, until they are golden brown and caramelized. Add the cinnamon, Szechuan peppercorns, and salt and stir to blend. Cover and transfer to the oven to cook for 35 minutes, or until the carrots are completely tender.

Make the Chimichurri Sauce:

Set a large pot of salted water over high heat and bring to a boil. Prepare an ice bath. Blanch the carrot greens for 2 to 3 minutes and transfer to the ice bath. Blanch the parsley for 1 minute and transfer to the ice bath. Once cool, squeeze out the parsley and carrot greens and put in a blender. Add the garlic, oil, red wine vinegar, salt, and piment d'Espelette and puree until smooth. Strain through a fine-mesh sieve.

Remove the carrots from the oven, cut into bite-sized pieces, and transfer to a serving bowl. Spoon some of the Chimichurri Sauce over the carrots and serve the rest alongside. Garnish with small carrot greens and serve family style.

Turnip and Rutabaga Salad

SERVES 10 TO 12

1 large rutabaga

6 large turnips

6 limes

1 jalapeño pepper, peeled and sliced

¼ **teaspoon** / 1 gram finely grated fresh ginger

2 **teaspoons** / 10 grams fish sauce

2 **teaspoons** / 10 grams soy sauce

1 **tablespoon** / 13 grams packed light brown sugar

1 **teaspoon** / 4 grams sesame oil

1½ **teaspoons** / 9 grams fine sea salt

1 bunch scallions

1 bunch red radishes

1 bunch mint, leaves only

1 bunch cilantro, leaves only

This is one of my go-to winter salads. Turnips and rutabagas are great because they don't oxidize when you cut them, they have a firm, crisp texture, and they can stand up to a flavorful vinaigrette. Rutabagas have a sweet, soft, earthy flavor. Turnips are sharper and a little peppery; their pungent flavor reminds me of fresh horseradish. Marinating them overnight serves two purposes: The vegetables absorb the sauce so the flavors have time to come together and the acid in the marinade tenderizes the vegetables, softening them just enough to give them a slightly silky texture as you chew. I add the herbs and radishes at the very last minute so there's contrasting texture and bright, fresh flavor from the greens.

Use a peeler or a sharp knife to peel the rutabaga. Cut it into 6 wedges. Use a peeler or a sharp knife to peel the turnips. Use a Japanese mandoline with the julienne attachment to cut the rutabaga and turnips into matchsticks.

Put them into a large bowl. Use a Microplane to zest 4 of the limes. Juice the zested limes into a small bowl. Add the zest, jalapeño pepper, ginger, fish sauce, soy sauce, brown sugar, sesame oil, and salt. Stir together and pour over the julienned rutabaga and turnips. Use a spoon to stir the marinade into the vegetables. Put the mixture into a large zip-top bag and refrigerate overnight.

When ready to serve, put the marinated rutabaga and turnip mixture in a large bowl. Thinly slice the scallions and radishes. Add the scallions, radishes, mint leaves, and cilantro leaves and mix gently to blend. Be sure to evenly distribute the herbs and radishes. Cut the remaining 2 limes into 8 wedges. Put the salad onto a serving platter and arrange the limes around the outside. Serve and invite everyone to add a fresh dose of lime juice if they enjoy extra zing.

Cast-Iron Pan-Fried Brussels Sprouts with Pickled Raisins and Sunflower Seeds

SERVES 10 TO 12

GOLDEN RAISIN PICKLE:

⅓ **cup** / 55 grams golden raisins

¼ **cup** / 56 grams water

2 **teaspoons** / 10 grams rice wine vinegar

2 **teaspoons** / 12 grams honey

¼ **teaspoon** / 1.5 grams fine sea salt

PIMENTÓN OIL:

6 **tablespoons** / 84 grams canola oil

½ **teaspoon** / 2 grams pimentón
(Spanish smoked paprika)

TOASTED SUNFLOWER SEEDS:

1 **teaspoon** / 5 grams Pimentón Oil

¼ **cup** / 25 grams unsalted raw sunflower
seeds

Tiny pinch of fine sea salt

CRISPY BRUSSELS SPROUTS:

4 **cups** / 900 grams Brussels sprouts

5 **tablespoons** / 70 grams Pimentón Oil

½ **teaspoon** / 3 grams fine sea salt

Every kitchen should have cast-iron pans. These heavy black pans are wonderful because they allow for consistent, even cooking. They are naturally nonstick and perfect for frying or sautéing. I have several in my kitchen of varying sizes and they are great for pan-roasting anything you can think of. I like cooking Brussels sprouts this way because I don't have to blanch them separately. They steam and fry in the skillet and are nicely balanced by the tangy golden raisins and the nutty sunflower seeds.

Make the Golden Raisin Pickle:

Put all of the ingredients in a microwave-safe bowl and stir to blend. Microwave on high for 2 minutes. Stir and let cool to infuse. Golden Raisin Pickle may be stored in a covered container in the refrigerator for up to 2 weeks.

Make the Pimentón Oil:

Put the canola oil and *pimentón* in a small pot set over medium heat. Stir well and let it cook for 2 to 3 minutes, until the oil warms and the spice becomes fragrant. Strain the mixture through a fine-mesh sieve lined with paper towels. Once all the oil has dripped into your container, squeeze the towels to yield any remainder. Cool and store in an airtight container.

Toast the Sunflower Seeds:

Put the Pimentón Oil in a small sauté pan set over medium heat. Once it warms enough to move rapidly across the pan, add the sunflower seeds and the salt. Cook, stirring, for 3 to 5 minutes, until the seeds are slightly browned and fragrant. Transfer to a plate lined with paper towels to cool.

Make the Crispy Brussels Sprouts:

Fill a large bowl with cold water and use it to thoroughly clean your Brussels sprouts in the sink. Drain and cut the hard stem off each sprout and slice in half lengthwise. Pat them dry with clean kitchen towels.

Take a sheet of aluminum foil and fold over the edges to make a lid for a large (14-inch) cast-iron skillet. Set the skillet over your largest burner and turn the heat up to medium. Add the Pimentón Oil, tilt the skillet to coat the bottom, and put your Brussels sprouts, cut side down, in the pan. Season with the salt and cover with the foil lid. Cook for 15 to 17 minutes, until the Brussels sprouts are tender on the inside and crisp on the outside. You may have to do this in batches or in 2 pans. Do not overcrowd the pan or the Brussels sprouts will not get crispy. Add the Toasted Sunflower Seeds and Golden Raisin Pickle and mix well. Transfer to a bowl and serve immediately.

Corn Bread Stuffing

When I worked at Aureole, we cooked Thanksgiving for 400 people. We made two different types of stuffing every year, bread stuffing and corn bread stuffing. The corn bread stuffing was always better. This recipe may seem like a lot of steps, but I really enjoy making my own corn bread. It's moist and flavorful, and since it is the foundation for the stuffing it makes sense to me to use homemade. The Quick Sausage really is just that, but in a pinch you could substitute your favorite store-bought brand. If you are planning ahead, you could make the corn bread 3 to 4 days in advance and let it dry out and make the Smoked Turkey Stock a week or two in advance and freeze it until you're ready to make the stuffing. I like to make my own poultry seasoning with fresh herbs to season the stuffing, and I mix it with bread crumbs to ensure a crispy topping.

CORN BREAD:

1 cup / 200 grams sugar

⅓ cup / 75 grams unsalted butter

1½ teaspoons / 9 grams fine sea salt

3 large eggs

1 cup plus 2½ tablespoons / 300 grams whole milk

1 cup / 240 grams buttermilk

2 teaspoons / 12 grams sorghum syrup or molasses

2⅔ cups / 400 grams all-purpose flour

2 cups / 276 grams cornmeal

¼ teaspoon / 0.6 gram ground nutmeg

SMOKED TURKEY STOCK:

1 medium sweet onion

2 medium carrots

4 celery ribs

4 smoked turkey tails or thighs (about **1⅓ pounds** / 600 grams)

8 cups / 1.8 kilograms cold filtered water

8 sprigs thyme

4 cloves garlic

QUICK SAUSAGE:

2 cups / 455 grams ground pork

½ small onion, minced

2 teaspoons / 4 grams minced or grated garlic

2½ teaspoons / 12.5 grams bourbon

1 teaspoon / 4 grams soy sauce

1 teaspoon / 0.75 gram chopped fresh flat-leaf parsley

1 teaspoon / 1 gram chopped fresh sage

½ teaspoon / 1 gram fresh thyme leaves

1 teaspoon / 6 grams fine sea salt

1 teaspoon / 0.75 gram black peppercorns, finely ground

¼ teaspoon / 0.5 gram ground coriander

ROYALE:

3 large eggs

1 cup / 240 grams heavy cream

VEGETABLES:

1 tablespoon / 14 grams canola oil

2 medium onions, cut into small dice

3 medium carrots, cut into small dice

6 celery ribs, cut into small dice

Fine sea salt, for seasoning

POULTRY SEASONING:

½ teaspoon / 1 gram fresh thyme leaves

2 teaspoons / 2 grams chopped fresh flat-leaf parsley

1 teaspoon / 1 gram chopped fresh sage

¼ teaspoon / 0.5 gram chopped fresh rosemary

¼ teaspoon / 0.5 gram fresh chervil leaves

2 teaspoons / 1.5 grams black peppercorns, finely ground

1 teaspoon / 2 grams onion powder

1 teaspoon / 2 grams ground coriander

1 teaspoon / 2 grams ground celery seeds

½ teaspoon / 3 grams fine sea salt

STUFFING:

1½ cups / 300 grams Quick Sausage

4½ cups / 345 grams freshly baked and crumbled Corn Bread

2 cups / 500 grams Smoked Turkey Stock or chicken stock

⅔ cup / 150 grams Royale

1¼ cups / 200 grams Vegetables

1½ teaspoons / 9 grams fine sea salt

CRUST:

⅔ cup / 50 grams panko bread crumbs

2½ tablespoons / 25 grams Poultry Seasoning (leftover seasoning can be used in stuffing)

SPECIAL EQUIPMENT:

6-quart pressure cooker (optional)

Make the Corn Bread:

Preheat the oven to 350°F (180°C).

Spray two 9-by-13-inch casserole pans or one 13-by-18-inch casserole pan with nonstick cooking spray.

Place the sugar, butter, and salt in a stand mixer with the paddle attachment and mix on medium speed until light and fluffy, 4 to 5 minutes. Add the eggs, one at a time, waiting until each one is fully incorporated before adding another. Stop the mixer and add the milk, buttermilk, sorghum, flour, cornmeal, and nutmeg. Turn the mixer on low speed and mix until everything comes together. Increase speed to medium and beat until the batter is fully hydrated, 2 to 3 minutes, making sure to scrape the sides of the mixing bowl a few times. Pour the batter onto the prepared pan(s) and bake for 30 minutes, or until the corn bread is cooked through and springs back lightly when pressed with a finger. Remove from the oven and let cool.

Make the Smoked Turkey Stock:

Cut the onion, carrots, and celery into uniform small dice. Put all of the stock ingredients in a pressure cooker. Cook at high pressure for 40 minutes. Alternatively, you can put all of the ingredients in a large pot set over high heat. Bring to a boil, reduce the heat to low, skim, and simmer for 2 hours, skimming occasionally. Strain through a fine-mesh sieve lined with cheesecloth or a paper towel.

Chill and reserve in a covered container in the refrigerator. Smoked Turkey Stock will keep in the refrigerator for up to 1 week or in the freezer for 3 months.

Make the Quick Sausage:

Place all of the ingredients in a medium bowl and use your hands or a spatula to mix gently to blend.

Make the Royale:

Crack the eggs into a blender. Put the cream in a medium saucepot set over medium-high heat and bring to 180°F (82°C). Start the blender on low speed and mix until the eggs are just blended. With the blender running, slowly pour in the cream. Blend until homogenized.

Make the Vegetables:

Set a large skillet over medium-high heat. Add the oil, and when it begins to shimmer, add the onions. Cook for 2 to 3 minutes, stirring, until the onions become tender and translucent. Add the carrots and celery, season lightly with salt, and cook, stirring, for another 3 to 5 minutes, until all the vegetables are just tender. Transfer to a large plate or baking sheet to cool and reserve.

Make the Poultry Seasoning:

Chop all the herbs very finely and put them in a small bowl. Add the pepper, onion powder, ground coriander, ground celery seeds, and salt and mix well to blend. Reserve.

Prepare the Stuffing:

Preheat the oven to 325°F (165°C).

Spray a 9-by-13-inch casserole dish with nonstick cooking spray. Set a small sauté pan heat over medium-high heat and sear the Quick Sausage, being sure to cook it through. Remove from the heat and let it cool slightly. Put the Corn Bread, Smoked Turkey Stock, Quick Sausage, Royale, Vegetables, and salt in a mixing bowl and fold everything together with a rubber spatula until the stuffing mix is fully incorporated and the stock has mostly been absorbed. The stuffing will look a little too wet before baking.

Make the Crust and Cook the Stuffing:

Prepare the crust by mixing the panko bread crumbs with the Poultry Seasoning. Fill the prepared casserole dish with the stuffing mixture and spread it evenly in the pan. Lightly tap the dish on the counter to even out the mixture in the pan. Sprinkle the crust over the top of the stuffing, letting it fall from your fingers in an even layer across the top. Bake for 30 minutes, or until the stuffing is fully cooked and very hot. Turn the broiler on high and broil the stuffing until the crust becomes GBD (Golden Brown and Delicious), 3 to 5 minutes. Serve family style, from the casserole dish.

Orange Creamed Butternut Squash

SERVES 10 TO 12

We don't have sweet potatoes with marshmallow topping on our Thanksgiving table. Instead I make this recipe, combining butternut squash with orange cream soda. My favorite brand is Frostop Orange & Creme soda, available online, but if you can't get that, Boylan's is another great brand. They're both made with real cane sugar and help accent the sweet flavor of the butternut squash without taking over the dish.

SQUASH BROTH:

8 cups / 1.8 kilograms water

3 cups / 680 grams orange cream soda (two 12-ounce bottles)

1 teaspoon / 6 grams fine sea salt

7 ounces / 200 grams butternut squash seeds, from the diced squash

SQUASH:

2⅔ pounds / 1.2 kilograms butternut squash, peeled and cut into bite-size triangular pieces

½ cup / 113 grams chilled unsalted butter, sliced

SPECIAL EQUIPMENT:

Pressure cooker (optional)

Make the Squash Broth:
Put the water, orange soda, salt, and butternut squash seeds in a pressure cooker and cook at high pressure for 15 minutes. Allow the pressure to dissipate naturally. Alternatively, you can put the ingredients in a medium pot. Set it over high heat, bring the mixture to a boil, reduce the heat to low, and simmer for 45 minutes. Strain the broth and discard the solids.

Make the Squash:
Preheat the oven to 350°F (180°C).

Put the squash and Squash Broth in a Dutch oven and cover with the lid. Bake for 30 minutes. Remove the lid and bake for 30 minutes more.

Remove from the oven and transfer the remaining Squash Broth to a small saucepot set over medium heat. Reduce by half, then whisk in the cold butter to thicken the sauce, and remove from the heat. Put the squash in a large serving bowl, pour the sauce over it, and serve immediately.

Cranberry Compote

MAKES 3½ CUPS

I love cooking with tea. Chamomile has a delicate, floral flavor that pairs beautifully with Riesling wine. Add the tart cranberries, sweet spices, and earthy jalapeño pepper and you've got a cranberry sauce to end all cranberry sauces. I caramelize the sugar to give it a deep flavor before deglazing the pan with the wine. Then I add the cranberries and let them simmer down with all the aromatics. The sauce is even better the next day and keeps well. Feel free to make it several days ahead of time and serve it warm or cold, as you prefer. I like it warm on Thanksgiving and cold the next day in my turkey sandwich.

1 medium orange

1 medium jalapeño pepper

½ cinnamon stick

1 bay leaf

2½ teaspoons / 3 grams dried chamomile

2 allspice berries

½ cup / 106 grams packed light brown sugar

½ cup / 100 grams granulated sugar

2 cups / 450 grams sweet Riesling

6 cups / 900 grams fresh cranberries

¼ teaspoon / 1.5 grams fine sea salt

Zest and juice the orange, reserving the zest and juice separately. Remove the seeds and the stem from the jalapeño pepper and soak the pieces of pepper in a small bowl of ice water for 2 to 3 minutes. Drain.

Cut a piece of cheesecloth into a 6-inch square. Put the cinnamon stick, bay leaf, chamomile, allspice berries, and the drained jalapeño pepper in the cheese-cloth and tie it shut with butcher's twine. Reserve the sachet.

Put the brown sugar and granulated sugar in a medium saucepot set over medium-high heat and let it caramelize to a light golden brown. Add the Riesling and stir to dissolve the sugar in the wine. Add the cranberries, orange zest, orange juice, and salt, and adjust the heat to low. Once the cranberries start to release their liquid, add the sachet. Cook for 15 minutes, or until the berries are soft and the flavors begin to marry, stirring occasionally. Remove from the heat and let cool.

Remove and discard the sachet. Cranberry Compote may be served warm or cold. It will keep in a covered container in the refrigerator for up to 2 weeks.

Thanksgiving Turkey

SERVES 12

When the food magazines come out the month before Thanksgiving, all you see on the covers are the huge, golden brown, perfect-looking turkeys. I have trouble believing that they taste as good as they look. Turkeys have a variety of different muscles that require different cooking methods to be served at their peak. As a chef, I prefer to break down my turkey and serve each part at the height of its flavor rather than carry a whole bird to the table. So I've broken it down for you here.

The drumsticks are smoked and then roasted for maximum tenderness and flavor. The thighs and wing flats are braised with a white mirepoix until they are so tender and juicy they practically melt in your mouth. Finally, the breasts are injected with a flavorful marinade made with mayonnaise. I love this technique because the mayonnaise doesn't liquefy and run out of the meat; it stays in there throughout the marination period and oven time, so you end up with moist, juicy, perfectly seasoned white meat. This is one turkey dinner that is much more than the sum of its parts.

TURKEY:

1 (**18- to 20-pound** / 8.2- to 9.1-kilogram) turkey

2 additional turkey wings

2 additional turkey thighs

You can break down the turkey yourself or ask your butcher to do it. A very sharp knife is helpful here. First cut through the skin at the side of the breast where it holds the leg against the body. Gently pull the leg away from the breast, stretching it out slightly to expose the joint at the thigh. Hold the thigh firmly near the joint that connects it to the body and gently press the thigh backward, so that the joint moves up toward the breast and out of its socket. Cut the leg away from the body, being sure to keep the oyster (the choice piece of meat above the thigh, in the backbone) attached, and repeat with the other leg. Separate the drumstick and thigh by cutting straight through the joint that connects them. Pull each wing slightly away from the breast and cut around and through the joint that connects them to the body. Remove the wing tips by cutting straight through the joint that attaches them to the flat part of the wing and reserve the tips for stock. Separate the flat and the drummette by cutting straight through the joint. Reserve the drummettes for stock. Cut along both sides of the backbone and remove it and the neck, and reserve them for the stock. Separate the tips, flats, and drummettes from the 2 additional turkey wings. Add the tips and drummettes to the reserved turkey parts for stock. Put the flats with the reserved flats and thighs from the whole turkey and the 2 additional turkey thighs. Reserve the breast separately. Keep the turkey parts in covered containers in the refrigerator until ready to cook, for up to 24 hours.

➔

TURKEY STOCK:

3 pounds / 1.36 kilograms turkey parts (reserved back, wing tips, necks, tails)

1 medium onion, roughly chopped

1 medium carrot, roughly chopped

1 celery rib, roughly chopped

3 cloves garlic

2 tablespoons / 32 grams soy sauce

8 cups / 1.8 kilograms cold water

SPECIAL EQUIPMENT:

Pressure cooker (optional)

Preheat the oven to 370°F (190°C). Lightly grease a baking sheet.

Lay the turkey parts on the baking sheet. Roast for 20 to 25 minutes, until the turkey pieces are golden brown. Let cool and transfer to a pressure cooker. Add the onion, carrot, celery, garlic, soy sauce, and water. Cook at high pressure for 15 minutes. Let the pressure dissipate naturally. Remove the lid and skim the stock. Alternatively, you can put the ingredients in a large pot set over high heat. Bring to a simmer, reduce the heat to low, skim, and cook, skimming occasionally, for 2 hours.

Strain the stock through a fine-mesh sieve. Turkey Stock may be used immediately or cooled down and chilled in the refrigerator for at least 4 hours and up to 24 hours. The fat will rise to the top as it chills and may be removed.

BRAISED TURKEY THIGHS AND WING FLATS:

2 tablespoons / 28 grams light olive oil

Reserved turkey thighs and wing flats (4 each)

1½ medium celeriac, cut into medium dice

1 rutabaga, cut into medium dice

1½ onions, cut into medium dice

3 carrots, cut into medium dice

4 cloves garlic

1 cup / 225 grams white wine

8 cups / 1.8 kilograms Turkey Stock

Preheat the oven to 300°F (150°C).

Set a large (6-quart) sauté pan over high heat and add the oil. When it begins to shimmer, add 2 of the wings and 2 of the thighs and cook for 5 to 7 minutes, until they are a deep golden brown. Flip the turkey parts and cook for another 5 minutes, or until browned on the bottom. Transfer to a large plate or platter to cool. Add the remaining 2 thighs and 2 wings to the skillet and brown on both sides in the same manner. Transfer to the platter with the other turkey.

Add the celeriac, rutabaga, onions, carrots, and garlic to the pan and stir them around to loosen the *fond* and deglaze the pan with their juices. Once the vegetables are translucent and tender, transfer them to a large plate or platter to cool. Once the vegetables are cool, transfer them to a covered container and reserve in the refrigerator.

Add the wine to the sauté pan. Let the wine come to a simmer and reduce to a glaze, about 10 minutes. Add the Turkey Stock to the wine and bring to a simmer. Return the turkey to the pan and cover with a lid. Transfer to the oven and cook for 2 hours, until the turkey is completely tender. Remove from the oven and stir in the reserved vegetables. Cover and refrigerate overnight.

The next day, gently rewarm the braised turkey just until the gelatin melts and you can easily remove the turkey pieces and the vegetables with a skimmer or slotted spoon and reserve them in a bowl. Set the braising liquid over medium-high heat, bring to a simmer, and reduce by half, 20 to 25 minutes. Reserve braising liquid and vegetables for Turkey Gravy (page 167).

➔

SMOKED TURKEY DRUMSTICKS:

Reserved turkey drumsticks (if available)

Reserve liver, gizzards, giblets, and hearts

Coffee BBQ Rub (page 118)

SPECIAL EQUIPMENT:

Stovetop or outdoor smoker

Wood chips

Rub the turkey drumsticks generously with the Coffee BBQ Rub. Season the liver, gizzards, giblets, and hearts on both sides with the Coffee BBQ Rub. Put everything on a rack set over a plate or baking sheet in the refrigerator overnight. Do not cover.

Preheat your smoker to about 225°F (107°C). Add wood chips, and when the smoke is going, put the turkey drumsticks and organ meats in the smoker and smoke for 15 minutes. Reserve the liver, gizzards, giblets, and hearts for the Turkey Gravy.

While the drumsticks are in the smoker, preheat the oven to 300°F (150°C). Lightly grease a baking sheet.

After smoking, put the drumsticks on the baking sheet and roast for 35 to 40 minutes, until juicy, golden brown, and cooked through. Let rest for 5 to 7 minutes before serving.

ROASTED TURKEY BREAST:

TURKEY BRINE:

1 cup / 225 grams Turkey Stock (page 165)

1 cup / 200 grams mayonnaise
(I prefer Duke's)

2 cloves garlic

1 tablespoon / 5 grams fresh thyme leaves

¾ **teaspoon** / 4.5 grams fine sea salt

½ **teaspoon** / 1 gram fennel seeds

¾ **teaspoon** / 0.9 gram coriander seeds

¼ **teaspoon** / 0.7 gram mustard seeds

½ bay leaf

Juice of 1 lemon

Reserved turkey breast

2 bunches broccoli rabe

2 tablespoons / 28 grams light olive oil

2 large onions, thinly sliced

1 teaspoon / 6 grams fine sea salt

4¼ cups plus 3 tablespoons / 1 kilogram apple cider

Preheat the oven to 400°F (200°C).

Make the Turkey Brine:
Put all of the ingredients in a blender and puree until smooth, about 1 minute.

Roast the Turkey Breast:
Use a syringe to inject the Turkey Brine into the turkey breast in various spots so that the seasoning is evenly distributed throughout both sides of the breast.

Cut the broccoli rabe into bite-size pieces. Put the oil in a roasting pan and rub it all over the inside of the pan. Put the broccoli rabe and the onions in the pan. Season with the salt and toss together to mix. Lay the turkey breast over the broccoli rabe. Pour the apple cider into the bottom of the pan. Roast, basting occasionally, for 2 hours, or until the breast is cooked through and the skin is golden brown.

Remove from the oven and let the turkey breast rest for 10 to 15 minutes. Transfer the breast to a cutting board and the broccoli rabe and onions to a serving platter. Slice the turkey and arrange over the broccoli rabe to serve family style.

Turkey Gravy

MAKES 3½ CUPS

There's no such thing as Thanksgiving without gravy. Instead of using flour to thicken my gravy, I use tapioca starch. It's a softer thickener that doesn't solidify, so I never run the risk of gravy that tastes like pudding. I like a judicious amount of cream in my sauce; I think it makes everything taste that much better. This gravy is smooth and delicious, especially if you take the time to make your own stock. Even better, it's easy to whip together, which is good because it's the last thing I make before I sit down at the table.

2⅔ cups / 600 grams turkey braising liquid (page 165)

1 cup / 240 grams heavy cream

1 teaspoon / 4 grams tapioca starch

Fine sea salt and freshly ground black pepper, for seasoning

Reserved vegetables from Turkey Thighs (page 165), diced

Reserved liver, gizzards, giblets, and hearts, diced

Chopped parsley for serving

Put the Turkey Stock in a medium pot set over medium-high heat and bring to a simmer. Whisk together the cream and tapioca starch to make a slurry and whisk it into the warm stock. Continue to cook, stirring, until the gravy thickens and comes to a simmer, 3 to 4 minutes. Add the reserved vegetables and organ meats and simmer 2—3 minutes to warm through. Add salt and pepper to taste. Transfer to a serving bowl and garnish with chopped parsley.

I have always been intrigued by the Feast of Seven Fishes. It's the only major holiday meal that is centered on seafood. That doesn't necessarily mean there is no meat on the table; at my house that would cause a rebellion. The meat in these recipes serves to support and elevate the fish, like the pepperoni in my Squid Bolognese or the bacon in my Clam Chowder Fritters, while the seafood retains the starring role. Here I've pulled together seven special dishes that can go together to create one extravagant seafood feast or be served on their own for a delicious lunch or dinner.

Clam Chowder Fritters

Squid Bolognese

Crispy Oysters with Collard
   Green Caesar Salad

Whole Roasted Bass and
   Cranberry Sea Beans

Smoked Shrimp and Grits

Artichokes Barigoule with
   Salt Cod

Monketta

The Feast of Seven Fishes

Clam Chowder Fritters

SERVES 12

STOCK:

24 middleneck clams

2 tablespoons / 28 grams unsalted butter

¼ fennel bulb, thinly sliced (about ½ cup)

3 shallots, thinly sliced

2 cloves garlic, sliced

1 cup / 225 grams white wine

1 lemon, thinly sliced

2 bay leaves

2 sprigs thyme

FILLING:

⅓ **cup** / 75 grams unsalted butter

½ **cup** / 60 grams bacon, cut into small dice

½ medium russet potato, peeled
and cut into small dice

¼ medium celeriac, cut into small dice

1 small leek, white and light parts only,
cut into small dice

⅓ **cup** / 46 grams onion, cut into small dice

¼ **cup** / 35 grams fennel bulb, cut into
small dice

1 clove garlic, minced

⅓ **cup** / 50 grams all-purpose flour

1 cup plus 2 tablespoons / 255 grams Stock

⅔ **cup** / 160 grams whole milk

¼ **cup** / 60 grams heavy cream

Zest and juice of 1 lemon

1 teaspoon / 5 grams malt vinegar

1 teaspoon / 6 grams Tabasco sauce

1½ teaspoons / 9 grams fine sea salt

½ **teaspoon** / 1.5 grams freshly ground
black pepper

1 tablespoon / 5 grams chopped
fresh flat-leaf parsley

1 tablespoon / 5 grams chopped
fresh chervil

1 sheet gelatin (soaked in ice water
for 3 minutes)

FRITTER COATING:

Vegetable oil, for your hands and for frying

½ (**1-pound** / 454-gram) box
saltine crackers

2 large eggs

½ **cup** / 120 grams buttermilk

½ **teaspoon** / 3 grams fine sea salt

½ **cup** / 75 grams all-purpose flour

Tartar Sauce (page 56), for serving

One of my favorite scenes in *Charlie and the Chocolate Factory* was when Violet ate the gum that turned into a three-course meal in her mouth. I love the idea of biting into something innocuous and discovering something delicious inside. At Table 21, the chef's table in my restaurant Volt, we focus on small portions and concentrated flavors. I took that philosophy and applied it to clam chowder. When you pop one of these fritters in your mouth and close your eyes, you'll swear you're enjoying a bowl of rich, creamy chowder. Of course, it's only one course of this meal, but I bet you, unlike Violet, won't turn into a blueberry when you finish eating it. You'll just want to reach for another one.

Make the Stock:
Soak the clams in cold water for at least 1 hour to remove the grit.

Set a medium pot over high heat and add the butter. When the butter melts, add the fennel, shallots, and garlic and sauté, stirring constantly. As soon as they begin to brown and become aromatic, add the clams, wine, lemon slices, bay leaves, and thyme. Cover with a lid and steam for 5 minutes, just until all the clams open. Do not overcook the clams. Remove from the heat and transfer the clams and liquid to separate large bowls to cool. Once they are cool enough to work with, strain the Stock and reserve. Remove each clam from its shell and chop it up.

Make the Filling:

Set a large stockpot over medium heat and add the butter and bacon. Once the bacon begins to brown, add the potato, celeriac, leek, onion, fennel, and garlic, and sauté for 2 minutes, stirring constantly. Sprinkle the flour over the vegetables and cook, stirring with a wooden spoon, for 1 minute. Whisk in the Stock, milk, and cream, bring to a simmer, then turn the heat to low and cook for 15 minutes to cook out the flour taste and thicken the mixture. Remove from the heat and stir in the lemon zest and juice, malt vinegar, Tabasco, salt, pepper, chopped clams, parsley, chervil, and gelatin. Stir until well blended and the gelatin dissolves, 1 to 2 minutes. Let the chowder cool, and then pour into a large casserole pan or other shallow container. Cover and chill in the refrigerator overnight to let it thicken into a scoopable mixture.

Form the Fritters:

Line a baking sheet with parchment paper. Use a 1-ounce ice cream scoop to portion fritters onto the prepared baking sheet. Place a few drops of oil on the palms of your hands and rub them together to lightly coat your palms so the fritters don't stick to your hands. Gently shape each scoop into a ball. Cover the pan loosely with plastic wrap and chill in the refrigerator for 1 hour.

Preheat a deep fryer or a large pot with 4 inches of oil to 350°F (180°C).

Make the Fritter Coating and Fry the Fritters:

Use a food processor to grind up the saltines into a fine crumb. Sprinkle a thin layer of cracker crumbs on a baking sheet. Transfer the remainder to a casserole pan or large bowl. Whisk together the eggs, buttermilk, and salt in a pie pan. Put the flour in another small bowl or pie pan.

Take the fritters from the refrigerator and roll each ball in the flour, shaking off any excess before transferring it to the egg mixture. Lightly coat each ball of filling with the egg mixture and then transfer to the container of cracker crumbs. Thoroughly coat each fritter with the cracker crumbs, and then return to the egg wash and the cracker crumbs once more so you have a nice coating of crumbs that won't break open when you fry. Once coated, lay each fritter on the prepared baking sheet in the cracker meal.

Fry the fritters for 5 minutes, or until golden brown and hot through. Serve immediately with Tartar Sauce alongside for dipping.

Squid Bolognese

BOLOGNESE SAUCE:

1 pound / 454 grams cleaned squid

12 ounces / 340 grams pepperoni

1⅔ cups / 375 grams Pinot Noir

1 tablespoon / 14 grams rice bran oil

1 medium onion, minced

½ fennel bulb, cut into small dice

3 celery ribs, cut into small dice

1 (**28-ounce** / 794-gram) can whole peeled San Marzano tomatoes

1 teaspoon / 5 grams fish sauce

1 teaspoon / 5 grams gochujang (Korean red pepper puree)

½ teaspoon / 1 gram fennel seeds

1 bay leaf

1 piece long pepper

1 clove garlic, smashed

½ cup / 113 grams unsalted butter

¼ cup / 56 grams extra-virgin olive oil

SQUID INK PASTA:

9 large egg yolks

2 large eggs

2 tablespoons / 30 grams squid ink

1 tablespoon / 16 grams whole milk

1 tablespoon / 14 grams olive oil

2¼ cups / 340 grams all-purpose flour

Grated Parmesan cheese, for serving

SPECIAL EQUIPMENT:

Meat grinder or grinding attachment for stand mixer

Pasta-rolling machine or attachment for stand mixer

On Season 5 of *Top Chef Masters*, I won a challenge using this Squid Bolognese sauce. We were cooking for four teachers from the Los Angeles Unified School District, and my teacher was known for progressive thinking. I knew I wanted to make something traditional and welcoming to draw diners in and then turn it on its head somehow to showcase a bit of innovation. Traditional Bolognese is the quintessential meat sauce, and it is on every Italian menu. This pasta looks like classic Bolognese, only it's made with calamari. It has a slightly lighter, sweeter flavor, with all of the richness and depth of the original. I use squid ink to make the pasta dough because I love layering flavors and the ink adds a hint of that briny, iodine flavor of the ocean. If you buy your squid cleaned, ask the fishmonger for some ink. To this day, it's one of my favorite sauces.

Make the Bolognese Sauce:

Cut the squid and pepperoni into 1-inch pieces, put them in a shallow baking dish, cover, and place in the freezer for 1 to 2 hours, until they are very firm (for easy grinding) but not frozen solid.

Pour the wine into a medium saucepan set over medium-high heat and bring it to a simmer. Reduce the wine by half, about 20 minutes, remove from the heat, and reserve.

Use a meat grinder with a medium die or the grinding attachment on a stand mixer to grind the squid and pepperoni.

Set a large pot over medium heat and add the rice bran oil. When it begins to shimmer, add the onion, fennel, and celery. Cook, stirring, until the vegetables are tender and translucent, 5 to 7 minutes. Add the ground calamari and pepperoni and cook, stirring continuously to break up any large clumps, until the mixture is smooth and comes to a simmer. Adjust the heat to maintain the simmer and continue to cook, stirring occasionally, for 7 to 10 minutes, making sure the bottom of the pan doesn't scorch.

Open the can of tomatoes and use a food mill to strain them into a large bowl. If you do not have a food mill, pulse the tomatoes in a food processor until they are finely chopped but not pureed, and then pass them through a mesh strainer to remove the seeds. Add the tomatoes, fish sauce, and *gochujang* to the pot and reduce the heat to low.

Use a small piece of cheesecloth to make a sachet with the fennel seeds, bay leaf, long pepper, and garlic. Tie it together with a long piece of butcher's twine. Tie the long end of the twine to the pot handle for easy removal and put the sachet in the pot. Cook over low heat for 1 to 1½ hours, stirring occasionally. The sauce will thicken and caramelize slightly.

Remove from the heat and stir in the butter and olive oil, mixing until it is absorbed into the sauce. Keep warm until ready to serve, or cool and refrigerate in a covered container. Leftover sauce will keep for up to 1 week in the refrigerator.

Make the Squid Ink Pasta:

Whisk together the egg yolks, eggs, squid ink, milk, and olive oil. Put the flour in a food processor and pulse while slowly drizzling in the egg mixture. Once all of the liquid has been absorbed, turn the dough out onto a clean countertop and knead until it forms a smooth ball, about 5 minutes. Wrap in plastic wrap and let the dough rest at cool room temperature for at least 1 hour and up to 4 hours.

Use a pasta machine and, following the manufacturer's directions, roll the pasta out to the second smallest setting. Cut it into 12-inch sheets, flour each one, fold into eighths, and slice into ¼-inch ribbons.

Set a large pot of salted water over high heat. When it comes to a boil, drop the pasta in the pot and cook for 2 to 3 minutes, until just tender, with a bit of resistance between your teeth. Transfer the pasta to the pot of sauce and cook for another 1 to 2 minutes, folding the pasta into the sauce so that it gets a nice glaze. Transfer the pasta and sauce to a large serving bowl. Set it on the table with a bowl of Parmesan cheese alongside.

Crispy Oysters with Collard Green Caesar Salad

SERVES 8 TO 10 AS A SIDE DISH

CAESAR DRESSING:

3 large egg yolks

2 ounces / 56 grams salted anchovies

5 cloves garlic

2½ tablespoons / 45 grams Dijon mustard

4½ tablespoons / 65 grams fresh lemon juice

1¼ cups / 280 grams extra-virgin olive oil

3½ tablespoons / 50 grams red wine vinegar

2 teaspoons / 12 grams Tabasco sauce

1 tablespoon / 14 grams Worcestershire sauce

2¾ cups / 620 grams olive oil

½ cup / 113 grams cold water

½ cup / 50 grams grated Parmesan cheese

1½ teaspoons / 3 grams freshly ground black pepper

¾ teaspoon / 4.5 grams fine sea salt

FOR THE SALAD:

2 bunches collard greens

1 cup Caesar Dressing

3 heads romaine lettuce

CRISPY OYSTERS:

Peanut or canola oil, for frying

2 cups / 60 grams cornflake cereal

12 oysters, shucked

½ cup / 70 grams all-purpose flour

½ batter recipe from Onion Rings (page 205)

Fine sea salt, for seasoning

Grated Parmesan cheese, for serving

People are often surprised to discover that Caesar salad is one of my favorite things to eat. Whenever I go out to a restaurant and it's on the menu, I order it, for myself or for the table. Everyone eats it. What's not to like about the contrast of the cool crunchy romaine lettuce, the rich creamy dressing, the snap of lemon, the crunch of well-made croutons, and the deep umami flavors from the anchovy and Parmesan cheese? Here I've combined the classic romaine with collard greens. They have great flavor and add a little more nutrition to the blend. The fried oysters stand in for the croutons, crispy, crunchy, and imbued with the flavors of the sea. It's Caesar salad my way, perfect for a seafood extravaganza. Because the greens marinate overnight, start the prep the day before you plan to serve.

Make the Caesar Dressing:

In a food processor, combine the egg yolks, anchovies, garlic, Dijon, and lemon juice; blend until smooth and frothy. While the processor is on, drizzle in the extra-virgin olive oil, red wine vinegar, Tabasco, and Worcestershire sauce. Once it's completely incorporated, start raining in the olive oil alternately with the water. Transfer to a container and whisk in the cheese, pepper, and salt. Refrigerate until ready to serve.

Prepare the Salad:

Remove the collard leaves from the stems. Finely slice the leaves and transfer to a large bowl. Toss with ¾ cup of the Caesar Dressing, cover, and place in the refrigerator to marinate overnight.

The next day, just before frying the oysters, finely chop the romaine lettuce and toss with the collard greens.

Fry the Oysters:

Preheat a deep fryer or pot with 4 inches of oil to 335°F (168°C).

Using a food processor, coarsely grind the cornflakes and place in a large bowl. Dredge each oyster in the flour, then dip in the batter; shake off any excess and completely coat with corn flakes. Fry for 3 to 5 minutes, until crunchy. Remove, drain, and season with salt.

Add the remaining dressing to the greens and toss. Garnish with grated Parmesan and the Crispy Oysters.

Whole Roasted Bass and Cranberry Sea Beans

SERVES 8

DASHI:

7 cups plus 1¾ tablespoons / 1.6 kilograms water

1¾ ounces / 50 grams kombu

1¾ ounces / 50 grams bonito flakes

5 dried shiitake mushrooms

CRANBERRY "SEA BEANS":

6⅔ cups / 1.5 kilograms Dashi

1 pound / 454 grams cranberry beans, soaked in cold water for at least 8 hours

9 ounces / 250 grams country ham, diced

1 ounce / 28 grams dried wakame

1½ teaspoons / 9 grams fine sea salt

BLACK SEA BASS:

1 (4- to 5-pound / 1.8- to 2.26-kilogram) whole black sea bass, cleaned

Fine sea salt, for seasoning

3 tablespoons / 42 grams Clarified Butter (page 57) or light olive oil

2 tablespoons / 28 grams unsalted butter, room temperature

4 sprigs thyme

Lemon wedges, for serving

SPECIAL EQUIPMENT:

Pressure cooker (optional)

This is a celebratory dish. I love serving whole roasted fish for a group. It's a dramatic presentation that draws the eye and encourages people to come forward and dig in. I make a Japanese dashi to cook the cranberry beans so that they are infused with the delicate flavor of the sea. I pan-roast the fish and employ an old chef's trick, basting it with fresh butter and herbs at the very end of cooking. You'll be amazed at how much flavor is absorbed with that one small step.

Make the Dashi:

Put the water, kombu, bonito flakes, and dried shiitake mushrooms in a medium stockpot. Set over low heat and bring the mixture to 155°F (68°C). Do not let it come to a boil. Remove from the heat and let cool to room temperature, about 1 hour. Remove the shiitake mushrooms, cut them into a fine dice, and reserve. Strain the Dashi.

Make the Cranberry "Sea Beans":

Put the Dashi, cranberry beans, ham, shiitake mushrooms, dried wakame, and salt in a pressure cooker. Cook at low pressure for 18 minutes. Let the pressure dissipate naturally. Alternatively, put everything in a medium pot set over high heat and bring to a boil. Reduce the heat to low, skim the froth, cover with a lid, and simmer for 1½ hours, or until the beans are tender.

Make the Black Sea Bass:

Pat the fish dry with paper towels and season with salt on both sides. Set a medium cast-iron pan large enough to hold your whole fish over medium-high heat. Add the Clarified Butter or light olive oil, and when it begins to shimmer, gently place the fish in the pan. Make sure it is not touching the sides of the pan. Sear until golden brown on the bottom, 4 to 5 minutes, and then carefully flip the fish. Sear on the top side until golden brown, another 4 to 5 minutes.

Add the softened butter and thyme to the pan and baste the fish continuously for 2 minutes, or until the butter stops foaming. Transfer to a warm plate to rest. Stir the Cranberry "Sea Beans" and spoon them onto a serving platter. Lay the fish on top of the beans and pour any juices from the plate over the fish. Garnish with the lemon wedges and serve immediately.

Smoked Shrimp and Grits

SERVES 8 TO 10 AS A SIDE DISH

1 pound / 454 grams U 16/20 whole shrimp

SHRIMP OIL:

Reserved shells and heads from shrimp

3 cups / 675 grams light olive oil, divided

1 medium onion, thinly sliced

5 medium shallots, thinly sliced

6 medium cloves garlic, thinly sliced

3 tablespoons / 24 grams smoked paprika

1 teaspoon / 6 grams fine sea salt

1 teaspoon / 2 grams cayenne pepper

1 tablespoon / 12 grams finely chopped fresh thyme

GRITS:

¾ cup / 170 grams Shrimp Oil, divided

2 cups / 450 grams unsalted butter, diced

4 cups / 680 grams stone-ground yellow grits

3 quarts / 2.7 kilograms Vegetable Stock (page 92) or store-bought

1 tablespoon / 18 grams fine sea salt

BEER-YEAST SAUCE:

1 cup / 225 grams unsalted butter

1¾ ounces / 50 grams compressed fresh yeast

2¼ teaspoons / 12 grams soy sauce

Zest and juice of ½ lemon

9 tablespoons / 130 grams light ale (like Pabst Blue Ribbon or Coors Light)

CHARRED LEMONS:

3 lemons

2 tablespoons / 18 grams Our Bay Seasoning Blend (page 35)

SPECIAL EQUIPMENT:

Stovetop smoker

Hickory wood chips

In the summertime there's nothing I like better than boiled shrimp and beer. In the wintertime I re-create that feeling with these shrimp and grits. I use the shells to make an aromatic shrimp oil that I use to season the grits. The shrimp are dusted with what I call Our Bay Seasoning Blend and grilled. The shrimp and grits are served with charred lemon wedges and a bright, tangy beer-yeast sauce. It transforms my favorite summertime dish into something delicious and warming for a winter feast.

Prepare the Shrimp:

Peel and remove the heads and tails from the shrimp and reserve to make the Shrimp Oil. Use a small paring knife to split open the backs of the shrimp to remove the vein. Make a small, shallow cut along the underside of the shrimp. This will help keep the shrimp straight during cooking. Skewer each shrimp using a 6-inch bamboo skewer and refrigerate in a covered container until ready to cook.

Make the Shrimp Oil:

Put the shrimp shells and heads in a medium pot and add ¼ cup (56 grams) of the olive oil, the onion, shallots, and garlic. Set over high heat and cook, stirring, for 5 to 7 minutes, to toast the shrimp shells and heads and soften the vegetables. Add the remaining 2¾ cups (619 grams) olive oil, the smoked paprika, salt, and cayenne pepper, and reduce the heat to medium. Cook for 10 minutes, or until the shells and onions are golden brown. Remove from the heat and cool for 20 minutes. Strain through a coffee filter and add the thyme. If not using immediately, reserve in a covered container in the refrigerator until needed.

Make the Grits:

Put ¼ cup (56 grams) of the Shrimp Oil and the butter in a medium stockpot or Dutch oven. Once the butter melts, add the grits and toast them, stirring constantly, for 3 to 4 minutes. Before the butter begins to brown, whisk in the stock and bring the mixture to a simmer, stirring constantly. Reduce the heat to low or transfer to a slow cooker and let the grits cook for at least 3 hours and up to 4 hours. Just before serving, whisk in the remaining ½ cup (114 grams) Shrimp Oil and the salt.

Make the Beer-Yeast Sauce:

Put the butter in a medium saucepot set over medium heat. As soon as the butter melts, whisk it until it browns and becomes nutty and aromatic. Add the fresh yeast and whisk to incorporate. Remove from the heat and add the soy sauce, lemon zest and juice, and beer. Transfer to a blender and puree until foamy.

Make the Charred Lemons:

Set a cast-iron skillet over medium-high heat and cut each lemon in half. Once the pan is hot, add the lemons, cut side down, and sear for 7 to 10 minutes, until they are a dark golden brown. Let cool slightly, and then cut into wedges.

Cook the Shrimp:

Take the shrimp from the refrigerator and season lightly with the Our Bay Seasoning Blend. Put ½ cup of hickory chips in a stovetop smoker and follow the manufacturer's directions to heat the smoker. Grease the inside tray of the smoker lightly with either nonstick cooking spray or oil and then line the skewered shrimp up inside. Once the chips begin to smoke, reduce the heat to low, put the shrimp inside, close the lid over the chips, and smoke for 12 to 15 minutes, until the shrimp are smoky and cooked through.

Spoon the grits into a large shallow serving bowl and arrange the shrimp in the center. Drizzle some of the Beer-Yeast Sauce over the shrimp and serve the rest alongside with a plate of Charred Lemon wedges.

Artichokes Barigoule
with Salt Cod

SERVES 8

2 pounds / 908 grams cod

¾ teaspoon / 4.5 grams fine sea salt

ARTICHOKES:

1 lemon

8 globe artichokes

9 tablespoons / 125 grams
extra-virgin olive oil

1 fennel bulb, thinly sliced

1 medium onion, thinly sliced

1 medium carrot, thinly sliced

3 cloves garlic, crushed

2 teaspoons / 12 grams fine sea salt

¼ teaspoon / 0.5 gram red pepper flakes

1⅔ cups / 375 grams Sauvignon Blanc

2 cups plus 3½ tablespoons / 500 grams
Vegetable Stock (page 92, or store-bought)
or water

8-inch square piece of kombu

PARSLEY-MINT OIL:

¾ cup / 30 grams fresh flat-leaf
parsley leaves

2 cups / 70 grams fresh mint leaves

7 ounces / 200 grams light olive oil

Espelette pepper for serving

When you're trained in classic French technique and work in progressive American restaurants like Aureole in New York City, you learn how to make artichokes *à la barigoule*. It's a classic technique that undergoes a variety of transformations in the hands of each chef. Artichokes are one of those vegetables that are well loved but not often cooked at home. Many home cooks find them intimidating, but this recipe will show you how easy and delicious they can be. *Baccalà* or salt cod is a staple at the Feast of Seven Fishes. I prefer to salt fresh cod rather than soaking the dried salted version because then I can control how it tastes. The contrast of the sweet juicy fish with the grassy, tender artichokes is something special.

Portion the cod into sixteen 2-ounce pieces. Set them on a large plate or tray, season with the salt, cover loosely with plastic wrap, and refrigerate.

Make the Artichokes:

Half-fill a large bowl with cold water and add the juice of the lemon. Peel the dark outer leaves off of the artichokes. Use a vegetable peeler to peel the outer layer from the stems. Cut off the tops, about 1 inch from the tips. Stand the artichokes on a cutting board, cut side down, and use a sharp knife to trim away the outer layers of leaves to expose the light green inner leaves. Cut the artichokes in half and use a small spoon or melon baller to scoop out the fuzzy choke in the center. Put the cut artichokes in the lemon water, being sure to coat each one with water to prevent browning. After you finish cleaning the artichokes, be sure to wash your hands thoroughly because they leave a very bitter residue on your fingertips.

Set a large pot over medium-high heat and add the olive oil. When it begins to shimmer, add the fennel, onion, and carrot. Cook, stirring, for 3 to 5 minutes, until the vegetables are tender and translucent. Add the garlic, salt, and red pepper flakes and stir. Drain the artichokes, and then add them, the wine, and the stock to the pot, and bring to a simmer. Lay the kombu directly on top of the simmering stock, reduce the heat to low, so that it slows down to a gentle bubble, and cook for 25 to 30 minutes, until the artichokes are tender when poked with a toothpick or cake tester.

Remove from the heat and let the vegetables cool in the liquid. Transfer them to a large container and then strain the liquid over them. They will keep in a covered container in the refrigerator for up to 3 days.

Make the Parsley-Mint Oil:

Put the parsley, mint, and oil in a blender and puree until smooth. Pour the mixture into a small pot, set it over medium heat, and bring to a boil. Immediately remove from the heat and strain through a strainer lined with a coffee filter into a metal bowl. Set the bowl of oil over an ice bath and stir to chill it down. This rapid cooling will help preserve the bright green color of the oil. Transfer to a covered container and refrigerate until needed, for up to 4 hours.

Cook the Cod:

When you're ready to cook the fish, pull the Parsley-Mint Oil out of the refrigerator to take the chill off. Put the artichokes in a medium pot with just enough of their liquid to cover them. Reserve the remainder of the liquid. Bring to a simmer and heat through. Meanwhile, put the cod in one layer in a large sauté pan and cover with the remaining artichoke liquid. Set over medium heat and bring to just below a simmer. Turn off the heat, cover, and leave the cod in the hot liquid for 5 minutes to finish cooking. Spoon the vegetables onto a platter. Slide pieces of fish around them. Drizzle with the Parsley-Mint Oil, sprinkle lightly with Espelette pepper, and serve.

Monketta

Every table has to have a centerpiece, one dish that really wows the crowd. This is that dish. Monkfish is perfect for roasting because it has a wonderful meaty texture and is a very juicy fish. Here I dust the monkfish tails with wakame powder to amplify the flavor of the sea and then wrap them in a home-made shrimp and pork sausage. Finally, I roll them in bacon, tie them, and roast them in the oven. The Monketta slices beautifully once it's cooked and has a wonderful play of textures and flavors. It's a dish that everyone will remember and ask for again and again.

SHRIMP AND PORK SAUSAGE:

1 pound / 454 grams shrimp, cleaned and deveined

1 pound / 454 grams ground pork

½ onion, minced

2 tablespoons / 28 grams dry vermouth

1 teaspoon / 4 grams soy sauce

½ **teaspoon** / 2 grams grated fresh ginger

1½ **teaspoons** / 9 grams fine sea salt

6 pieces cleaned monkfish tails (about **3 pounds** / 1.36 kilograms)

2 ounces / 56 grams dried wakame, ground to a fine powder

2 pounds / 908 grams bacon slices

Dijon Mustard Vinaigrette (page 84)

Make the Shrimp and Pork Sausage:
Put the shrimp in a food processor and pulse until it is finely ground but not pureed. Transfer the shrimp to a bowl and add the ground pork, onion, vermouth, soy sauce, ginger, and salt. Mix gently with your hands or a rubber spatula until well blended. Divide the sausage into 3 equal portions.

Dust the monkfish tails evenly with the wakame powder, coating them complete-ly. Group the tails into pairs, keeping pieces of approximately the same size and shape together. Take an 8-by-10-inch piece of plastic wrap and spread 1 portion of sausage in a rough rectangle, approxi-mately 9 inches wide, in the center of the plastic wrap. Take 2 pieces of monkfish and lay them head to tail in the center of the sausage rectangle. Lift the plastic wrap up and over the fish, pulling a layer of sausage up and over the monkfish tails. Gently squeeze the sausage against the fish and pull the plastic wrap out and away from it. Continue to roll the fish in the sausage until it forms a compact log. Wrap the log in the plastic wrap, twisting the ends to tighten the compression evenly around the fish, and refrigerate. Repeat with the remaining 2 portions of sausage and 2 sets of monkfish tails. Refrigerate for at least an hour so that the sausage has time to chill and set around the fish.

Lay an 8-by-10-inch piece of plastic wrap on the counter. Lay 14 or 15 slices of bacon on the plastic wrap, slightly overlapping them. Pound them lightly with a meat mallet so they adhere to one another. Unwrap 1 monkfish log and lay it on the bottom third of the bacon strips. Use the bottom of the plastic wrap to help lift the bacon over and around the fish and then roll everything up into a tight log. Wrap the log in the plastic wrap, twisting the ends to tighten the compression evenly around the bacon, and refrigerate. Repeat with the remain-ing 2 monkfish logs. Refrigerate the bacon-wrapped fish for at least 1 hour and up to 24 hours to seal the Monkettas before cooking.

Preheat the oven to 375°F (190°C).

Set up a stovetop steamer large enough to hold the Monkettas.

Cut twelve 12-inch lengths of butcher's twine. Lay them out vertically on a cutting board, leaving 1 inch of space between them. Gently unwrap 1 Monk-etta log and lay it horizonatally across the butcher's twine, seam side down. Tie the strings around the log and trim off the long ends. Repeat with the remaining 2 Monketta logs.

Steam the Monkettas for 10 minutes. Transfer to a roasting pan. Put them in the oven and roast for 10 minutes. Without opening the oven, increase the temperature to 425°F (220°C) and roast for 10 minutes. Reduce the temperature to 325°F (165°C), remove the Monkettas from the oven, brush each generously with Dijon Vinaigrette, and then return the pan to the oven. Roast for 10 more minutes, until the Monkettas are cooked through and the bacon is golden brown and crisp. Transfer the Monkettas to a platter and let rest for 10 minutes before slicing. Cut the logs into slices approxi-mately 1 inch thick, arrange on a platter, and serve immediately.

Super Bowl Sunday may not be an official holiday, but to my mind it should be. It has all of the elements of a perfect day: a great game, tons of appetizers, and my favorite chili, all while surrounded by the family and friends. There's no holiday pressure to give gifts or create that perfect moment; there's only a good time to be had by all. People can come and go, it's completely laid back, and there's always lots of good food.

Shrimp-Stuffed Mushrooms

Crab and Artichoke Dip

Chicken Wings with Kimchi Caramel and Wing Sauce

Potpie Fritters

Pimento Cheese Hush Puppies

Deviled Ham with Eggs

Sweet Potato and Chickpea Fries with Thousand Island Dressing

Onion Rings with Bacon-Horseradish Dip

Chili with the Fixings

Super Bowl Sunday

Shrimp-Stuffed Mushrooms

MAKES 25 MUSHROOMS

MARINADE:

2 tablespoons / 28 grams rice wine vinegar

5 teaspoons / 25 grams fish sauce

1½ tablespoons / 22 grams soy sauce

1 clove garlic, grated

3 sprigs thyme

¾ cup / 165 grams olive oil

25 large button mushrooms, stems removed

SHRIMP STUFFING:

¼ cup / 56 grams Clarified Butter (page 57)

1¾ ounces / 50 grams saltine crackers, ground into fine crumbs

1 clove garlic, minced

1 pound / 454 grams peeled shrimp

1 teaspoon / 6 grams fine sea salt, divided

2 scallions, minced

1 teaspoon / 4 grams minced or grated fresh ginger

1 tablespoon / 14 grams dry vermouth or Sauvignon Blanc

1 teaspoon / 4 grams soy sauce

½ teaspoon / 2.5 grams fish sauce

1 large egg, lightly beaten

Barbecue sauce, to finish

SPECIAL EQUIPMENT:

Meat grinder or grinding attachment for stand mixer

Stuffed mushrooms are one of my guilty pleasures. They always seemed to be on the table at parties when I was growing up. This is probably because they taste so good. As a restaurant chef, I feel as though I should make something fancier, but when I'm watching the Super Bowl or any other big game, these mushrooms are what I want with my beer. I marinate the mushroom caps, stuff them with little shrimp cakes, and roast them in the oven. You can prepare them ahead of time and pop them in the oven when the game starts. You will not find these on the menu at any of my restaurants, but if you ever come to a party at my house, these sizzling stuffed mushrooms will definitely be on the buffet.

Make the Marinade:

Put the vinegar, fish sauce, soy sauce, garlic, and thyme in a bowl and whisk to blend. Slowly whisk in the olive oil. Put the mushrooms in a large zip-top bag and pour the marinade over them; seal the bag, set it in a bowl, and marinate in the refrigerator for at least 2 hours and up to 12 hours.

Make the Shrimp Stuffing:

Preheat the oven to 350°F (180°C).

Set a small sauté pan over medium heat and add the Clarified Butter. Once the pan is hot, add the cracker crumbs and garlic and cook, stirring, until the crackers are golden brown and aromatic, 5 to 7 minutes. Remove from the heat and transfer to a bowl to cool.

Coarsely chop half of the shrimp, put in a medium bowl, and mix with ¾ teaspoon (4.5 grams) of the salt. Put the remaining shrimp in a clean bowl and add the scallions, minced ginger, vermouth, soy sauce, fish sauce, and the remaining ¼ teaspoon (1.5 grams) salt. Use a meat grinder or grinding attachment on a stand mixer to grind the marinated shrimp through a medium die into the bowl with the chopped pieces in it. Fold in the cracker mixture and the egg and mix thoroughly.

Cook the Mushrooms:

Line a baking sheet with parchment paper. Drain the mushrooms and line them up on the pan. Fill each mushroom cap with the shrimp mixture, mounding it slightly into a dome on top. Bake for 8 minutes, rotate the baking sheet, and bake for 8 minutes more, or until the mushrooms are golden brown and sizzling. Brush with your favorite barbecue sauce and serve.

Crab and Artichoke Dip

SERVES 8 TO 12

4½ cups / 1 kilogram cold water

5 lemons

1 pound / 454 grams artichokes

2 tablespoons / 28 grams
extra-virgin olive oil

1 leek, cut into small dice

1 medium shallot, minced

6 cloves garlic, minced

1 jalapeño pepper, seeded and thinly sliced

7 ounces / 200 grams white wine

1 pound / 454 grams crabmeat, picked
through for shells and cartilage

8 ounces / 227 grams crème fraîche

1 tablespoon / 14 grams extra-virgin olive oil

¼ teaspoon / 1.5 grams fine sea salt

1 tablespoon / 4 grams chopped
fresh flat-leaf parsley

1 tablespoon / 2 grams chopped fresh
rosemary

TOPPING:

2 ounces / 60 grams saltine cracker crumbs
(ground in food processor)

1½ tablespoons / 3 grams chopped
fresh rosemary

2½ teaspoons / 3 grams chopped
fresh flat-leaf parsley

¼ teaspoon / 1.5 grams fine sea salt

2 tablespoons / 28 grams unsalted butter,
melted

This is another family staple. We love to dip and we love crab. Artichokes are actually one of my favorite vegetables, and their presence in the dip lets you pretend you're eating something healthy. In fact, I made this recipe specifically so that some people, and they know who they are, would have a great-tasting crab-and-artichoke dip to bring to our next party. The best thing about this dip is that there is a balance between the crabmeat and the artichokes, so that they are both present in equal amounts in every bite. It's addictive, and somehow it all disappears by halftime.

Put the water in a bowl and add the juice from the lemons. Pull off the outer dark leaves of the artichokes, turning as you go. Using a stainless-steel serrated knife, cut off the very top of the artichokes. One at a time, invert each artichoke on a cutting board so that the stem side is up and begin to pare off the outer layer, cutting about ½ inch off the outer circumference of the leaves of each artichoke to expose the inner soft green leaves. You can hold the stem as you do this and cut from the base to the top, rotating the artichoke on the cutting board to make it easier. When you're done, use a peeler or a paring knife to remove the outer layer of the stem, which is very fibrous. Finally, use a teaspoon to scoop out and discard the choke, and drop the trimmed artichoke into the bowl of lemon water, being sure it gets submerged at least once to coat the vegetable with liquid. This will stop the artichoke from oxidizing, which happens almost immediately. After you finish cleaning the artichokes, be sure to wash your hands thoroughly because they leave a very bitter residue on your fingertips.

Put the olive oil in a medium pot set over medium-high heat. When the oil begins to shimmer, add the leeks and shallot. Reduce the heat to low, stir well to blend the vegetables, cover, and cook for 15 minutes, or until the leeks are tender. Add the garlic and jalapeño pepper and cook for 2 to 3 minutes, until they are tender and aromatic. Meanwhile, cut each artichoke into quarters and then thinly slice them. Add the artichokes to the vegetables, stir, cover, and cook for 10 minutes.

Put the white wine in a small saucepot and bring to a simmer. Let the wine reduce by half while the artichokes are cooking. Add the wine to the pot with the artichokes and remove from the heat.

Preheat the oven to 350°F (180°C).

Transfer the artichoke mixture to a bowl. Add the crabmeat, crème fraîche,

olive oil, salt, parsley, and rosemary and gently mix everything together with a rubber spatula. Transfer the crab-artichoke mixture to a 7-by-11-inch casserole dish.

Make the Topping and Bake the Dip:
Put the cracker crumbs, rosemary, parsley, and salt in a small bowl and mix well with a spoon. Pour in the melted butter and stir everything together. Sprinkle the crumb topping over the crab-artichoke casserole. Bake for 20 to 25 minutes, until the top is golden brown and the dip is bubbling. Serve hot.

Chicken Wings with Kimchi Caramel and Wing Sauce

MAKES 24 WINGS

MARINADE:

3 large egg whites

2 teaspoons / 10 grams baking soda

1¾ teaspoons / 10.5 grams fine sea salt

24 whole chicken wings

KIMCHI CARAMEL:

1 cup / 200 grams sugar

1½ tablespoons / 30 grams corn syrup

½ cup / 112 grams water, divided

7 ounces / 200 grams kimchi liquid
(from the jar)

2 teaspoons / 10 grams red wine vinegar

½ teaspoon / 3 grams fine sea salt

WING SAUCE:

⅔ cup / 150 grams crème fraîche

3 tablespoons / 55 grams ketchup

1½ tablespoons / 25 grams gochujang
(Korean red pepper puree)

3½ ounces / 100 grams crumbled
blue cheese

1 tablespoon / 15 grams minced
bread-and-butter (sweet) pickles

½ teaspoon / 3 grams fine sea salt

WINGS:

½ cup / 65 grams unsalted
chopped peanuts

4 scallions, thinly sliced

This is a great way to make crispy chicken wings without using a fryer. That keeps it free for the Potpie Fritters (page 195) and any other goodies you might want to fry up. The wings are moist and tender, with a crackling skin. I make a kimchi-caramel sauce inspired by the flavors of Korean fried chicken, and fold some crumbled blue cheese inspired by Buffalo wings into the wing sauce, and somehow it all harmonizes. The sauce is so good that you'll find yourself dipping in French fries when all the wings are gone.

Make the Marinade:

Combine the egg whites, baking soda, and salt together in a bowl with a wire whisk until frothy. Toss with the wings and place them on a stainless-steel rack set over a baking sheet. Refrigerate uncovered for 14 to 18 hours or overnight.

Make the Kimchi Caramel:

Put the sugar and corn syrup into a medium saucepot. Pour ¼ cup (56 grams) of the water over them and mix everything together. Wipe down the sides of the pot with a damp paper towel to eliminate any stray grains of sugar that may cause the caramel to crystallize. Cover the pot with plastic wrap; this allows you to see the caramel cooking. Set over medium heat and cook until the caramel becomes light amber. Carefully remove the plastic wrap, as there will be steam, and slowly whisk in the kimchi liquid, the remaining ¼ cup (56 grams) water, and the vinegar. The sugar will hiss and bubble rapidly. Once it settles down, stir in the salt. Remove from the heat and let the caramel cool.

Make the Wing Sauce:

Put all of the ingredients in a food processor. Pulse 3 times to blend but not puree; you want a slightly chunky sauce. Transfer to a bowl, cover, and reserve in the refrigerator until ready to serve.

Roast the Wings:

Preheat the oven to 450°F (230°C).

Spray a clean rack with nonstick cooking spray, set it over a baking sheet, and transfer the wings to the prepared rack. Roast the wings for 10 minutes, remove from the oven, and flip the wings over. Roast for 15 minutes, remove from the oven, and flip the wings again. Roast for a final 10 minutes, or until the wings are caramelized and crisp. Sprinkle the peanuts and scallions over the wings just before serving. Serve with Wing Sauce.

Potpie Fritters

SERVES 12 TO 16

POACHED CHICKEN:

2 tablespoons / 28 grams light olive oil

1 medium leek, roughly chopped

4 carrots, roughly chopped

1 onion, roughly chopped

2 cloves garlic, smashed

2 cups / 450 grams white wine

3 quarts / 2.7 kilograms water

2 bunches sage

4 thyme sprigs

2 bay leaves

2 teaspoons / 12 grams fine sea salt

1 (**3½- to 4-pound** / 1.5- to 1.8-kilogram) whole chicken

FILLING:

2½ cups / 650 grams whole milk

1 cup / 240 grams heavy cream

1⅓ cups / 300 grams unsalted butter, diced

1 medium celeriac, minced in food processor

4 carrots, minced in food processor

2 onions, minced in food processor

1 head garlic, peeled and minced in food processor

1½ cups / 225 grams all-purpose flour

½ cup / 24 grams chopped fresh chives

4 sprigs thyme

5¾ teaspoons / 34.5 grams fine sea salt

1 teaspoon / 2 grams freshly ground black pepper

¼ teaspoon / 0.25 gram grated nutmeg

3 sheets gelatin, soaked in ice water for 5 minutes and squeezed dry

Juice of 1 lemon

Peanut or canola oil, for frying

COATING:

1 (**13.7-ounce** / 388-gram) box Ritz crackers

4 large eggs

1 cup / 240 grams buttermilk

1 tablespoon / 6 grams fine sea salt

1 cup / 150 grams all-purpose flour

I wanted to create chicken potpie in one bite. You break through the fine, crispy crust to release the creamy chicken and vegetables inside. The secret ingredient is the Ritz crackers. They make the perfect crust. If you prefer an actual potpie, you can pour this filling into a savory piecrust and bake one off. I like my pie in one bite because that leaves room to try everything else. It may seem a little excessive to start by poaching a whole chicken, but the results will be worth the small amount of effort. Once you taste these, you'll want to make sure there are leftovers. Extra filling can be turned into a pie, or it can be warmed and served over pasta with a topping of Ritz cracker crumbs.

→

Make the Poached Chicken:

Set a large soup pot over medium-high heat and add the oil. Once the oil begins to shimmer, add the leek, carrots, and onion and cook, stirring occasionally, until the vegetables begin to caramelize, about 10 minutes. Add the garlic and cook until it softens and begins to become aromatic, about 5 minutes. Add the wine and stir to dissolve all of the *fond* on the bottom of the pot. Add the water, sage, thyme, bay leaves, and salt and stir until the salt dissolves. Bring the mixture to a simmer. Remove and discard the bag of innards from inside the chicken and slide the bird into the pot. Turn the heat down to low, cover, and cook for 1 hour. Remove from the heat and let the chicken cool completely in the stock, about 2 hours.

Transfer the chicken to a large platter and strain the stock. Reserve the chicken stock in a covered container in the refrigerator. Remove the skin from the chicken, finely chop it, and put it in a bowl. Use your hands to pull all of the meat from the bird. Discard the bones. Roughly chop the meat and add it to the bowl with the skin. Reserve.

Make the Filling:

Put 4 cups (900 grams) of the reserved chicken stock, the milk, and cream in a medium saucepot set over medium-high heat and bring to a simmer. Reduce the heat to low and keep warm. Put the butter in a large stockpot set over medium heat. Once the butter melts, add the minced celeriac, carrots, onions, and garlic. Sauté for 2 minutes, and then sprinkle the flour over the vegetables. Stir everything together and cook for 1 minute. Whisk in the warm chicken stock mixture and then reduce the heat to low and cook for 15 minutes; the flour flavor will cook out and the mixture will thicken. Remove from the heat and stir in the chives, thyme, salt, pepper, nutmeg, and gelatin. Stir until the salt and gelatin dissolve. Add the reserved chicken meat and skin and the lemon juice. Stir well and then pour into a large casserole dish to cool and set. Once the mixture cools, cover and refrigerate overnight, or for at least 8 hours.

Prepare the Fritters:

Line a baking sheet with parchment paper. Use a 1-ounce ice cream scoop to portion the batter onto the baking sheet. You can easily freeze half for another time or to use as filling in a potpie. Rub a few drops of oil into the palms of your hands so the filling doesn't stick, roll each portion into a ball, and return it to the baking sheet. Cover loosely with plastic wrap and refrigerate for 1 hour to set up.

Make the Coating and Fry the Fritters:

Preheat a deep fryer or a large pot with 4 inches of oil to 350°F (180°C).

Put the crackers in a food processor and grind them into fine crumbs. Transfer to a shallow baking dish. Put the eggs, buttermilk, and salt in a medium bowl and whisk to blend. Put the flour in a separate bowl. Remove the fritters from the refrigerator and set the flour next to the fritters, the egg mixture next to the flour, the cracker crumbs next to the eggs, and sprinkle a thin layer of cracker crumbs in a baking sheet and set it at the end. Roll each fritter in flour, shaking off any excess, and then coat with the egg mixture and then the cracker crumbs. Then go back the egg mixture and the cracker crumbs once more to make a solid coating. Put the finished fritter on the baking sheet lined with cracker crumbs and repeat until all of the fritters are coated. Fry in small batches, being careful not to crowd the fryer, for 5 minutes, or until the fritters are golden brown. Serve hot.

Pimento Cheese Hush Puppies

SERVES 8 TO 12

PIMENTO CHEESE:

12 ounces / 340 grams cheddar cheese, shredded

8 ounces / 227 grams cream cheese, diced

3½ ounces / 100 grams mozzarella cheese, shredded

¾ cup / 100 grams diced piquillo peppers

1 cup plus 2 tablespoons / 225 grams mayonnaise (I prefer Duke's)

1 tablespoon plus ½ teaspoon / 21 grams smooth Dijon mustard

2 tablespoons / 18 grams Worcestershire sauce

1 tablespoon / 16 grams soy sauce

2½ teaspoons / 15 grams Tabasco sauce

1½ teaspoons / 8.5 grams malt vinegar

1½ teaspoons / 8 grams paprika

HUSH PUPPY BATTER:

2½ cups / 350 grams cornmeal

½ cup / 75 grams all-purpose flour

1 teaspoon / 6 grams baking powder

1½ teaspoons / 6 grams sugar

1½ teaspoons / 9 grams fine sea salt

1½ teaspoons / 3 grams freshly ground black pepper

½ teaspoon / 1 gram cayenne pepper

3 large eggs

2 cups / 480 grams buttermilk

½ cup / 130 grams whole milk

Peanut or canola oil, for frying

1 cup / 150 grams all-purpose flour

¾ cup / 24 grams chopped fresh chives

Here I've married two staples of Southern cuisine, hush puppies and jalapeño poppers. Poppers are one of those appetizers that usually promises more than it delivers. I wanted to take the sweet, earthy flavor of a hush puppy with its crispy coating and stuff it with a seriously good pimento cheese. The nutty cornmeal batter complements the flavor of the peppers and the cheddar. It's tempting to eat them right out of the fryer, but I can tell you from experience that it's a good idea to let them rest for 5 minutes or so before you take that first molten bite. Once they've cooled a bit, the flavors explode across your palate, and you may even forget there's a game on, they're so good.

Make the Pimento Cheese:
Place all of the ingredients in a stand mixer with the paddle attachment and mix on low speed until everything comes together. Transfer to a covered container and refrigerate until completely cold, at least 2 hours and up to 24 hours.

Make the Hush Puppy Batter:
Put the cornmeal, flour, baking powder, sugar, salt, black pepper, and cayenne in a medium bowl and whisk until combined. In a separate bowl, whisk together the eggs, buttermilk, and milk until completely smooth. Pour the wet ingredients into the cornmeal mixture, whisking slowly until smooth. Cover and refrigerate until ready to use, for up to 4 hours.

Line a baking sheet with parchment paper. Use a 1-ounce ice cream scoop to portion all of the Pimento Cheese and lay the scoops out on the prepared baking sheet. Roll each scoop into a ball, and return to the baking sheet. You can rub a few drops of oil into the palms of your hands to keep the cheese from sticking. Cover the pan loosely with plastic wrap and chill for 30 minutes.

Fry the Hush Puppies:
Preheat a deep fryer or large pot with 4 inches of oil to 370°F (190°C).

Line a baking sheet with paper towels. Put the flour in a medium bowl. Roll each ball of cheese in the flour and shake off any excess. Add the chives to the Hush Puppy Batter and stir to blend. Use a spoon to dip each cheese ball into the batter and then transfer them to the hot oil. You will want to fry these in small batches so as not to crowd the oil. Fry each hush puppy until golden brown and cooked through, about 3 minutes. Transfer to the prepared baking sheet to drain and serve hot.

Deviled Ham with Eggs

MAKES 48 DEVILED EGGS

EGGS AND FILLING:

24 large eggs

¾ cup plus 1½ tablespoons / 170 grams mayonnaise (I prefer Duke's)

4½ teaspoons / 27 grams yellow mustard

1 tablespoon / 16 grams soy sauce

2 teaspoons / 10 grams apple cider vinegar

1½ teaspoons / 7 grams pickle juice (from a jar of your favorite pickles)

½ teaspoon / 3 grams Tabasco sauce

¼ teaspoon / 1.5 grams fine sea salt

DEVILED HAM:

1 tablespoon / 14 grams light olive oil

½ onion, minced

2½ cups / 380 grams diced honey ham

2 tablespoons / 6 grams finely sliced fresh chives

Grated zest of ½ orange

1 cup / 200 grams mayonnaise (I prefer Duke's)

2 tablespoons / 36 grams whole-grain mustard

2 teaspoons / 12 grams Tabasco sauce

1 teaspoon / 5 grams sherry vinegar

½ teaspoon / 3 grams fine sea salt, plus extra for seasoning

½ teaspoon / 1 gram freshly ground black pepper

2 celery ribs, minced

Peanut or canola oil, for frying

Leaves from 1 bunch celery

I prepare these in the morning, store the filling in a pastry bag or plastic bag, and pipe them out just before kickoff. They are one of the first things on the buffet table and are just as indulgent as the Chicken Wings with Kimchi Caramel and Wing Sauce (page 192). Deviled ham seems to be one of those dishes that is falling by the wayside, but in some circles it will never disappear. The secret is the pickle juice. It makes everything taste better, especially if you make my Bread-and-Butter Pickles (page 115) and use the pickle juice from those. If you have a fear of frying, you can chop up the celery leaves and sprinkle them over the eggs, though I like the contrast of the fried ones against the creamy filling and tender egg whites.

Cook the Eggs:

Put the eggs in a single layer in a large pot and cover with at least 2 inches of cold water. Set the pot over high heat and, once it comes to a boil, reduce the heat to medium and cook for 7 minutes; use a timer. When the time is up, remove from the heat, strain, and cover the eggs with ice water. Let them cool in the pot, about 15 minutes, and then peel the eggs.

Make the Filling:

Cut a small slice off the bottom of each egg so that it will stand up without rolling. Cut the tops off of each egg, scoop out the yolks, and put them in a food processor with the mayonnaise, mustard, soy sauce, vinegar, pickle juice, Tabasco, and salt. Process until smooth. Transfer the mixture to a piping bag fitted with a large star tip. Reserve in the refrigerator while you make the Deviled Ham.

Make the Deviled Ham:

Put the olive oil in a small sauté pan set over medium-high heat. When the oil begins to shimmer, add the onion and cook, stirring, for 3 to 5 minutes, until tender and translucent. Let cool for 10 minutes.

Put the ham, chives, orange zest, mayonnaise, mustard, Tabasco, vinegar, salt, and pepper in a food processor and pulse 4 or 5 times, until smooth. Transfer to a bowl and stir in the onions and celery. Transfer to a piping bag fitted with a large plain tip. Store in the refrigerator until ready to serve.

Just before you are ready to serve the eggs, set a small pot with 2 inches of oil over medium-high heat and bring it to 350°F (180°C). Line a plate with paper towels. Rinse the celery leaves, pat them dry gently but thoroughly, and drop them in the oil. Let them fry for 10 to 15 seconds, until the oil stops bubbling and they are crisp and translucent. Transfer to the paper towels, season lightly with salt, and let them cool.

Take the piping bag with the ham and fill each egg almost to the top with the Deviled Ham. Take the bag with the deviled egg yolks and pipe them over the ham, mounding them slightly over the top of each egg. Garnish each egg with a piece of fried celery leaf and serve immediately.

Sweet Potato and Chickpea Fries with Thousand Island Dressing

SERVES 6 TO 8

THOUSAND ISLAND DRESSING:

2 shallots, minced

1 tablespoon / 14 grams olive oil

¼ teaspoon / 1.5 grams fine sea salt

3 tablespoons / 55 grams ketchup

½ cup / 60 grams capers

2 tablespoons / 50 grams tahini

1 cup / 200 grams mayonnaise
(I prefer Duke's)

1 teaspoon / 5 grams sesame oil

SWEET POTATO AND CHICKPEA FRIES:

2 medium sweet potatoes

1¾ cups plus 1½ tablespoons / 500 grams whole milk

1 medium leek, white part only, finely chopped

¼ cup / 56 grams unsalted butter

3 tablespoons / 42 grams olive oil

1 teaspoon / 6 grams fine sea salt

Zest and juice of 1 lemon

2¼ cups / 225 grams chickpea flour

Peanut or canola oil, for frying

This recipe is a twist within a twist. I've taken *panisses*, classic chickpea cakes that resemble French fries, and added roasted sweet potatoes to the base. Instead of serving them with ketchup, I made "Thousand Island Dressing" with tahini and sesame oil to serve with my fries. The dressing is deeper and nuttier than the classic version and pairs nicely with the sweet, earthy flavors of the sweet potatoes and chickpeas. The fries themselves are crisp and crunchy on the outside and warm and creamy on the inside. It's an irresistible combination, perfect alongside a cold beer and a big game.

Make the "Thousand Island Dressing":
Put the shallots, olive oil, and salt in a small microwave-safe bowl. Cover the bowl with plastic wrap and microwave on high for 30 seconds. Remove the bowl from the microwave and remove the plastic wrap. Add the ketchup, capers, tahini, mayonnaise, and sesame oil and stir well to combine. Cover and refrigerate until needed.

Make the Sweet Potato and Chickpea Fries:
Preheat the oven to 350°F (180°C).

Put the sweet potatoes on a baking sheet. Use the tip of a knife to poke several shallow holes into each potato. Roast the potatoes for 45 minutes, or until they are tender and easily pierced with a cake tester. Remove the sweet potatoes from the oven and let cool for 10 to 15 minutes, until they are easily handled when held with a kitchen towel.

❯

Use a paring knife to peel off the skins. Cut the sweet potatoes into small dice.

Weigh out 35 ounces (1 kilogram) of diced sweet potato and put them in a large pot. Set aside the rest for another use. Add the milk, leeks, butter, olive oil, salt, and lemon zest and juice. Set the pot over medium heat, bring the mixture to a simmer, and cook for 5 minutes, or until the leeks are tender and the sweet potatoes are falling apart. Add all of the chickpea flour and use a wooden spoon to stir it into the mixture. The potatoes will continue to break down as you stir the batter. Reduce the heat to low and cook for 5 more minutes, or until the mixture begins to pull away from the sides of the pot. Remove from the heat.

Pour the hot batter into the bowl of a food processor. Process the mixture until smooth, occasionally stopping to scrape down the sides of the food processor. Work quickly so the sweet potato mixture does not begin to thicken and set. When the puree is smooth, pour it into a 9-by-13-inch baking dish. Press a piece of plastic wrap against the surface and chill the mixture for 4 hours, or until firm and set.

When the chickpea base is firm, invert it onto a cutting board. Cut the dough in half horizontally and then cut each half into ½-inch batons. Fry immediately or refrigerate in a covered container for up to 3 days.

Cook the Fries:
Preheat a deep fryer or large pot with 4 inches of oil to 350°F (180°C).

Preheat the oven to 200°F (95°C). Set a wire rack over a baking sheet.

Cook the fries in batches of 6 to 8 (depending on the size of your fryer; you don't want to crowd them in the oil) for about 5 minutes. They should be crisp, golden brown, and hot. Transfer to the wire rack and set in the oven to keep warm as you continue to fry. Once you've finished cooking all of the chickpea fries, serve immediately with the "Thousand Island Dressing" in a bowl alongside.

Onion Rings with Bacon-Horseradish Dip

SERVES 8

BACON-HORSERADISH DIP:

14 ounces / 400 grams bacon, minced in a food processor

½ medium onion, minced

½ medium shallot, minced

1 clove garlic, minced

1½ tablespoons / 23 grams sherry vinegar

3½ tablespoons / 58 grams maple syrup

14 ounces / 400 grams ricotta cheese

3½ ounces / 100 grams fresh horseradish, grated

6½ tablespoons / 100 grams crème fraîche

10 tablespoons / 30 grams finely sliced fresh chives

2 scallions, thinly sliced

1 teaspoon / 6 grams fine sea salt

ONIONS:

Peanut or canola oil, for frying

6 cups / 180 grams cornflakes

3 large white onions

½ cup / 75 grams all-purpose flour

BATTER:

1 large egg, separated

1 cup / 260 grams whole milk

1 tablespoon / 14 grams light olive oil

1 teaspoon / 5 grams malt vinegar

1 cup / 150 grams all-purpose flour

1 tablespoon / 4.5 grams onion powder

2 teaspoons / 12 grams fine sea salt

1½ teaspoons / 9 grams baking powder

Battered onion rings are too soggy and floured onion rings are too dry. I use a three-step breading technique here: flour, batter, and then a coating of cornflake crumbs. This is to get the crispiest onion rings possible that are still sweet and tender on the inside. The breading works so well that any stray onion rings will still be crispy when the game ends. I serve these with the world's best bacon and horseradish dip. The bacon jam that is the base for this dish is one of the most requested recipes at my restaurant Range. I serve it with steak there, but at home I add crème fraîche and fresh horseradish to make the best dip in the world. Any leftovers are great on sandwiches or alongside steak or roasted fish.

Make the Bacon-Horseradish Dip:

Set a large sauté pan over medium heat and add the bacon, onion, shallot, and garlic, and cook, stirring continuously, until the bacon is a deep golden brown, about 15 minutes. Deglaze the pan with half of the sherry vinegar, let it come to a simmer, and reduce until almost dry, 3 to 5 minutes. Add the remaining vinegar and the maple syrup, reduce the heat to low, and cook for 10 minutes. Remove from the heat and transfer to a medium bowl to cool completely. This bacon jam can be made a day ahead and refrigerated in a covered container until needed.

Put the ricotta cheese and horseradish in a food processor and process for 2 minutes, or until completely smooth. Add the bacon jam, pulse a few times to blend, and transfer to a bowl. Whisk in the crème fraîche, chives, scallions, and salt. Serve at room temperature.

Prepare the Onions:

Preheat a deep fryer or large pot with 4 inches of oil to 335°F (168°C).

Put the cornflakes in a food processor and pulse until they are ground into coarse crumbs, about 1 minute. Transfer to a large bowl. Take a handful of crumbs and sprinkle them in an even layer on a baking sheet; set aside. Slice the onions into ¼-inch-thick rounds, discard the root end, and separate the slices into rings. Put them in a bowl and sift the flour over the onions, tossing them gently in the flour so that each ring is thoroughly coated.

Make the Batter:

Whisk the egg white in a bowl until it becomes light and foamy, with very soft peaks. Put the egg yolk, milk, olive oil, and vinegar in a large measuring cup and whisk until smooth. Put the flour, onion powder, salt, and baking powder in a medium bowl and whisk to blend. Pour in the milk mixture and whisk it into the flour. Finally, add the egg whites and use a rubber spatula to gently fold them in.

Batter and Fry the Onions:

Dip a floured onion ring into the batter, shaking off any excess, and then drop it into the bowl of cornflake crumbs. Once you have 3 rings in the cornflake bowl, toss them lightly to thoroughly coat them with crumbs, and transfer to the prepared baking sheet so they are resting on a bed of cornflake crumbs. Repeat until all of the onion rings are coated.

Line a baking sheet with paper towels. Fry the onion rings in small batches for 1 minute, flip them over, and fry them for 1 minute on the other side, or until they are golden brown and crisp. Transfer the onion rings to the paper towels to drain, and continue to fry. Serve the onion rings while they are still warm with the Bacon-Horseradish Dip.

Chili with the Fixings

SERVES 12

CHILI:

1 **tablespoon** / 14 grams rice bran oil or light olive oil

2 **pounds** / 908 grams ground beef chuck

2 **pounds** / 908 grams ground venison (preferably leg)

1⅔ **pounds** / 750 grams first-cut brisket, ground

5 medium red bell peppers, cut into medium dice

5 medium yellow bell peppers, cut into medium dice

3 medium onions, cut into medium dice

8 cloves garlic, minced

¼ **cup** / 30 grams dark chili powder

5 **teaspoons** / 10 grams ground cumin

5 **teaspoons** / 8 grams dried oregano

1 **tablespoon** / 18 grams smoked paprika

2 **teaspoons** / 12 grams fine sea salt

1½ **teaspoons** / 3 grams freshly ground black pepper

9 **ounces** / 250 grams beef jerky, finely chopped

2 (**15-ounce** / 425-gram) cans red kidney beans

12⅓ **ounces** / 350 grams porter beer

1 **tablespoon** / 16 grams soy sauce

2 (**28-ounce** / 794-gram) cans diced fire-roasted tomatoes

2 (**14½-ounce** / 411-gram) cans crushed fire-roasted tomatoes

CHARRED LIME CREMA:

½ **cup** / 120 grams crème fraîche or sour cream

1 **cup** / 240 grams heavy cream

4 **ounces** / 113 grams cream cheese, diced, room temperature

1 lime

¼ **teaspoon** / 1.5 grams fine sea salt

BACON JAM:

14 **ounces** / 400 grams bacon, minced in food processor

1 medium onion, minced

1 medium shallot, minced

2 cloves garlic, minced

3 **tablespoons** / 45 grams sherry vinegar

7 **tablespoons** / 105 grams maple syrup

2 **teaspoons** / 12 grams fine sea salt

CHARRED SCALLION RELISH:

3 bunches scallions, divided

1 jalapeño pepper, cut into fine dice

1 **teaspoon** / 5 grams honey

2 dashes of Tabasco sauce

2 **teaspoons** / 10 grams extra-virgin olive oil

2 **teaspoons** / 10 grams sherry vinegar

Juice of 1 lemon

SERVE WITH:

½ **cup** / 20 grams fresh cilantro leaves

3 limes, cut into wedges

2 jalapeño peppers, cut into fine dice

Aerated Cheese Sauce (page 51)

Chili is the classic Super Bowl dish. No game party would be complete without it. I make mine with a blend of ground venison and beef. I also add some chopped-up beef jerky for even more flavor. My favorite brand of jerky is Krave, but use your favorite jerky for this recipe. The flavors will permeate the stew and help intensify its rich, beefy flavor. I set up a mini buffet of condiments so that everyone can dress their own bowl. Good chili has to have fixings. My Aerated Cheese Sauce (page 51) is like Cheez Whiz for a new generation, with the same creamy texture as the original, only lighter and better tasting. I won't say how I know this, but a whipped-cream canister shoots cheese sauce just as well as any of those cans in the supermarket. ➲

Make the Chili:

Set a large heavy-bottomed Dutch oven over medium-high heat and add the rice bran oil. When it begins to shimmer, add the ground chuck, ground venison, and ground brisket. Cook, stirring occasionally, until well browned, 10 to 12 minutes. Add the red peppers, yellow peppers, onions, garlic, chili powder, cumin, oregano, smoked paprika, salt, and pepper, and cook, stirring, until the vegetables are tender, about 5 minutes. Stir in the beef jerky, kidney beans, beer, and soy sauce and stir to blend. Add all of the tomatoes and stir to blend. Bring the mixture to a simmer, reduce the heat to low, and simmer for 1½ to 2 hours. The meat will be completely tender and the flavors will have blended.

Make the Charred Lime Crema:

Half an hour before you want to make the Charred Lime Crema, pull the crème fraîche, heavy cream, and cream cheese from the refrigerator to take the chill off. Set a grill pan over your highest heat until it begins to smoke. Grate the zest from the lime with a Microplane and reserve. Slice the lime in half and place the 2 pieces, cut side down, on the grill pan and char until a deep black crust forms. Remove from the heat and let cool slightly. Juice the charred lime over a strainer to catch any citrus cells or pith. In a stand mixer with the paddle attachment on medium-low speed, mix the

lime juice, lime zest, crème fraîche, heavy cream, cream cheese, and salt. Once combined, increase the speed to high and beat for 2 to 3 minutes, until light and fluffy. Transfer to a covered container and refrigerate until ready to serve.

Make the Bacon Jam:

Set a large sauté pan over medium heat and add the bacon, onions, shallot, and garlic, and cook, stirring continuously, until the bacon is a deep golden brown, about 15 minutes. Deglaze the pan with half of the sherry vinegar, let it come to a simmer, and reduce until almost dry, 3 to 5 minutes. Add the remaining vinegar and the maple syrup, reduce the heat to low, and cook for 10 minutes. Remove from the heat, season with the salt, and transfer to a medium bowl to cool completely. Bacon Jam can be made a day ahead and refrigerated in a covered container until needed.

Make the Charred Scallion Relish:

Preheat a grill or grill pan over high heat. Thinly slice 1 bunch of the scallions and reserve. Sear the remaining 2 bunches of scallions on the grill or in the grill pan until they are nicely charred and tender. Transfer to a large bowl and cover so the scallions steam as they cool. Once cool, finely chop the scallions and put them in a large bowl.

Put the Bacon Jam in a small saucepot set over low heat. Add the jalapeño, honey, and Tabasco, and stir to blend. Cook for 5 minutes, then remove from the heat and add to the bowl with the charred scallions. Add the sliced scallions, olive oil, vinegar, and lemon juice. Stir to blend. Transfer to a serving bowl.

To Serve:
Put the cilantro leaves in a small bowl and set on the table. Put the lime wedges in a bowl and set on the table. Put the diced jalapeño peppers in a small bowl and set on the table. Transfer the chili to a soup tureen and set on the table with bowls of Charred Lime Crema and Scallion Relish alongside. Keep the canister of Aerated Cheese Sauce in a warm water bath nearby. Serve family style so that everyone can dress his or her own chili.

Sometimes I like to eat dessert before dinner. In my kitchen, I take traditional desserts and reinvent them, like serving Red Velvet Cake with Cream Cheese Semifreddo, or adding parsnips to a moist ginger cake. I like to layer textures and flavors, especially when I make ice cream sundaes, so that every bite is different: warm, cold, creamy, and crunchy, in infinite combinations. Dessert is the course where I can really play with my recipes and reach out to the kid who still lives inside me. Whether I'm revisiting illicit breakfasts of chocolate cake and orange juice or re-creating Cracker Jack, these recipes are all about having a little fun with my food.

Moist Chocolate Bundt with Orange Glaze

Red Velvet Cake with Cream Cheese Semifreddo

Ginger-Parsnip Cake

Goat Cheesecake with Blueberry-Gin Compote

Applesauce-Apple Pie

Chess Pie with Sweet Curry Crust

Banana Pudding Parfaits

Maple-Pecan Tart

Peach Crisp

Rocky Road Cookies

Cornmeal Thumbprint Cookies

Lemon Cookies

Quadruple-Chocolate Brownie Sundaes

Caramel-Popcorn Sundaes

Dessert

Moist Chocolate Bundt with Orange Glaze

CAKE:

2 cups / 455 grams canola oil, plus extra for the pan

4½ cups / 675 grams all-purpose flour

3¾ cups / 750 grams granulated sugar

½ cup / 60 grams unsweetened cocoa powder

2 tablespoons / 30 grams baking soda

¾ teaspoon / 4.5 grams fine sea salt

1 cup plus 2 tablespoons / 293 grams whole milk

1 cup plus 2 tablespoons / 270 grams buttermilk

9 large eggs

1½ teaspoons / 6 grams vanilla extract

2 cups plus 2 tablespoons / 480 grams hot brewed coffee

ORANGE GLAZE:

3 cups plus 2 tablespoons / 625 grams granulated sugar

¼ cup / 56 grams water

¼ cup / 75 grams light corn syrup

10 tablespoons / 140 grams fresh orange juice

¼ cup / 56 grams white verjus

¼ cup / 56 grams Muscat wine

¼ cup / 32 grams powdered sugar

2 teaspoons / 10 grams fresh lemon juice

1 orange, for zesting

Don't tell my kids, but one of my guilty pleasures is eating chocolate cake with a glass of orange juice for breakfast. I love the way the cocoa in devil's food cake gives it that faint hint of bitterness, but I don't love the fact that the cake is often dry. So here I've added cocoa to a super-moist chocolate cake infused with orange. It's almost like a pudding cake, so good it's hard to stop after just one slice.

Make the Cake:

Preheat the oven to 325°F (165°C). Use canola oil to grease the inside of a 10-inch Bundt pan.

Sift together the flour, granulated sugar, cocoa powder, baking soda, and salt, letting them fall into the bowl of a stand mixer. Put the canola oil, milk, buttermilk, eggs, and vanilla in a medium bowl and whisk until smooth. Using the paddle attachment, turn the mixer on low speed and slowly pour half of the liquid into the flour. Once it is absorbed, slowly pour in the remainder. Once all of the liquid has been absorbed, slowly pour in the coffee and mix for 30 seconds. Pour into the prepared Bundt pan and bake for 45 minutes. Rotate the pan, and bake for another 10 to 15 minutes, until a cake tester inserted into the center of the cake comes out clean. Let cool for 15 minutes, and then invert onto a wire rack set over a baking sheet to cool completely.

Make the Orange Glaze:

Put the granulated sugar, water, and corn syrup, in that order, in a medium saucepot set over medium high heat and cook until the mixture comes to a simmer. Continue to cook, undisturbed, until the mixture turns golden brown. Remove from the heat; the sugar will continue to darken. Stir in the orange juice, verjus, and Muscat. If the caramel hardens, set it back over low heat and cook, stirring, just until the sugar melts back into the sauce. Remove from the heat and let cool. Reserve at room temperature until you are ready to glaze the cake.

Just before glazing, add the powdered sugar and lemon juice and stir until smooth. Leave the cake on the wire rack set over the baking sheet to catch the excess glaze, and slowly pour the glaze over the cake, letting it run down the sides. Use a Microplane to zest the orange over the top. Slide the cake onto a serving plate.

Red Velvet Cake with Cream Cheese Semifreddo

MAKES 1 (10-INCH) BUNDT CAKE

SEMIFREDDO BASE:

1 pound / 454 grams cream cheese, room temperature

8 ounces / 227 grams mascarpone cheese

Seeds from 1 vanilla bean

ITALIAN MERINGUE:

1½ cups / 300 grams sugar

1 tablespoon / 14 grams fresh lemon juice

5 large egg whites, room temperature

RED VELVET CAKE:

½ cup / 113 grams unsalted butter, room temperature, plus extra for the pan

1½ cups / 300 grams sugar

1 teaspoon / 4 grams vanilla extract

2 large eggs, room temperature

2 cups plus 2 tablespoons / 333 grams cake flour, sifted

2 tablespoons / 12 grams unsweetened cocoa powder

1 teaspoon / 6 grams baking powder

1 teaspoon / 5 grams baking soda

½ teaspoon / 3 grams fine sea salt

1 cup / 240 grams buttermilk

1 tablespoon / 14 grams red food coloring

1 teaspoon / 5 grams distilled white vinegar

WHITE CHOCOLATE GLAZE:

1 medium beet, peeled and grated

½ cup / 120 grams heavy cream

7 ounces / 200 grams white chocolate, chopped

2 tablespoons / 28 grams coconut oil

⅛ teaspoon / 0.75 gram fine sea salt

Any celebration with my wife Jennifer's family has to have red velvet cake. It's just not a party without one. I always feel the need to change things up and make classics like this my own. Here I've changed that luscious cream cheese frosting into ice cream, because I love to eat my cake with ice cream. The cream cheese *semifreddo* steals the show. It's so rich and creamy that I sometimes even make it without the cake.

Make the Semifreddo Base:
Mix all of the ingredients in a stand mixer with the paddle attachment on low speed until smooth. Reserve.

Make the Italian Meringue:
Put the sugar and lemon juice in a medium saucepot and mix until the sugar becomes a paste. Set over high heat and bring to a boil. Cook until the sugar reaches 235°F (113°C). Remove from the heat. Whip the egg whites in a stand mixer with a whisk attachment, starting on low speed. Once the whites are light and foamy, after 1 to 2 minutes, increase the speed to medium-high and whip until they form soft peaks. With the mixer running, slowly and carefully pour in the hot sugar syrup. Continue to whip until the bowl is cool to the touch, 5 to 7 minutes. The meringue will have formed stiff, shiny peaks. Use a rubber spatula to fold the Semifreddo Base into the Italian Meringue in 3 additions. Transfer to a deep casserole dish or loaf pan, cover, and freeze for at least 8 hours before scooping.

Make the Red Velvet Cake:
Preheat the oven to 325°F (165°C). Generously butter a 10-cup swirled Bundt pan.

Mix the butter, sugar, and vanilla in a stand mixer with the paddle attachment, starting on low speed and gradually increasing the speed to medium-high, until the butter is light and fluffy, 3 to 4 minutes. Add the eggs one at a time, waiting until each one is absorbed before adding the next. Put the flour, cocoa powder, baking powder, baking soda,

➲

and salt in a bowl and whisk to blend. Put the buttermilk, food coloring, and vinegar in a large measuring cup and stir well to blend. Alternately add the flour and buttermilk to the cake batter, beating well after each addition. Pour the batter into the prepared Bundt pan and bake for 45 minutes. Rotate the pan, and bake for another 15 to 20 minutes, until a cake tester inserted into the middle of the cake comes out clean. Let cool for 15 minutes, and then invert onto a wire rack set over a baking sheet to cool completely.

Make the White Chocolate Glaze:
Once the cake is cool, put the grated beet and cream in a small pot set over medium heat and bring to a simmer. Put the chocolate, coconut oil, and salt in a medium microwave-safe bowl. Once the cream comes to a simmer, strain it over the bowl of white chocolate and whisk until smooth. If the chocolate doesn't melt completely, microwave on high for 20 seconds and whisk again. Repeat if necessary to melt all of the white chocolate. Let the glaze cool slightly so that it has the texture of cold maple syrup.

Slowly pour the glaze over the cake in a steady stream, moving back and forth over the top as you go around the cake, until you have used up the glaze. Let the glaze set completely, about 30 minutes, before cutting the cake. Serve with a scoop of the *semifreddo* alongside.

Ginger-Parsnip Cake

MAKES 1 (9-INCH) LAYER CAKE

CAKE:

3½ **cups** / 525 grams all-purpose
flour, sifted

5 **teaspoons** / 25 grams baking soda

1 **teaspoon** / 6 grams fine sea salt

1 **tablepoon** / 6 grams ground ginger

2½ **teaspoons** / 5 grams ground cinnamon

1½ **teaspoons** / 3 grams curry powder

4¼ **cups plus 2 tablespoons** / 875 grams
granulated sugar

4 large eggs

2½ **cups** / 562 grams canola oil

1⅓ **pounds** / 600 grams parsnips, shredded

1¾ **cups** / 300 grams hazelnuts,
toasted and chopped

7 **tablespoons** / 100 grams Greek yogurt

CREAM CHEESE FROSTING:

1 **pound** / 454 grams unsalted butter,
room temperature

8 **cups** / 1 kilogram powdered sugar

Seeds from 2 vanilla beans

1 **teaspoon** / 6 grams fine sea salt

1½ **tablespoons** / 21 grams fresh lemon juice

8 **ounces** / 227 grams cream cheese

8 **ounces** / 227 grams ricotta cheese

Toasted hazelnuts, for garnish

To toast hazelnuts (or any nuts), I lay them out in a single layer on a sheet pan and bake them at 350°F (180°C) for 8-12 minutes, stirring them halfway through, until they are a deep golden brown. Cool completely before using.

Parsnips are an often overlooked vegetable. People just don't seem to find them as interesting as carrots, but this is a mistake. Parsnips may not be as sweet and colorful, but they have a wonderful flavor of their own, soft and earthy, sweet and surprisingly delicate. I love ginger cake. Adding grated parsnips makes the cake even moister and gives it a more balanced sweetness to counter the spice. The frosting is a blend of cream cheese and ricotta; it's almost like cheesecake in frosting form. You end up with moist, spicy cake and rich, creamy frosting—total indulgence on a plate.

Make the Cake:

Preheat the oven to 325°F (165°C). Butter two 9-inch round cake pans.

Mix the flour, baking soda, salt, ginger, cinnamon, and curry powder in the bowl of a stand mixer with the paddle attachment on low speed until fully blended. Put the sugar and eggs in a medium bowl and whisk until the sugar has completely dissolved. Slowly drizzle in the oil while continuing to whisk. Pour the wet mixture into the flour mixture and mix on low speed until combined. Add the parsnips, hazelnuts, and yogurt and mix until well blended. Divide equally between the prepared cake pans. Bake for 10 minutes. Rotate the pans, and bake for another 10 minutes, or until the cakes are set and a toothpick inserted in the center of each one comes out clean. Let the cakes cool completely on a rack.

Make the Cream Cheese Frosting:

Cream together the butter, powdered sugar, vanilla seeds, salt, and lemon juice in a stand mixer with the paddle attachment on medium speed until light and airy. Put the cream cheese and ricotta in a food processor and process until smooth. Fold together the two with a rubber spatula and use immediately.

Frost the Cake:

Split the cake layers in half horizontally so you end up with 4 layers. Put the first layer (a bottom piece) on your serving platter and add about ¾ cup frosting. Spread the frosting in an even layer on top of the cake, leaving a ¼-inch border all the way around the circumference. Invert the top half of that layer over the frosting and gently press it so that you have a flat, even layer on top. Put another ¾ cup frosting on top of this layer. Spread the frosting in an even layer on top of the cake, leaving a ¼-inch border all the way around the circumference. Repeat with the next 2 cake layers. Use the rest of the frosting to coat the cake. Wipe the rim of the serving plate and grate a few hazelnuts over the top. Rim the bottom circumference of the cake with whole roasted hazelnuts and chill the cake for at least 1 hour so the frosting can set before serving.

Goat Cheesecake with Blueberry-Gin Compote

MAKES 2 (9-INCH) CHEESECAKES

CRUST:

½ **cup** / 113 grams unsalted butter, melted, browned, and cooled slightly

4¾ **ounces** / 136 grams chocolate graham crackers

4¾ **ounces** / 136 grams honey graham crackers

½ **cup** / 106 grams packed light brown sugar

¼ **teaspoon** / 1.5 grams fine sea salt

FILLING:

24 **ounces** / 700 grams goat cheese

20 **ounces** / 570 grams ricotta cheese

16 **ounces** / 454 grams cream cheese

2¾ **cups plus 2 tablespoons** / 575 grams granulated sugar

⅓ **cup** / 80 grams sour cream

8 large eggs

3 large egg yolks

¾ **teaspoon** / 3 grams vanilla extract

1 **teaspoon** / 6 grams fine sea salt

⅓ **cup** / 50 grams all-purpose flour, sifted

BLUEBERRY-GIN COMPOTE:

15 **ounces** / 425 grams blueberries, divided

Grated zest from ½ orange

1 **tablespoon** / 15 grams agave syrup

1 **teaspoon** / 5 grams gin

¼ **teaspoon** / 1.5 grams fine sea salt

GOAT CHEESE CREAM:

2 **ounces** / 56 grams goat cheese

1 **cup** / 240 grams heavy cream

¼ **teaspoon** / 1.5 grams fine sea salt

Cherry Glen Farm in Boyds, Maryland, is the place where I fell in love with goat cheese. They make some of the best cheeses that I've ever tasted. The fact that it's a local farm made it taste even better. I knew that this goat cheese would make a cake that was truly special. It has a nice tang and the flavor of the fields and meadows. Combined with smooth cream cheese and sweet, soft ricotta, it makes a unique and delicious cheesecake that is nothing like you've ever tasted before. I serve it with a compote of fresh blueberries folded into blueberry puree.

Make the Crust:

Preheat the oven to 325°F (165°C).

Put the butter in a small saucepot set over medium heat. When it starts to melt, whisk the butter until it starts to brown and smell nutty. Remove from the heat and leave on the stovetop. Put the chocolate graham crackers, honey graham crackers, brown sugar, and salt in a food processor and pulse until the crackers are ground into fine crumbs.

Pour the brown butter into the food processor and pulse 3 to 5 times, until the mixture becomes like wet sand and the butter has been absorbed. Divide the crumbs evenly between two 9-inch springform pans and firmly press the crumbs into an even layer on the bottom of the pan. You can use the bottom of a measuring cup to do this. Cover and reserve in the refrigerator until needed.

Make the Filling:

Mix the goat cheese, ricotta, cream cheese, granulated sugar, and sour cream in a stand mixer with the paddle attachment on low speed until fully blended, 2 to 3 minutes. Add the eggs one at a time, waiting until each one is fully incorporated before adding the next, followed by the yolks in the same manner. Add the vanilla and salt. When they are absorbed, stop the mixer and add the flour. Mix on low speed just until the flour is absorbed into the batter.

➔

Bake the Cake:

Set a teakettle full of water over high heat and bring to a boil. Remove from the heat. Take our your prepared pans and wrap the bottoms with aluminum foil to prevent any water from getting into the pans and any batter from leaking out. Divide the filling evenly between the 2 pans. Put each cake in a large baking dish or roasting pan and add hot water from the kettle until the water comes halfway up the sides of the cake pans. Bake for 10 minutes, then turn the oven temperature down to 225°F (105°C) and bake for 1 hour more.

Carefully remove the cakes from their water baths and let them cool to room temperature. Cover and refrigerate overnight so the cakes can set up before serving.

Make the Blueberry-Gin Compote:

Put 10 ounces (285 grams) of the blueberries, the orange zest, agave syrup, gin, and salt in a medium pot set over medium-high heat and bring to a simmer. Turn the heat down to low and cook for 5 minutes, or until the blueberries are completely tender and soft. Transfer to a blender and puree until smooth. Strain the puree through a fine-mesh sieve. Add the remaining blueberries and mix well. Reserve in a covered container in the refrigerator until ready to serve. Blueberry-Gin Compote may be stored in a covered container in the refrigerator for up to 3 days.

Make the Goat Cheese Cream:

Put all of the ingredients in a deep bowl. Use a handheld mixer or whisk to whip them into soft peaks. Cover and reserve in the refrigerator until needed. If the cream falls a bit, you can whisk a few times by hand to lighten it up again.

Serve slices of cheesecake with a spoonful of Blueberry-Gin Compote and a dollop of Goat Cheese Cream.

Applesauce-Apple Pie

MAKES 1 (9-INCH) PIE

DOUBLE-CRUST PIE DOUGH:

3 cups / 450 grams all-purpose flour

¼ cup / 50 grams sugar

¾ teaspoon / 4.5 grams fine sea salt

3 ounces / 85 grams chilled unsalted butter, diced

3 ounces / 85 grams vegetable shortening

1 chilled large egg

3 tablespoons / 42 grams ice-cold water

FILLING:

7½ cups / 850 grams apples (I like to use half Gala and half Granny Smith), peeled, cut into medium dice

3½ ounces / 100 grams Baked Applesauce (page 95) or store-bought

2 tablespoons / 28 grams apple cider

2 teaspoons / 10 grams fresh lemon juice

1½ teaspoons / 8 grams bourbon

1 tablespoon / 21 grams cornstarch

1½ teaspoons / 9 grams tapioca starch

¾ teaspoon / 4.5 grams fine sea salt

EGG WASH:

1 large egg

1 tablespoon / 14 grams water

2 tablespoons / 30 grams heavy cream

Sugar, for sprinkling

The best apple pies are sweet and juicy. You have to add thickeners to apple pie filling or once it's cut the juices soak through the crust, making the bottom soggy. Sadly, many people use too much thickener, causing the pie to be gummy and unpleasant. My solution was to fold the thickener, in this case cornstarch, into applesauce so it could add flavor and absorb the juices in a way that would make the pie taste even better. I dice my apples instead of slicing them, so the filling ends up being like chunky applesauce, with soft, tender, chunks suspended in the Baked Applesauce.

Make the Double-Crust Pie Dough:
Put the flour, sugar, and salt in a food processor and pulse 2 or 3 times to blend. Add the butter and pulse 3 or 4 times, until the butter is broken up into small pebbles in the flour. Pour the mixture into a bowl and put the bowl in the freezer for 15 minutes.

Pour the chilled flour and butter into the bowl of a stand mixer and add the shortening. Mix with the paddle attachment on low speed, and add the egg while the mixer is running. Once the egg is absorbed, add the ice water. Stop the mixer as soon as the dough comes together. Divide the dough into 2 flattened rounds, wrap each in plastic wrap, and refrigerate for at least 30 minutes and up to 24 hours.

Preheat the oven to 325°F (165C).

Remove 1 round of pie dough from the refrigerator, unwrap it, and roll it out on a lightly floured surface, giving the dough a 90-degree turn after each pass with the rolling pin until you have a rough circle approximately 13 inches wide and ¼ inch thick. Lay it on a baking pan, cover with plastic wrap, and refrigerate. Remove the second round of pie dough from the refrigerator, unwrap it, and roll it out on a lightly floured surface, giving the dough a 90-degree turn after each pass with the rolling pin until you have a rough circle approximately 13 inches wide and ¼ inch thick. Fit this circle of dough into a 9-inch pie pan and trim the edges so there is ¼ inch of overhang all around the perimeter. Cover with plastic wrap and refrigerate.

Make the Filling:
Put all of the ingredients in a large bowl and mix thoroughly.

➡

Make the Egg Wash and Bake the Pie:
Put the egg and water in a small bowl. Whisk with a fork until smooth.

Remove the pie pan lined with dough from the refrigerator and uncover. Pour the filling into the shell. Remove the circle of dough from the refrigerator, lay it over the top, and trim it so that there is about ½ inch of dough hanging over the edge of the pie plate along the circumference. Gently pinch the two layers of dough together and fold the extra bit of top layer over the bottom layer, tucking it under the edge of the dough. Gently pinch and crimp the circumference of the pie dough. Slide the pie onto a baking sheet and brush the Egg Wash over the top in an even coating. Bake for 45 minutes.

Remove from the oven and brush the cream over the top of the pie. Sprinkle sugar over the top, and return to the oven. Bake for another 15 minutes, until the pie is a deep, even golden brown. Let cool on a rack.

Chess Pie with Sweet Curry Crust

MAKE 1 (9-INCH) PIE

CURRY PIECRUST:

1⅔ **cups** / 250 grams all-purpose flour

¾ **cup** / 95 grams powdered sugar, divided

2 **teaspoons** / 5 grams curry powder

¼ **teaspoon** / 1.5 grams fine sea salt

⅛ **teaspoon** / 0.25 gram ground ginger

⅔ **cup** / 150 grams chilled unsalted butter, diced

1 large egg

1 large egg yolk

CHESS FILLING:

6 large eggs, room temperature

1½ **cups** / 300 grams granulated sugar

4 **teaspoons** / 12 grams cornmeal

3 **tablespoons** / 45 grams fresh lemon juice

3 **tablespoons** / 45 grams fresh lime juice

4 **teaspoons** / 20 grams white wine vinegar

½ **teaspoon** / 2 grams vanilla extract

10 **tablespoons** / 140 grams unsalted butter, melted

I love the flavors of curry. The warm spices are so aromatic and addictive. One of the interesting things about working with curries is how the spices bloom when combined with fresh citrus. It's one of those combinations that is always so much more than the sum of its parts. Chess pie is a classic Southern dessert, a sweet citrus filling thickened with cornmeal that rises to the top and creates a delicate crust on top of the pie. I used a combination of lemon and lime in my filling and created a curry piecrust to bring the flavors together. It's a hint of the exotic in a very traditional dessert.

Make the Curry Piecrust:

Sift the flour, ½ cup (65 grams) of the powdered sugar, the curry powder, salt, and ginger together. Mix the butter and remaining powdered sugar in a stand mixer with the paddle attachment on low speed until smooth. Add the egg and mix until incorporated. Add the egg yolk and mix until it is absorbed. Stop the mixer and add the sifted flour mixture. Mix on low speed just until a dough forms. Turn off the mixer, turn out the dough, shape it into a flattened disk, wrap with plastic wrap, and refrigerate for at least 1 hour and up to 24 hours.

Preheat the oven to 300°F (150°C).

Remove the pie dough from the refrigerator, unwrap it, and roll it out on a lightly floured surface, giving the dough a 90-degree turn after each pass with the rolling pin, until you have a rough circle approximately 13 inches wide and ¼ inch thick. Fit the circle of dough into a 9-inch pie pan and trim the edges so there is 1 inch of overhang all around the perimeter. Fold the edges and tuck them under the rim of the pie pan and then pinch it together and crimp the edges all the way around the pie. Line the dough with parchment paper and fill it with pie weights. Blind-bake for 10 minutes.

Make the Chess Filling:

While the piecrust is in the oven, mix the eggs, sugar, and cornmeal in a stand mixer with the paddle attachment on low speed until smooth. Add the lemon juice, lime juice, vinegar, and vanilla and mix until smooth. With the mixer running, slowly pour in the melted butter and mix until fully incorporated.

Take the piecrust from the oven and remove the parchment paper and pie weights. Pour the filling into the hot piecrust, cover with aluminum foil, and bake for 45 minutes. Remove from the oven, uncover, and let cool completely on a wire rack.

Banana Pudding Parfaits

MAKES 8 PARFAITS

BUTTERSCOTCH PUDDING:

¾ **cup** / 150 grams granulated sugar

¼ **cup** / 56 grams water

¼ **cup** / 60 grams heavy cream

2 **tablespoons** / 28 grams butterscotch schnapps

½ **cup** / 106 grams packed light brown sugar

⅓ **cup** / 37 grams cornstarch

2 **teaspoons** / 12 grams fine sea salt

3 **cups** / 720 grams half-and-half

4 large eggs

¼ **cup** / 56 grams unsalted butter, sliced

1 **teaspoon** / 4 grams vanilla extract

CHEESECAKE "MOUSSE":

8 **ounces plus 1¾ tablespoons** / 250 grams cream cheese, diced, room temperature

Seeds from ½ vanilla bean

13 **tablespoons plus 1 teaspoon** / 200 grams heavy cream

1 **teaspoon** / 4 grams vanilla extract

6½ **tablespoons** / 50 grams powdered sugar

¼ **teaspoon** / 1.5 grams fine sea salt

BANANA JAM:

2½ **cups** / 500 grams granulated sugar

1 **cup plus 1¾ tablespoons** / 250 grams water

6 ripe bananas, sliced

3 **tablespoons** / 42 grams fresh lemon juice

½ **teaspoon** / 3 grams fine sea salt

SPICED SHORTBREAD:

1 **pound** / 454 grams unsalted butter, diced, room temperature

1 **cup plus 2 tablespoons** / 225 grams granulated sugar

4½ **cups** / 675 grams all-purpose flour

½ **teaspoon** / 3 grams fine sea salt

¾ **teaspoon** / 1.5 grams ground cinnamon

½ **teaspoon** / 1 gram ground ginger

Sliced bananas, for serving

Granulated sugar, for sprinkling

SPECIAL EQUIPMENT:

Propane torch

Banana pudding is on the menu at almost every BBQ joint I've ever had the pleasure of visiting. It's practically a requirement. Southern banana pudding usually consists of layers of vanilla pudding, sliced bananas, and vanilla wafer cookies. The banana flavor infuses the pudding and the cookies soften, becoming almost cakelike. It's an American trifle. I knew I could take things up a level. I started with butterscotch pudding and layered it with banana jam and cream cheese mousse in a mason jar. You can put the lids on and store them in the fridge until you're ready to serve them. Then top them with sliced bananas sprinkled with sugar and use a butane torch to caramelize them. It's the best banana pudding you'll ever eat.

Make the Butterscotch Pudding:
Put the granulated sugar and water in a medium saucepot set over medium heat and bring to a boil. Let it cook, undisturbed, until the sugar turns a deep golden brown. Remove from the heat and carefully add the heavy cream and butterscotch schnapps. Stir until everything melts and comes together. Return to medium heat and whisk in the brown sugar, cornstarch, salt, and half-and-half. Bring to a simmer.

Put the eggs in a medium bowl and whisk until smooth and well blended. Slowly temper in the pudding base and then return the mixture to the pot to finish cooking. Set over medium heat and cook, stirring constantly, until it reaches 170°F (77°C). Remove from the heat and strain the mixture through a fine-mesh sieve. Stir in the butter and vanilla and mix until the butter melts and is absorbed. Press plastic wrap against the surface of the pudding and refrigerate for at least 4 hours and up to 24 hours.

Make the Cheesecake "Mousse":

Mix the cream cheese and vanilla seeds in a stand mixer with the paddle attachment on low speed until smooth. Stop the mixer and change to the whisk attachment. Add the cream, vanilla extract, powdered sugar, and salt and whip until light and fluffy, 2 to 3 minutes. Transfer to a covered container and refrigerate for at least 3 hours to chill and set.

Make the Banana Jam:

Put the sugar and water in a medium pot and bring to a boil. Cook, without stirring, until the sugar turns a deep golden brown. Remove from the heat and carefully add the bananas. Set over medium-low heat and cook, stirring, for 5 minutes, or until the caramel melts, the bananas break down, and the mixture becomes soft and jammy. Remove from the heat and stir in the lemon juice and salt. Let cool. Banana Jam may be stored in a covered container in the refrigerator for up to 1 month.

Make the Spiced Shortbread:

Cream the butter and sugar in a stand mixer with the paddle attachment on medium speed until light and fluffy, 2 to 3 minutes. Stop the mixer. Add the flour, salt, cinnamon, and ginger and mix on low speed until all of the flour is absorbed. Turn out onto a lightly floured surface.

Shape the dough into a rough rectangle, cover with plastic wrap, and refrigerate for at least 30 minutes and up to 24 hours.

Preheat the oven to 350°F (180°C).

Roll the dough out ¼ inch thick, cut out 2-inch rounds, and lay them out on a baking sheet, leaving at least 1 inch of space between each cookie. Bake for 10 to 12 minutes, until the cookies are just set and golden brown around the edges. Cool for 5 minutes, and then transfer to a wire rack to cool completely. Cooled cookies may be stored in an airtight container at room temperature for up to 1 week.

Make the Parfaits:

Put ½ cup Butterscotch Pudding in the bottom of eight 8-ounce mason jars or other similar serving containers. Add 2 tablespoons Banana Jam, 2 tablespoons Cheesecake "Mousse," and top with 1 cookie, gently pressing it down into the mousse. Repeat the layers, ending with a cookie on top. Parfaits may be covered with lids and refrigerated until ready to serve, for up to 3 days. To serve, arrange 5 or 6 slices of banana over the top of each parfait. Sprinkle a light, even layer of granulated sugar over the tops of the bananas and use a propane torch to caramelize the sugar. Let cool for 3 to 5 minutes before serving.

Maple-Pecan Tart

TART DOUGH:

2½ **cups** / 375 grams all-purpose flour

½ **cup** / 50 grams almond flour

1 **cup plus** 2 **tablespoons** / 140 grams powdered sugar, divided

1 **cup** / 225 grams unsalted butter, room temperature, diced

Seeds from ½ vanilla bean

1 large egg

FILLING:

1 **ounce** / 28 grams unsweetened chocolate, chopped

¾ **cup** / 160 grams packed light brown sugar

½ **cup** / 156 grams light corn syrup

¼ **cup** / 60 grams maple syrup

¼ **cup** / 56 grams unsalted butter

1 **tablespoon** / 9 grams all-purpose flour

½ **teaspoon** / 3 grams fine sea salt

1 **teaspoon** / 4 grams vanilla extract

1 **teaspoon** / 4 grams espresso extract

1½ **tablespoons** / 21 grams bourbon

4 chilled large eggs

1 **cup** / 128 grams chopped roasted pecans

Most people make pecan pie, but I prefer a tart. The filling is so rich and intense that I like the smaller bites, and this way there's enough crust to balance things out. Pecans are sweet and earthy. They are a natural match for maple syrup and brown sugar. This is one of my favorite fall desserts. It's always on the dessert buffet for Thanksgiving dinner. I like to serve it with just a little whipped cream. It's so indulgent that it doesn't need anything more than that.

Make the Tart Dough:

In a medium bowl, sift together the all-purpose flour, almond flour, and ⅓ cup of the powdered sugar. In a stand mixer with the paddle attachment on low speed, cream together the butter, the remaining powdered sugar, and the vanilla seeds. Add the egg and mix until smooth. Stop the mixer, add the flour mixture, and mix on low speed just until it is absorbed. Do not overmix. Turn the dough out of the bowl and pull it together into a flattened round. Wrap with plastic wrap and refrigerate for at least 3 hours and up to 24 hours.

Preheat the oven to 425°F (220°C).

Butter a 10-inch tart pan with a removable bottom and place it on a baking sheet lined with parchment paper or aluminum foil. Take the tart dough out of the refrigerator and roll it out onto a lightly floured surface. Gently dust the top with flour and give the dough a quarter-turn after every roll. Roll the dough out into a 14-inch circle, roughly ¼ inch thick. You can do this on a piece of parchment paper to make it easier to move the dough. Fit the dough inside the tart pan and trim the dough so there is roughly ½ inch of excess dough above the rim of the pan. Gently press the dough against the bottom and sides of the pan and then fold the excess dough inward and down, gently pressing it against the sides so that the walls of the crust are slightly thicker. Line the inside of the tart dough with foil and fill with pie weights or dried beans. Bake on the middle rack for 12 to 15 minutes, until the bottom is set. Remove the foil with the pie weights and bake the crust for another 5 to 7 minutes, until the bottom turns a light golden brown. Remove from the oven and let cool for at least 15 minutes.

Reduce the oven temperature to 325°F (165°C).

Make the Filling:

Put the chopped chocolate in a large heatproof bowl. Put the brown sugar, corn syrup, maple syrup, and butter in a medium saucepot set over medium-high heat and bring to a simmer. Pour the hot mixture over the chocolate and let it rest for 2 minutes to give the chocolate time to melt. Add the flour and salt and whisk just until smooth. Whisk in the vanilla extract, espresso extract, and bourbon. Finally, whisk in the eggs, one at time, making sure each egg is fully absorbed before adding the next. Scatter half of the pecans on the bottom of the tart pan and pour in the filling. Sprinkle the remaining pecans over the top and bake for 12 to 15 minutes, until the filling is just set. Remove from the oven and let cool for at least 30 minutes before serving.

Peach Crisp

PEACHES:

6 cups / 1 kilogram peeled and sliced peaches

3¾ cups / 750 grams granulated sugar

1¾ cups plus 2½ tablespoons / 213 grams cornstarch

5 teaspoons / 10 grams ground ginger

½ teaspoon / 3 grams fine sea salt

Juice of 1 lemon

½ teaspoon / 2 grams white verjus or apple cider vinegar

STREUSEL TOPPING:

6¼ cups / 624 grams rolled oats

5 cups / 567 grams cake flour

2⅔ cups / 567 grams packed light brown sugar

1 cup plus 2 tablespoons / 225 grams granulated sugar

2 tablespoons / 12 grams ground cinnamon

1 tablespoon / 6 grams fine sea salt

1 pound / 454 grams unsalted butter, diced

1½ tablespoons / 18 grams vanilla extract

Every year Jennifer and I travel up to Pryor's Orchard to get peaches. The Red Haven peaches are my favorite, and I drop some off at each of my restaurants so they can use them. But I always take some home and make a peach crisp. Pies need to cool before you can eat them. Having a crisp is like eating hot pie, only better, because the fruit-to-crust ratio is skewed in favor of the fruit. I serve this with vanilla ice cream or a dollop of fresh whipped cream. Nothing more is needed.

Prepare the Peaches:
Put all of the ingredients in a 9-by-13-inch casserole dish and mix gently to blend. Cover and let macerate at room temperature for 20 minutes.

Preheat the oven to 350°F (180°C).

Make the Streusel Topping:
Put the oats, flour, brown sugar, granulated sugar, cinnamon, and salt in a food processor and pulse 4 or 5 times to blend. Add the butter and vanilla and pulse until the mixture becomes moist and crumbly. Let rest for 20 minutes, and then sprinkle the streusel evenly over the top of the casserole. Line a baking sheet with parchment paper or aluminum foil, in case the crisp bubbles over, put the casserole on the baking sheet, and bake for 1 hour, or until the top is a deep golden brown and the fruit is bubbling up around the edges. Let cool for 10 minutes and serve hot.

Rocky Road Cookies

MAKES ABOUT 4 DOZEN COOKIES

Rocky road is one of my favorite ice creams. I love the combination of chocolate, marshmallow, and almonds. It was one small step to turn them into a cookie. These are indulgent enough to be a satisfying dessert. I must admit, though, that in the summertime I've been known to sandwich them around a small scoop of vanilla or chocolate ice cream. Either way, you'll find it hard to eat just one.

COOKIES:

6½ ounces / 185 grams dark chocolate (70% cacao), chopped

6 tablespoons / 85 grams unsalted butter, sliced

2⅓ cups / 350 grams all-purpose flour

½ cup / 60 grams unsweetened cocoa powder

1½ tablespoons / 27 grams baking powder

½ teaspoon / 3 grams fine sea salt

6 large eggs

3¾ cups / 750 grams granulated sugar

1 tablespoon / 12 grams vanilla extract

4 cups / 199 grams mini marshmallows

2½ cups / 420 grams chocolate chunks

1½ cups / 255 grams white chocolate chunks

7¼ ounces / 206 grams almonds, chopped

COATING SUGAR:

½ cup / 65 grams powdered sugar

3 tablespoons / 21 grams unsweetened cocoa powder

Make the Cookie Batter:

Preheat the oven to 325°F (165°C).

Put the chocolate and butter in a microwave-safe bowl and microwave on high for 30 seconds. Stir and microwave for 30 seconds more. Repeat until the chocolate and butter are completely melted, 1 to 2 minutes total.

Sift together the flour, cocoa powder, baking powder, and salt. In a medium bowl, whisk together the eggs, granulated sugar, and vanilla until smooth. Pour the egg mixture into the flour mixture and stir with a rubber spatula until they are just blended. Fold in the mini marshmallows, chocolate chunks, white chocolate chunks, and almonds.

Make the Coating Sugar:

Put the powdered sugar and cocoa powder in a medium bowl and whisk them together.

Bake the Cookies:

Use a 1¾-ounce ice cream scoop to portion balls of dough. Roll each ball of dough in the Coating Sugar and put them on baking sheets, leaving 2 inches of space between each one. Bake for 9 to 11 minutes, until the cookies are just set. Cool for 5 minutes and then transfer to a wire rack to cool completely.

Cornmeal Thumbprint Cookies

MAKES ABOUT 2 DOZEN COOKIES

Thumbprint cookies are fun to make. I add a little bit of cornmeal to my dough for flavor and because it gives them an extra bit of crunch. Instead of using walnuts or pecans, I use pine nuts. I love their unique buttery flavor and the way they blend in with and support the taste of the fruit preserves. We get the kids in the kitchen to make these, and everybody helps out. They can all press their thumbs into the cookies and choose their own flavors of jam. Everybody gets to make some his or her way, and later we all sit down to eat them together. It's a great way to spend an afternoon at home.

1 cup / 225 grams unsalted butter

½ cup / 100 grams sugar

2 large eggs, separated

1 teaspoon / 4 grams vanilla extract

1¼ cups / 188 grams all-purpose flour

½ cup / 70 grams fine cornmeal

¼ teaspoon / 1.5 grams fine sea salt

1 cup plus 2 tablespoons / 156 grams chopped pine nuts

1 cup / 340 grams fruit preserves, stirred

Preheat the oven to 300°F (150°C).

Cream the butter and the sugar in a stand mixer with the paddle attachment on low speed until light and fluffy, 2 to 3 minutes. Add the egg yolks one at a time, making sure that the first one is fully incorporated before adding the next. Add the vanilla and mix until it is absorbed. Stop the mixer, add the flour, cornmeal, and salt, and mix on low speed just until the dough comes together.

Put the egg whites in a small bowl and whisk until frothy. Put the chopped pine nuts in a separate bowl. Use a ¾-ounce ice cream scoop to form balls of dough, and then roll them first in the egg whites and then in the pine nuts. Lay them out on baking sheets, leaving 2 inches of space between each one. Use the back of a ½-teaspoon measuring spoon or your thumb to press a rounded indentation into the center of each one. Put ½ teaspoon jam in each indentation. Bake for 8 to 11 minutes, until the cookies are just set and the pine nuts have turned a light golden brown. Let cool completely before serving. Thumbprint Cookies may be stored in an airtight container at room temperature for up to 1 week.

Lemon Cookies

I love lemon at the end of a meal. It's refreshing and helps me shake off any drowsiness that can be a side effect from enjoying eating well. These little lemon cookies are on the dessert cart at Range. They are like little lemon cakes dipped in icing, perfect when you want just a small bit of something sweet after dinner.

COOKIES:

1½ **cups** / 225 grams all-purpose flour

¼ **cup** / 28 grams cornstarch

⅛ **teaspoon** / 0.75 gram fine sea salt

¾ **cup** / 170 grams unsalted butter, room temperature

⅓ **cup** / 65 grams granulated sugar

1 **teaspoon** / 4 grams vanilla extract

Grated zest of 1 lemon

GLAZE:

3 **tablespoons** / 42 grams water

2½ **tablespoons** / 35 grams fresh lemon juice

¼ **teaspoon** / 1.5 grams fine sea salt

2½ **cups** / 315 grams powdered sugar

Freshly grated lemon zest, for sprinkling

Make the Cookies:

Sift the flour, cornstarch, and salt together. Cream the butter and sugar in a stand mixer with the paddle attachment on low speed until light and fluffy, 3 to 5 minutes. Add the vanilla and lemon zest and mix until smooth. Stop the mixer and add all of the flour mixture. Mix on low speed until the dough pulls away from the side of the bowl, 2 to 3 minutes. Put the dough in a covered container and refrigerate for at least 4 hours or preferably overnight.

Preheat the oven to 300°F (150°C). Line a baking sheet with parchment paper.

Use a ¾-ounce ice cream scoop to portion the dough into balls, and lay them out on the baking sheet, leaving 2 inches of space between each cookie. Bake for 8 minutes, or until the cookies are set and slightly golden brown around the edges. Transfer the cookies to a wire rack to cool completely, about 30 minutes.

Make the Glaze:

Put the water, lemon juice, and salt in a medium bowl and whisk until the salt dissolves. Add the powdered sugar and whisk until smooth. Set a wire rack over a baking sheet. Dip the tops of each cookie into the glaze and then set them on the rack. Sprinkle the cookies with freshly grated lemon zest and leave them on the rack until the glaze hardens, about 20 minutes.

Quadruple-Chocolate Brownie Sundaes

MAKES 8 SUNDAES

CHOCOLATE-STOUT ICE CREAM:

8 ounces / 227 grams dark chocolate (70% cacao), chopped

3 cups / 675 grams stout beer

2 cups / 480 grams heavy cream

12 large egg yolks

½ **cup** / 100 grams granulated sugar

¼ **cup** / 75 grams light corn syrup

¼ **cup** / 60 grams malt syrup

FUDGE BROWNIES:

8 ounces / 227 grams semisweet chocolate (61% cacao), chopped

¾ **cup** / 170 grams unsalted butter, diced

¼ **cup** / 60 grams malt syrup

3¼ **cups** / 406 grams powdered sugar

1½ **cups** / 225 grams all-purpose flour

¼ **cup** / 30 grams unsweetened cocoa powder

1 teaspoon / 6 grams baking powder

½ **teaspoon** / 3 grams fine sea salt

4 large eggs

4 teaspoons / 16 grams vanilla extract

½ **teaspoon** / 1 gram freshly grated orange zest

HOT FUDGE:

1 cup / 240 grams heavy cream

¾ **cup** / 225 grams light corn syrup

¼ **cup** / 56 grams water

½ **cup** / 60 grams unsweetened cocoa powder

½ **teaspoon** / 3 grams sea salt

Seeds from ½ vanilla bean

6 ounces / 170 grams dark chocolate (70% cacao), chopped

6 ounces / 170 grams milk chocolate, chopped

¼ **cup** / 56 grams unsalted butter

Bittersweet chocolate, for grating

This is my "death by chocolate" dessert. Every element has chocolate, and I grate a little more over the top. I love the combination of chocolate and stout. The beer adds a hint of bitterness and deep complexity to the natural flavors of the chocolate. Pair that with chewy hot fudge and a soft, moist brownie and you've got chocolate to the nth degree. For chocolate lovers, there is no better dessert.

Make the Chocolate-Stout Ice Cream:
Put the chopped chocolate in a large heatproof bowl. Put the stout and heavy cream in a medium saucepot set over medium-high heat and bring to a simmer. Meanwhile, whisk together the egg yolks, granulated sugar, corn syrup, and malt syrup. Once the liquid comes to a simmer, slowly whisk 2 tablespoons at a time into the egg yolks until you have added about 1 cup and the mixture is warm. Whisk the egg mixture into the remaining liquid in the pot and set over medium heat. Cook until the mixture

➔

reaches 162°F (72°C) and then immediately pour it into the bowl with the chopped chocolate. Let it rest for 1 minute to melt the chocolate, and then slowly whisk until smooth. Try not to incorporate too much air into the mixture. Let it cool and then refrigerate in a covered container for at least 4 hours to chill the ice cream base.

Freeze in an ice cream machine according to the manufacturer's directions. Then transfer to a covered container and let harden in the freezer for at least 4 hours before scooping.

Make the Fudge Brownies:
Preheat the oven to 325°F (165°C). Butter a 9-by-13-inch baking dish.

Put the chopped chocolate and butter in a microwave-safe bowl and microwave on high for 30 seconds. Stir with a silicone spatula and return to the microwave for another 30 seconds. Stir again, and, if the mixture isn't smooth and completely melted, return to the microwave one more time. Whisk in the malt syrup. Let cool slightly and reserve.

In a medium bowl, sift together the powdered sugar, all-purpose flour, cocoa powder, baking powder, and salt. In a stand mixer with the paddle attachment, mix the eggs on low speed until smooth. With the mixer running, slowly pour in the chocolate mixture. Once it is absorbed, stop the mixer and add the flour mixture.

Turn the mixer back on low speed and mix until smooth. Stir in the vanilla and orange zest. Pour the batter into the prepared pan and bake for 30 to 35 minutes, until a cake tester inserted into the center of the brownies comes out almost clean. Remove from the oven and let cool completely before cutting.

Make the Hot Fudge:
Put the heavy cream, corn syrup, water, cocoa powder, salt, and vanilla seeds in a medium saucepot and whisk until smooth. Set over medium-high heat and bring to a simmer. Reduce the heat to medium-low and simmer for 5 minutes. Whisk in the dark chocolate. Once the chocolate melts, remove from the heat. Whisk in the milk chocolate and butter. Let the mixture cool for 15 minutes, stirring occasionally; it will thicken as it cools. Serve warm. Extra Hot Fudge may be stored in a covered container in the refrigerator for up to 1 month.

To build a sundae, take a shallow ice cream dish and lay a Fudge Brownie in the bottom. Top with a generous scoop of Chocolate-Stout Ice Cream. Ladle warm—not hot—Hot Fudge over the top. Grate some bittersweet chocolate over the top using a vegetable peeler or Microplane and serve immediately.

Caramel-Popcorn Sundaes

MAKES 8 SUNDAES

PEANUT BUTTER ICE CREAM:

13½ ounces / 380 grams smooth peanut butter

1 (**13.4-ounce** / 380-gram) can sweetened condensed milk

1½ cups / 360 grams heavy cream

1½ cups / 390 grams whole milk

1 teaspoon / 4 grams soy sauce

¼ teaspoon / 1.5 grams fine sea salt

CARAMEL POPCORN:

4 quarts / 150 grams air-popped popcorn (from ½ cup kernels)

2 cups / 400 grams sugar

¾ cup / 170 grams water

3 tablespoons / 42 grams unsalted butter

1 tablespoon / 18 grams fine sea salt

1 teaspoon / 5 grams baking soda

JACK DANIEL'S CARAMEL SAUCE:

2¼ cups plus 2 tablespoons / 475 grams sugar

2 tablespoons / 39 grams light corn syrup

¾ cup / 170 grams water

¾ cup / 170 grams Jack Daniel's whiskey

¼ cup / 60 grams heavy cream

2 tablespoons / 28 grams unsalted butter

As a kid, I loved going to baseball games. It should come as no surprise that one of the things I liked best about going to the games was the food. I always got a box of Cracker Jack, caramel popcorn with roasted peanuts, and would sit there munching away while I watched the game. Those flavors were the inspiration for this sundae. Intense peanut butter ice cream, smooth caramel sauce, and caramel popcorn—it's warm and cold, creamy and crunchy, everything you need in an ice cream sundae.

Make the Peanut Butter Ice Cream:
Put all of the ingredients in a blender and puree until smooth. Refrigerate in a covered container for at least 4 hours to chill the ice cream base.

Freeze in an ice cream machine according to the manufacturer's directions. Then transfer to a covered container and let the ice cream harden in the freezer for at least 4 hours before scooping.

Make the Caramel Popcorn:
Put the popcorn in a large bowl. Put the sugar in a medium saucepot. Be sure to use a large enough pot because the caramel will bubble vigorously and rise. Pour the water over the top and mix it together so that all of the sugar is hydrated, then wipe down the sides of the pot

with a paper towel to make sure there are no clinging sugar granules, and cover with plastic wrap. Set over medium heat and cook until the sugar turns light amber. Remove from the heat, carefully remove and discard the plastic wrap—there will be extremely hot steam—and slowly whisk in the butter. Next, add the salt and baking soda. Pour over the popcorn immediately and toss with a heatproof spatula to coat every kernel. Allow to cool completely before serving. The popcorn will crisp up as it cools. Caramel Popcorn can be stored in an airtight container at room temperature for up to 1 week.

Make the Jack Daniel's Caramel Sauce:
Put the sugar and corn syrup in a medium saucepot. You need a good-size pot because the caramel will bubble vigorously and rise. Pour the water over the top and mix it together so that all of the sugar is hydrated, then wipe down the sides of the pot with a paper towel to make sure there are no clinging sugar granules, and cover with plastic wrap. Set over medium heat and cook until the sugar turns light amber. Remove from the heat, carefully remove and discard the plastic wrap—there will be extremely hot steam—and slowly whisk in the Jack

❯

Dessert

Daniel's and then the cream and butter. If the caramel crystallizes, set the pot over low heat and cook until it melts back into the sauce. Use warm. Extra Jack Daniel's Caramel Sauce may be cooled and stored in a covered container in the refrigerator for up to 3 months. If it separates, just stir it back together when you warm it up.

To build a sundae, put a generous scoop of Peanut Butter Ice Cream in a dish. Spoon warm Jack Daniel's Caramel Sauce over the ice cream and sprinkle at least ¾ cup Caramel Popcorn over the top. Serve immediately.

toping

Garlic powder

POPPY seeD

FenneL
seeD

FanATTseeD

Alepo
chiliy

6 potatoes red
or more
ethr sise

toping

coddcola

PineNuts

extra
salt sea

Acknowledgments

To my family—without them there would be no HOME. Jennifer, my wife and high-school sweetheart; and my three beautiful children, Thacher, Piper, and Ever: Thank you for supporting the life of a cook and, most important, for your love.

To my parents, for believing in me even if you thought my ideas were unattainable, because without your unconditional love and support I could not have accomplished them anyway.

To my brother, Michael, and sister, Staci, thanks for all the memories at the dinner table. Sorry, Michael, you had to stay longer than us to finish the brussels sprouts.

To my longtime friend and chef de cuisine at Volt, Graeme Ritchie, thank you for your handiwork and dedication to making all of our ideas a reality.

To my partners, for also believing in me even if your gut told you otherwise; you stayed the course and for that I will always be grateful.

To Michael Sand, Garrett McGrath, and the team at Little, Brown, thank you for your guidance to make this book not only a reality, but also a beautiful piece of work.

To Aki Kamozawa and Alex Talbot from Ideas in Food, thank you for your patience and for your ability to take our ideas and transform them into very easy-to-follow and tasty recipes, which is an accomplishment and craft in itself. Without you we would still be staring at my torn-up Moleskines, ragged-looking legal pads, and a few typed recipes.

To Ed Anderson—your amazing photography made it so easy to tell the story behind the food from my home. You are a true talent and friend, and thank you.

To all of the cooks, chefs, and anyone who has ever carried a serving in my restaurants, thank you for all you have done to make us who and what we are today.

Thank you to the team at Williams-Sonoma for being the perfect source for all of the tools and pieces necessary to translate the professional kitchen experience into the home.

Also, thank you to all of the local supporters of my restaurants and this book: Flying Dog Brewery, Big White Barn, Cherry Glen Farm, Whitmore Farm, Rappahannock Oysters, Relish Decor, and Heritage Antiques.

To you, the reader, for supporting, reading, and, I hope, cooking from this book: Without your curiosity about understanding what it is like to cook at home from a chef's perspective, we never would have met, and I like meeting new people, so thank you.

Index

About the Author

Bryan Voltaggio is the executive chef and owner of the restaurants Volt, Lunchbox, Family Meal, Range, and Aggio, in Washington, DC, and Maryland. As a finalist on season 6 of *Top Chef* and season 5 of *Top Chef Masters*, Voltaggio was the first chef to compete on both programs. The James Beard Foundation Award finalist co-authored the cookbook *VOLTink.* with his brother Michael Voltaggio and lives with his wife, Jennifer, and their three children in Frederick, Maryland.